ELITES & CHANGE IN THE KENTUCKY MOUNTAINS

ELITES & CHANGE IN THE KENTUCKY MOUNTAINS

H. Dudley Plunkett
& Mary Jean Bowman

The University Press of Kentucky

ISBN: 0–8131–1275–3

Library of Congress Catalog Card Number: 76–160049

A statewide cooperative scholarly publishing agency serving Berea College, Centre College of Kentucky, Eastern Kentucky University, Kentucky Historical Society, Kentucky State University, Morehead State University, Murray State University, University of Kentucky, University of Louisville, and Western Kentucky University.

Editorial and Sales Offices: Lexington, Kentucky 40506

Contents

Tables

Figures

Preface

Over the last decade the people of Appalachia have become better known to the rest of their countrymen, as have the frustrating social and economic problems faced by mountain residents. Nevertheless, the subculture of these people, and of the eastern Kentucky mountains in particular, continues vigorously to resist erosion of its central values. At the same time, human problems in the mountains have become so numerous and so severe as to evoke even in the most obtuse outside observer an awareness that change is long overdue.

In this study we are concerned less with particular policies than with the development of capacities in the regional society to effect its modernization. We adopt a case-study approach, covering only a short span of years in the experience of a society that has long suffered from periodic crises; though each wave may seem to have been unprecedented and unique, the economic disequilibria and cultural disjunctions vis-à-vis the wider society are chronic. Our intent in this research is to provide some insights with respect to this area and its subculture and to contribute to the filling of a serious void with respect to empirical studies of the transmission of modernization to the lagging parts of generally developed societies.

We view Appalachian Kentucky and its broader national environment as "inner" and "outer" social systems. In our terminology the "interstitial person" is the individual who, by reason of his achieved qualifications, experiences, and opportunities, has access to both inner and outer societies. The relevance of such persons to the modernization process in the region lies in the communication, or "cultural bridge" role that they may be able to perform, linking the two cultures of the traditional "inside" and the modern "outside."

For the purposes of this study, interstitial persons are empirically identified with certain key occupations. The local society will be likely to develop in a modernizing direction if large proportions of those holding interstitial positions in its occupational and social structure are competent and willing to serve this cultural intermediary function. It should go without saying that this does not presuppose an elitist theory of social change. However broad, this study constitutes only part of a fully rounded analysis of cultural bridge functions in development. In Appalachian conditions, at least, modernization will have to be chosen by the people at large, but the role of men who are sensitive to both mountain traditions and broader forces of social and economic change must surely prove crucial in how that choice evolves.

It is now well over a decade since one of the authors (Bowman) began to work on a detailed assessment of the economic problems and potentials of the Kentucky mountains. That research was begun without any predisposition to focus upon human resources, let alone upon mountain culture, people, and institutions more broadly conceived. Nevertheless, a book that started out to treat mountain problems and prospects in a relatively conventional economist's approach ultimately required heavy emphasis upon people and the effects of geographic isolation on mountain society. Subsequently Bowman became very much interested in some of the work of human geographers and others on communication and the diffusion of innovations, including changes in practices, institutions, and attitudes —work with wide applicability to development problems, particularly those of eastern Kentucky.

Plunkett first became interested in eastern Kentucky as an area and a subculture sharing in significant respects many of the attributes of developing countries. From the start his orientation was sociological rather than economic, and his first work on Appalachia was an empirical study involving determinants of the geographical diffusion of school continuation rates in Appalachian Kentucky, Tennessee, Virginia, and West Virginia. Still using an ecological framework, he next undertook a study of the elementary schoolteacher as an interstitial person in order to assess potentials of teachers to serve as cultural bridges between their local communities and the larger society. Almost from the start, his research was viewed as preliminary to this collaborative study of mountain elites.

We would like to record our appreciation for the advice and help given us by large numbers of Kentuckians—first of all by the respondents to our various survey inquiries and by those who carried out field interviews. Many colleagues at the University of Kentucky gave us their time and their ideas. We extend special thanks to Harry Schwarzweller, James Brown, Richard Miller, and William Carse. Among others with long experience and deep interest in Kentucky who contributed ideas, information, and indispensable practical help to our research were John Whisman of the Appalachian Regional Commission, William Miller and Chris Maxwell of the Eastern Kentucky Resources Development Project, Frank Glass and others of the state education department, Tom Gish of the *Mountain Eagle*, Whitesburg, Kentucky, and numerous other officials, local citizens, and friends living and working in the Kentucky mountains. We also valued the painstaking help in data processing by Mary Anton and Stephanie Abeshouse. Finally, we owe a particular debt to Professor C. A. Anderson of the University of Chicago, who went over the manuscript with a sharp eye for both broad problems and critical details; his comments led to many improvements. We alone, however, are responsible for faults that remain.

CHAPTER 1

Modernization: A Case Study

The two decades following World War II witnessed an unflagging concern with the development of economically backward nations and depressed areas within highly developed nations. With these concerns has come an intensification of activities in the various social sciences that directs attention increasingly toward people, whether as direct human-resource inputs into productive processes, as transmitters of information and attitudes conducive to change and modernization, or as carriers of attitudes that dampen or block such processes. These developments have touched every one of the traditional social science disciplines and have also given rise to essentially new interdisciplinary specializations —among them "regional science," "urban studies," and a new sort of human geography. The theoretical base of the present study lies at an intersection of these various streams of thought. Empirically the focus is upon the occupational elites of the Kentucky mountains as potential carriers and diffusers of modernization, both to the mountain communities and to those of their residents (young and old) who will migrate to other parts of the nation.

Although this is a case study of one particular area, which in many respects is unique, it is our contention that such case studies are essential if we are to understand the common and the disparate aspects of development processes in a variety of socioeconomic contexts. Such indeed is the rationale of the so-called comparative method in the social sciences; if they are to be other than superficial, comparisons must derive from a better knowledge of each of the entities ultimately to be compared.

In this introductory chapter we will undertake: (1) to propose a working definition of the term "modernization," relying upon a variety of disciplinary approaches, but at the same time posing many problems that arise from the unavoidable judgments of value involved; (2) to specify those essential environmental and other socioeconomic characteristics of eastern Kentucky that justify its selection for a case study; and (3) to delineate the theoretical sources upon which the communication focus of the interstitial person construct is based.

Concerning Modernization

Economists have an initial advantage over other social scientists in defining what may be meant by "development." They have two measures—"growth" in the aggregate (or regional) product and increase in per capita income—both of which would conventionally be regarded as objective indicators of desirable societal trends, other things equal. However, this seeming tidiness begins to crumble when we look further. In the first place the measures are not always as unambiguous as they may seem to be: this is probably better recognized by economists than by other social scientists who criticize a "too narrowly economic" view of things. A long line of thoughtful men from Sir William Petty through Adam Smith, John Stuart Mill, and Alfred Pigou to Simon Kuznets and younger national-income econometricians have wrestled with problems of what elements in the national income should be counted and how—and even with how far measured income marches in step with satisfactions or (not quite the same thing) with the quality of life.

Other problems also arise for the economist, such as the correlation of the aggregate and the per person indicators of growth in a particular case and, crucially in some instances, the "shape" of the distribution of income among a population as opposed to average or per capita values. Increasingly economists who have concerned themselves with this latter problem have emphasized the importance of what happens to the middle or (as in the case of the recent high out-migration area of the Appalachians) the bottom of the distribution of incomes. Whether as a normative goal in itself or as an indicator of solid foundations for sustained progress, a wider diffusion of income gains may be essential for development in many backward areas. Regional economic development entails diffusion of economic benefits and opportunities among the population of the area, including both individuals who will remain and those who will leave to work elsewhere.[1] But development is not just an economic phenomenon.

In an earlier article, in which the concepts of regionalism and development were jointly discussed, development was defined as "the enlargement and cumulative diffusion among a population of opportunities to widen the range of experiences and satisfactions and to participate in an on-going national life."[2] The authors went on to point out that, "by this criterion, declining regions with limited economic potentials could still experience 'development' provided there is *creatively adaptive* community planning and an increase of communication with more dynamic centers."

This view of development challenges the economist's propensity to set aside ignorance after a few caveats, to disregard the processes by which values and tastes are formed and changed, and to neglect the importance of human interactions in socioeconomic development processes. But when measured economic ends are perceived as means to more subjectively defined ends or satisfactions (as basic economic theory would require), and when economists incorporate "spillover" or "neighborhood effects" in their models, economic development takes on broader connotations. It is then more nearly commensurate with modernization as that concept has been used by social scientists who stress the "socio" in their analysis of socioeconomic change.

Modernization, as the term is currently used,[3]

---

1. A more detailed discussion of the effects of migration upon the Kentucky mountains may be found in Mary Jean Bowman and W. Warren Haynes, *Resources and People in East Kentucky: Problems and Potentials of a Lagging Economy* (Baltimore: Johns Hopkins Press, 1963), especially Chapters 10 and 12.

2. C. Arnold Anderson and Mary Jean Bowman, "Interdisciplinary Aspects of a Theory of Regional Development," in *Problems of Chronically Depressed Areas* (Agricultural Policy Institute, North Carolina State University, in cooperation with the Tennessee Valley Authority, November 1965).

3. Examples of such usages will be found in the writings of several authors in Myron Weiner, ed., *Modernization: The Dynamics of Growth* (New York:

refers to a process of change rather than an end. This process is ultimately societal even if, as usually happens in practice, it first affects, or is activated among, an elite or another minority within a society. Types of change in the culture and socioeconomic structures of a society that are seen as progressive are termed modernization, and normally these changes are responsive to elements of change located in or emerging from a "lead" society.[4] However, each society or subsociety has its own baseline configuration of established and emergent values, institutions, and resources; and it therefore both carries and combats a particular set of strains in its culture, social structure, and economy. Modernization will never be merely imitative diffusion; the adaptive changes that occur are also in greater or lesser degree creative. Because of this process, with its mixing of imitative diffusion and creativity (including creative conflict), the details of modernization cannot be specified in advance. A problem central to the understanding of modernization and basic to the theoretical and empirical analysis in this study involves identifying and understanding the interplay among diffusive acceptance, conflict, and creative adaptation—and recognizing the possibility that outcomes of this interplay can be stagnation and even retrogression as well as progress.[5]

For the purposes of discussion the main types of changes that may be said to characterize modernization may be conveniently categorized as changes in scale, in social organization,[6] and in access of individuals to satisfying participative roles in a society. Important changes of scale include, for example, nationwide demographic growth, increases in both urban density and spread, and enlargement of the geographic areas over which there is frequent social contact (both face to face and via mass media). These changes are closely interwoven with other aspects of modernization and what it means for an area lagging in material and cultural resources.

The changes in social organization tend to be in the direction of a growing complexity in structure and in communications, with concurrent regularizing of economic and administrative processes, specialization of tasks and roles, and upgrading of skills. These can be seen as virtually unidirectional changes in society, though the speed with which they progress is related not only to the means of their diffusion but also to cultural resistances they may encounter. We would nonetheless expect that in most societies there would be a steady diffusion of changes of this type—changes that are incompatible with the persistence in their full traditional meanings of opposing values such as the familism and personalism of Appalachia.[7]

Inclusion of the third type of change, which we will term "social mobilization,"[8] as a component of modernization is more problematic. Certain normative questions pose themselves in more or less similar fashion in all societies, whatever the particular stage of socioeconomic development. In any society, opinions will be widely divided upon our proposition that progressive

---

Basic Books, 1966); Charles E. Black, *The Dynamics of Modernization* (New York: Harper and Row, 1966); S. N. Eisenstadt, *Modernization: Protest and Change* (Englewood Cliffs, N.J.: Prentice Hall, 1967).

4. See the discussion of the relationship of modernization and westernization in Daniel Lerner, *The Passing of Traditional Society* (New York: Free Press, 1958); or see the characterization of westernization as a world culture in Lucian Pye, *Politics, Personality, and Nation-Building* (New Haven: Yale University Press, 1962), p. 10.

5. S. N. Eisenstadt, "Breakdowns of Modernization," *Economic Development and Cultural Change* 12 (July 1964): 345–67.

6. These changes do not seem necessarily to be sequentially related, but Philip M. Hauser speaks, for example, of the "social morphological revolution" that is based upon increasing population density. See "Urbanization: An Overview," in Hauser and Leo F. Schnore, eds., *The Study of Urbanization* (New York: John Wiley, 1965), p. 12.

7. This assumption or conclusion is to be found in dispassionate (as opposed to polemical or tendentious) writings about the Appalachian area; see, for example, Harry K. Schwarzweller and James Brown, "Education as a Cultural Bridge between East Kentucky and the Greater Society," *Rural Sociology* 27 (December 1962): 357–73, and Jack E. Weller, *Yesterday's People: Life in Contemporary Appalachia* (Lexington: University of Kentucky Press, 1965).

8. Karl Deutsch, "Social Mobilization and Political Development," *American Political Science Review* 55 (September 1961): 493–514. Other writers have made use of the same concept: for example, Fred Riggs, "Political Aspects of Developmental Change," in Art Gallaher, Jr., ed, *Perspectives in Developmental Change* (Lexington: University of Kentucky Press, 1968).

social change involves the increased access of individuals to participative roles—whether this comprises increased consultation and communication across sectors of the society, or a shift in the levels of active involvement in the society's affairs, or both. Examples of the former would be an extension of the franchise (or effective voting rights) to illiterate black people in the United States or to women in Switzerland, or a modification of attitudes leading to new forums for the legitimate discussion and resolution of group conflicts. Active involvement expands with the opening of access to previously monopolized economic opportunities through the widening of apprenticeship openings or with a thrust by newly formed elites or nonelites toward an effective voice in diverse sociopolitical activities.

Clearly, new commitments to propositions about mobilizational changes and the implementation of accompanying value choices in the modernization process present the greatest problems of conflict. While norms of sociopolitical participation are diffused from one society or subsociety to another, any changes in supporting predominant values or institutional arrangements must involve a redistribution of power, to the disadvantage of established decision-makers. Such changes will be subject to dispute according to the intensity or violence of the conflict of interests involved in a particular social context.[9] The extent and nature of mobilization is a matter of peculiar interest for Appalachian Kentucky, where it may prove to be the acid test of the modernization process.

The Kentucky Mountains

Whether one draws the boundaries of eastern Kentucky narrowly, to incorporate only the central subsistence-farming counties and the coal complexes at the river headwaters, or more broadly, to include some or all of the relatively more accessible counties to the north and along the southwestern edge of the eastern coalfield, he is not looking at what the modern regional scientists usually consider a region. This is not a functionally integrated economic area. On the other hand it is decidedly a cultural region with a self-conscious identity, however divided the institutions and subpopulations of that region may be.

Economic & Social Change in the Mountains

The early development of the timber and coal industries in the Kentucky mountains, although it brought employment opportunities for a wave of migrant jobseekers, never gave a stable economic footing to the mountain population as a whole. The purely physiographic characteristics of the area were decisive. Topography militated first against the laying of asphalt roads, then against the building of railways, and now against the construction of airports. The connections that were established followed the physical contours through the tortuous mountain valleys and passes (Figure 1). Railways, for example, illustrate the geographic problem. Just before World War I, lines were built up the Cumberland Valley through Harlan, from Lexington up the Kentucky River to its headwaters, and from Ashland in the north up the Levisa Fork of the Big Sandy into Pike County, at the extreme southeastern corner of the state. These rail lines were not connected with each other, and each stopped as it reached the headwaters; the system did little to cut through the internal geographic compartmentalization of the mountains. However, the railroads did bring in thousands of workers and profit seekers whose descendants have more recently been leaving the coal valleys with the decline of employment in the mines.

In 1956–1957 eastern Kentucky was just emerging from the shock of a postwar coal boom-and-bust that overlaid long-term economic problems.[10] As though that were not enough, the greastest flood in the area's recent history came in 1957. A surge of national concern with backward regions in general and with Appalachia in particular,[11] similar in many ways to that of the

9. See the typology of conflict presented in Ralf Dahrendorf, *Class and Class Conflict in Industrial Society* (Stanford: Stanford University Press, 1959), especially Chapter VI.

10. Bowman's work commissioned by Resources for the Future Inc., in preparation of *Resources and People in East Kentucky*, began at that time.

11. A significant official review of these problems

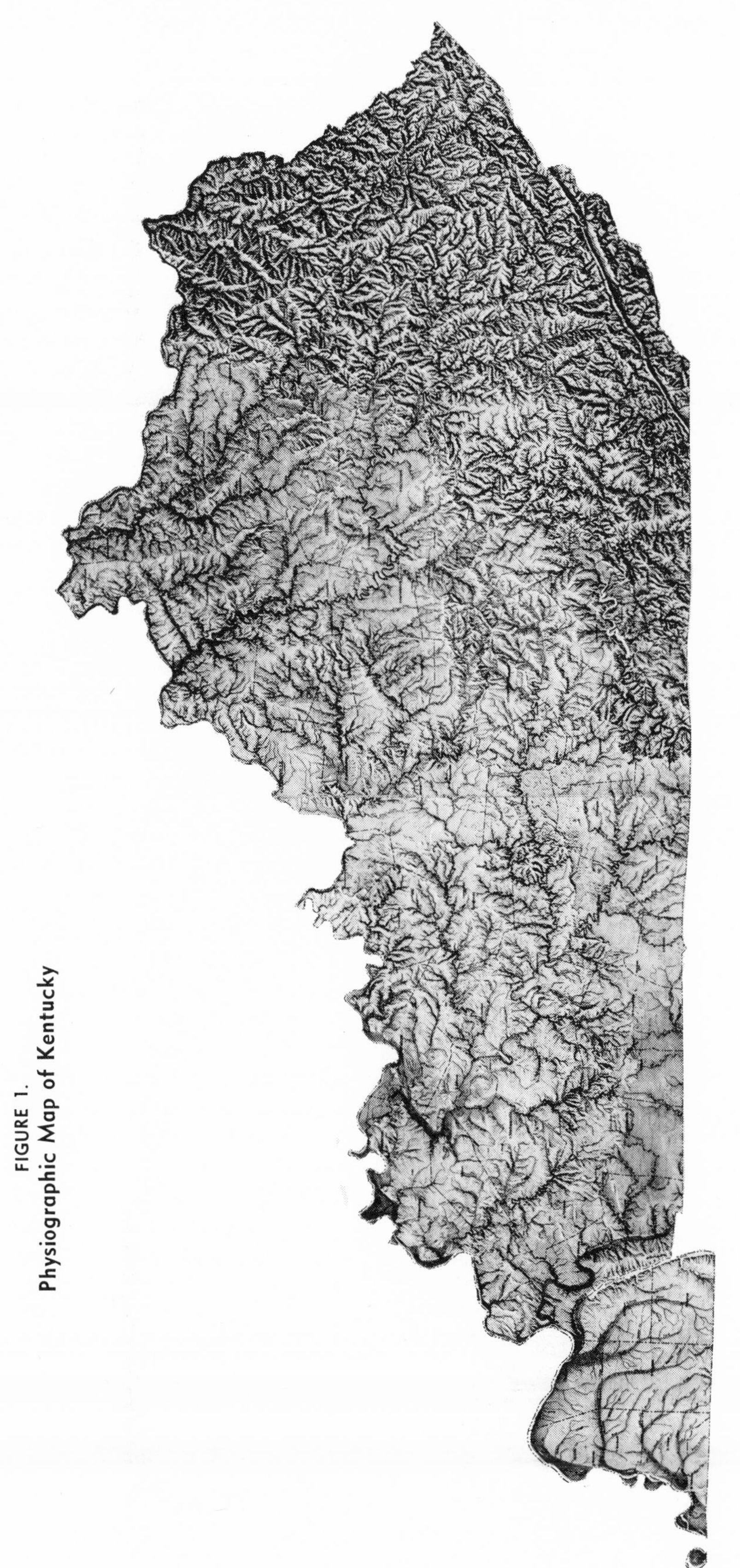

FIGURE 1.
Physiographic Map of Kentucky

FIGURE 2.
Population Density, Eastern Kentucky Extended

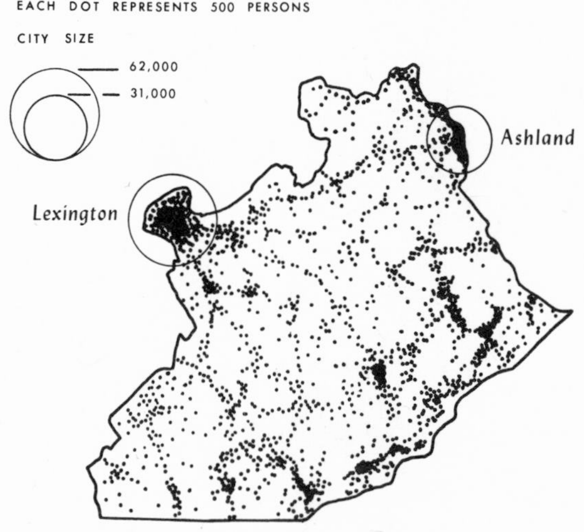

1930s, began at this time to stir the national Congress. In the years since, the Area Redevelopment Act, the Appalachian Development Act, the manpower acts, and the antipoverty legislation have successively been advertised with a fanfare as key measures for the Appalachian area.

Despite all this legislation the past decade has seen strip mines and huge augers piling their refuse on small hillside farms and poisoning the streams. The short-run effects have included profits but no jobs; the long-run effects are, of course, neither profits nor jobs, but the discouragement of community improvement and stultification of the tourist industry. The same decade has brought interstate highways across northern Kentucky and across the southwestern counties on the routes from Lexington to Knoxville and Chattanooga, along with the state-built eastern Kentucky Mountain Parkway—the latter being the only major road offering mountain people the possibility of greater contact with outside regions. A steady rationalization of local industry has also led to the demise of many small or inefficient manufacturing firms. Community efforts to establish or to encourage new enterprises to employ mountain people have met with almost universal disappointment and frustration, although several enterprises still hang on.[12] Meanwhile the rate of out-migration has slowed slightly as employment in the coalfields has been stabilized, and as would-be migrants found gloomy prospects for employment in northern cities.

The very starkness of the economic situation in eastern Kentucky (which has made it an extreme case even within the Appalachian context) provides a setting all the more fitted for the study of the diffusion of information and attitudes that may induce or block change and for the identification of human resource potentials in the communication of modernization. Problems and needs common to other depressed areas are here starkly evident, despite the complexities which characterize human interaction patterns in this and other settings.

Mountain Ecology & Isolation

It must already be apparent that eastern Kentucky as a physiographic-cultural area is at once both one and many. Various sections of the mountains differ in their degree of physical and cultural isolation from outside contacts, and within the mountains there is physical and social separation of one valley from another. The broad human context for these communication problems is illustrated by Figures 2 and 3, especially when these are compared to the physiographic structure detailed on Figure 1. The population dot map shows clearly the population clusters of the coal counties, extending in a double tier along the southeastern boundary of the state. The sparser populations of central eastern Kentucky (though still dense relative to the resources of the land on which they live) dwell along the narrow river valleys, which also trace out the roads. This pattern is broken, however, across the

found expression in the report of the President's Appalachian Regional Commission, *Appalachia* (Washington: Government Printing Office, 1964).

12. For further information concerning the fortunes of mountain manufacturers over the past decade see Mary Jean Bowman and H. Dudley Plunkett, *Communication and Mountain Development*, Part II, contained in the final Report to the Economic Development Administration U.S. Department of Commerce, Project No. 6–147–66 (December 1968), pp. 11–98.

FIGURE 3.
Traffic Flow, Eastern Kentucky & Adjacent Bluegrass

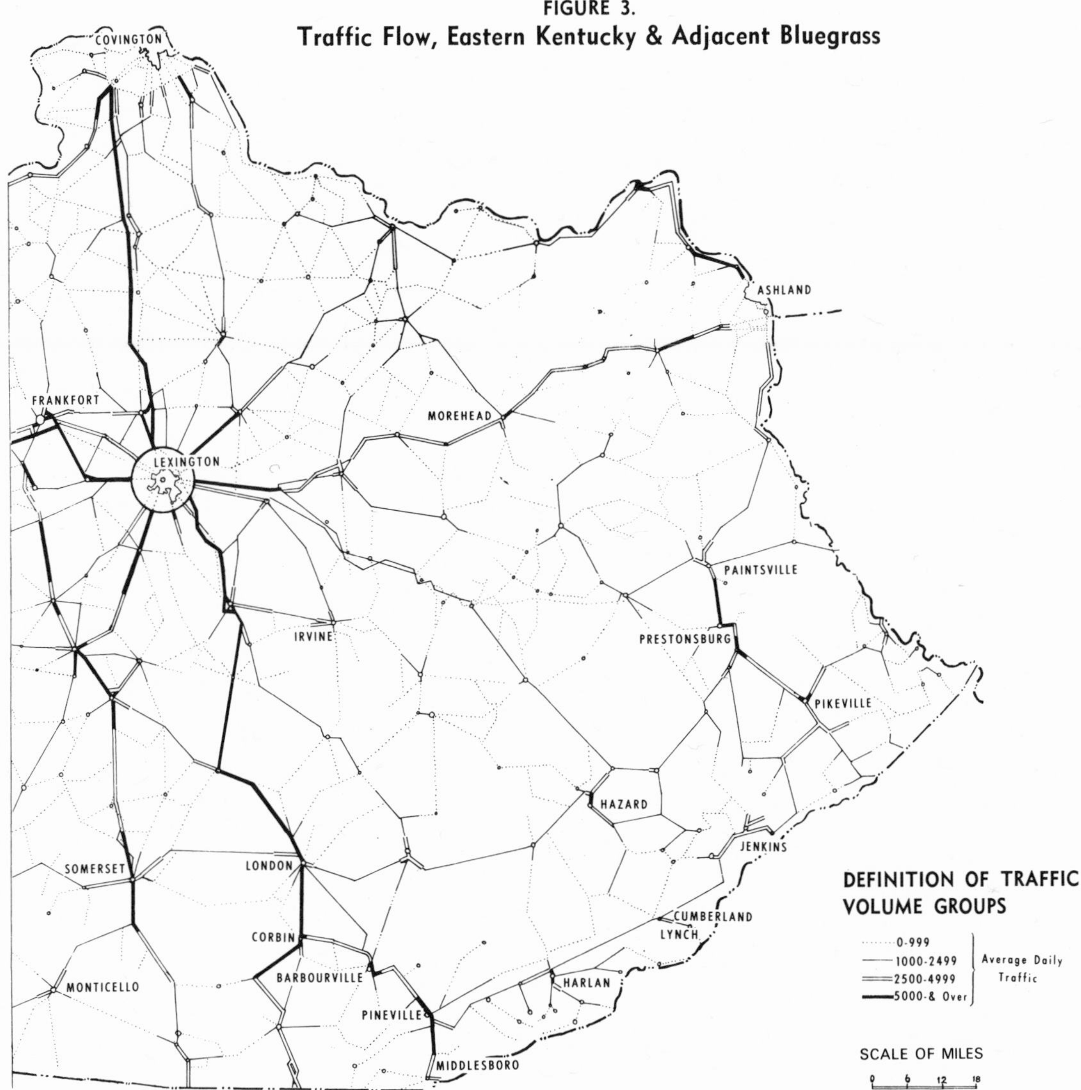

northern and southwestern parts of the area. Lexington, in the heart of the Bluegrass, is of course outside of eastern Kentucky and, despite its proximity to the mountains, Ashland is also a place apart and has not been included in our study of eastern Kentucky elites. What the dot map cannot show is the continuing movement down out of the hollows and into the relatively larger mountain settlements, a movement that has long gone on, but one which has accelerated recently and is reducing the most severe incidence of isolation among mountain people.

Figure 3, which depicts the flow of traffic in 1965, underscores the sparsity of communication in the area between the interstate highways across the northern and the southwestern margins of eastern Kentucky. (Effective mountain communication along those highways should not be overestimated: much of the traffic merely traverses the area, but the people of the northern and the southwestern counties are in closer communication with outside urban centers than are those in other mountain counties.) The flow of traffic between the Bluegrass area around Lexington and the eastern mountain region becomes slight at the Cumberland escarpment, though the flow along the new Mountain Parkway (from Lexington to the vicinity of Hazard) was sufficient to show up as a solid line on the 1965 map. The modest scale of this traffic will be better appreciated if it is compared with the population density patterns shown in Figure 2; this is light traffic relative to the densities of resident populations at the terminus of the parkway and in the coal towns that lie beyond it.

In his first study,[13] Plunkett undertook a factor analysis of variables selected initially to explain local differences in the proportions of youth continuing into and completing high school instead of dropping out after elementary school or failing to complete the twelfth grade. Using the county as the unit of observation, he did this analysis for eastern Kentucky alone, for eastern Kentucky including the Lexington area (hereafter called "eastern Kentucky extended"), and separately for Appalachian parts of West Virginia and Tennessee. The Tennessee and the West Virginia results conformed to the central place patterns hypothesized, but neither of the Kentucky analyses came out in that way. For Kentucky three distinct factors showed up: the first Plunkett labeled modernization, the second selected out areas with high population density (Lexington and the coalfields), and the third combined his three school continuation rates while also giving a moderate weight to out-migration.

Table 1* lists the variables used and their factors for eastern Kentucky extended. The Factor I (county modernization) scores for eastern Kentucky extended are shown by quarters on Figure 4, which matches to the finest detail an isolation contour map drawn by Bowman ten years ago and included in *Resources and People in East Kentucky*.[14] The map had been based solely on travel time and frequencies of trips to the nearest major city, together with frequency and extent of contacts of local manufacturers with people in cities outside the mountains.[15] The clustering of economic, cultural, and communication variables is strikingly displayed in this mapping of Plunkett's Factor I, which sums up a number

FIGURE 4.
Modernization Scores, Eastern Kentucky Extended

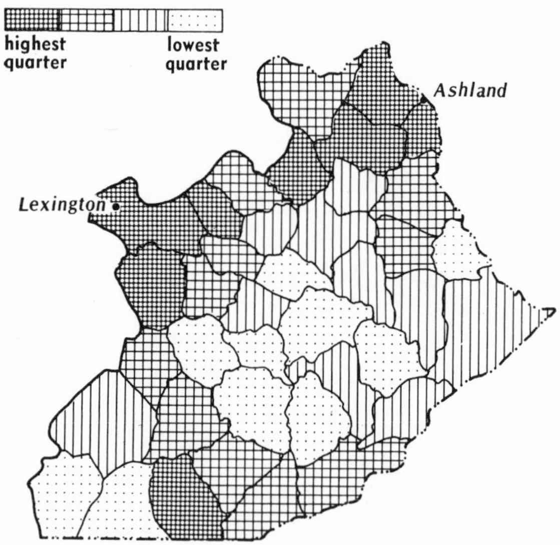

of important facets of the social ecology of the mountains.

The handicap to an area's society and economy inherent in geographic dispersion and inaccessibility has been often noted, and there can be no question that for eastern Kentucky this has long been a serious problem. The clustering of traits in Factor I (Table 1) is sufficient evidence of the interplay of physical isolation, economic poverty, and cultural backwardness—mutually reinforcing phenomena. For example, high birth rates lead, despite high out-migration, to high dependency ratios, to low per capita and family incomes, to malnutrition, school dropouts, more unemployed and more out-migrants, and so on. The isolation that allows these processes to remain unchanged by events in the larger economy contributes to the frustration and alienation of

---

* Tables begin p. 95.

13. H. Dudley Plunkett, "Determinants and Limiting Factors in the Diffusion of Educational Components of Social Change," a paper read at the Annual Meeting of the Society for Applied Anthropology, Lexington, Ky., 1965.

14. Bowman and Haynes, *Resources and People in East Kentucky*, p. 30.

15. Nevertheless, at that time it was almost a perfect match for a map of human fertility rates.

disadvantaged elements of the population, to the typically low level of financial support given to education, to a general limitation of perceptions and aspirations, and to the rejection of national agencies or even extrafamilial local community associations. Nineteenth-century stereotypes hang on, together with an extreme political localism. Government is felt to be dysfunctional in direct relation to the scope of its activities and the threat it may hold for the status and influence of the county-seat establishment. A personalized, small-scale society, suffering both physical and social isolation from the wider national scene, provides a haven for those who stay home; but the associated psychic isolation from the norms and values of the national society leaves men more fearful than prepared, more insecure than confident in any situation that requires interaction with that wider society.

The same factors constraining the development of national institutions within Appalachian Kentucky—namely its ecological fragmentation and its culturally insulated attitudes[16]—also foster a segmental structure that seems to typify institutions within the area.[17] The valley settlements, still frequently separated by long, winding, and ill-paved (or unpaved) roads, harbor many churches, school systems, civic and political groups that confine their separate interests within narrow physiographic bounds. In eastern Kentucky a man can set up his own church in competition with his neighbor's without benefit of any wider affiliation. The very closeness and the inward character of local life have evoked bitter personal conflicts along family, religious, and local political lines. Yet at the same time there is a common defensiveness against the outside world, and strong local commitments and loyalties are deeply entrenched among the mountain people.

Whatever the starting point, conditions such as these must surely force a reconsideration of development policies to give more heed to the development of people and to the quality of life in the mountains despite many economic handicaps. How can the mountain communities of the future be made better places for those who remain, and how can they come to provide enlarged opportunities in life for both those who will stay and the many who will leave? No matter how much may be done to subsidize physical aspects of community development, the critical concern must certainly be with people—the development of people as individuals and as members of a community. If these assumptions are sound, obviously we must seek to understand the avenues of communication within the mountains and between the mountains and the outside world.

Theories of Communication in Modernization

A study of the potential modernizing roles of elites in Appalachian Kentucky seems to require an interdisciplinary approach. Accordingly the theoretical framework of this study lies at the convergence of diverse streams of thought in the social sciences, and certain themes are most relevant. 1. The "human investment revolution" in economic thought[18] has precipitated a widening range of concerns about productive roles of human beings and the determinants of their productivity, including, in recent work, a human-resource view of change agents. 2. Studies of the patterning of social interaction that are of direct interest to us have appeared in several disciplines, but primarily in the work of human geographers and sociologists on diffusion and communication. 3. Also relevant are the investigations of power relationships, conflict, and sociopolitical mobilization in the literature of political science.

This study of mountain elites as interstitial persons who potentially can function as cultural bridges[19] derives from these sources. We are

16. These localist attitudes are vividly described in Harry M. Caudill, *Night Comes to the Cumberlands* (Boston: Little, Brown, 1960).

17. A collection of related studies supports this observation, along with Caudill's conclusions: see Thomas Ford, ed., *The Southern Appalachian Region: A Survey* (Lexington: University of Kentucky Press, 1962).

18. Mary Jean Bowman, "The Human Investment Revolution in Economic Thought," *Sociology of Education* 39 (Spring 1966): 111–37.

19. The term "cultural bridge" and its application in this study in communication is owed to the article by Schwarzweller and Brown; the interstitial person and cultural bridge constructs were developed by Plunkett and originally applied in a study of Appalachian Ken-

concerned with assessing the availability of human resources and observing the extent of their mobilization both for the development of the productive potentials of mountain youth and for the modernization of mountain communities or institutions. We will be concerned empirically with exploring how far the attitudes and community participation of interstitially placed individuals are compatible with their effective transmission of ideas and the involvement of increasing proportions of the population in the modernizing process.

A New Economics of Human Resources for Development

Only by identifying what human resources do (or, better, what they have the potential of doing in alternative uses) can we determine what they are. And only when we can say something about what they are can we proceed to analyze how human resources are formed.

Practical men have long known that in any advancing enterprise the most valuable men were those able to communicate, to search for solutions, and to adapt rapidly and creatively to change. But only recently have economists concerned with investment in human capital or with the productive contributions of "embodied education" begun to take hard looks in this direction and to introduce a dynamic view into economic models that was missing from the initial static formulations concerning schooling and on-the-job learning.[20]

In searching for determinants of growth and in studying the nature of technical change, economists have had to come to a more systematic examination of how human resources jointly contribute and adapt to dynamic growth processes. Richard Nelson, for example, in his research into the economics of research and development, has argued that the critical role of schooling in an advanced economy is the formation of the ability to adjust quickly when innovations are introduced.[21] Given the increasing awareness of the importance of organizational innovation in the sum of so-called technical change, such inferences have a wide application; but this also points up the fact that the interplay betwen human-resource development and innovation includes communication and dimensions of human interaction that are normally ignored when technical change is visualized as primarily a change in physical capital. It would seem that here again we must give more attention to the information and communication potentials associated with more widely diffused human-capital resources, and to the importance of communication networks linking subpopulations both geographically and in social space.

Social Interaction & Modernization

Communication facilities, whether we see these in relation to physical separation or to the social structure, are a distinguishing feature of modern societies. Macrosocial theorists, from Durkheim to Parsons, have stated the widely observable principle of social evolution: social (or "moral") density is imposed upon physical density in human settlements.[22] The structural-functionalist sees large-scale change in society as essentially the differentiation of social institutions—movement away from institutions with diffuse functions toward those with specific functions.[23]

To take a concrete example, the company town (which flourished during the coal booms of eastern Kentucky as well as in the industrial development of many other parts of the nation) was a

tucky elementary teachers. See H. Dudley Plunkett, "The Elementary School Teacher as an Interstitial Person: An Essay in Human Ecology and the Sociology of Communication" (Ph.D. diss., University of Chicago, 1967).

20. For the accepted theoretical formulation see Gary S. Becker, "Investment in Human Capital; A Theoretical Analysis," and Jacob Mincer, "On-the-Job Training: Costs, Returns and Some Implications," both in *Investment in Human Beings*, ed. T. W. Schultz (a special supplement to the *Journal of Political Economy*, Vol. 70, No. 5, Part 2, October 1962).

21. See especially Richard R. Nelson and Edmund S. Phelps, "Investment in Humans, Technological Diffusion, and Economic Growth," *American Economic Review* 56 (May 1966): 69–76.

22. The terms physical and moral density are those used by Emile Durkheim in *The Rules of the Sociological Method* (New York: Free Press, 1964), pp. 113–14.

23. A succinct statement of this theoretical framework is contained in Talcott Parsons, "Some Considerations on the Theory of Social Change," *Rural Sociology* 26 (September 1961): 219–39.

multifunctional institution within a particular subculture in a segmentally ordered society. In the process of modernization the company town is being displaced by unifunctional institutions that cut across multiple residential and other structural features of the community. Thus the umbrella institution of the company town, with its pervasive involvement with the work, home, and commercial dealings of the miner, is replaced by the specialized plant, the variety of stores, the estate agent or municipal housing agency, state and private medical facilities, and so forth.

In suggesting that modernization consists of enlargement of scale and differentiation of social organization, deferring for the present the question of social mobilization, we adopt Durkheim's distinction between physical and social density. As the diffuseness of traditional institutions (family, church, or company town) is reduced, there may be some reduction in the density of internal communication within the local or primary enclave. Correlative with the differentiation and specialization of institutional functions, however, will be an extension of the scope of interactions, which in turn fosters increased contacts with the larger society, hence greater social density and cultural integration in a wider context. Although we make no attempt to analyze the institutional structures in Appalachian Kentucky, this inexorable acculturation process, in which changing institutions condition social communication, forms the social context within which the interstitial person operates and which he alters by his cultural-bridge function.

Regional scientists have probably provided the closest approximations to empirical tests of macrosocial theories such as those of Durkheim and Parsons—a contribution that reflects their concern with changes in scale and social organization as observed in a variegated human ecology. The concepts of urbanization (as the ordering of human life in compact settlements, the functional approach to central places, intercity relations, and hierarchies of dominance,[24] or systems of cities[25]) have been extensively operationalized.[26] At the same time the concept of hierarchical systems of cities and applications of this idea to analysis of communication have limited relevance to the peculiar spatial, socioeconomic structure of Appalachian Kentucky.[27] Our attention is centered more on a microlevel of analysis, with individuals as the units of observation.

The cultural geography of Torsten Hägerstrand[28] stands between the more aggregative analyses of most regional scientists and our micro approach. He has analyzed the diffusion of a variety of items and practices, both among individuals and as community goods (such as schools, public baths, and sports halls). Ignoring substantive details and the more technical aspects of his research, we confine our comments here to Hägerstrand's basic concepts: (1) "information fields" as spatial (and also social-status) communication networks through which new practices, institutions, and attitudes are diffused; (2) "resistances" which explain why, with any given intensity of "tellings," given traits are or are not taken up, and with what speed.

Hägerstrand's main emphasis is on the development and empirical testing of the "information field" in his theoretical framework, which he has done with finely detailed evidence demonstrating the stability of paths of influence or "tell-

24. Donald Bogue, *The Structure of the Metropolitan Community: A Study of Dominance and Subdominance* (Ann Arbor: University of Michigan Press, 1951).

25. Brian Berry, "Cities as Systems within Systems of Cities," in *Regional Development and Planning*, ed. John Friedmann and William Alonso (Cambridge: M.I.T. Press, 1964).

26. See, for example, Otis Dudley Duncan and Albert J. Reiss, *Social Characteristics of Urban and Rural Communities* (New York: John Wiley, 1956) or the major attempt to provide a statistically validated functional map of the U.S.: Donald Bogue, *State Economic Areas: A Description of the Procedure Used in Making a Functional Grouping of the Counties of the United States* (Washington: G.P.O., 1951).

27. Evidence as to the inapplicability of such ecological models to the study-area was presented in Plunkett, "The Elementary School Teacher as an Interstitial Person," Chapter 1, and was summarized earlier *supra*, (p. 8).

28. For a recent application of Hägerstrand's approach, see his "Quantitative Techniques for Analysis of the Spread of Information and Technology," in *Education and Economic Development*, ed. C. Arnold Anderson and Mary Jean Bowman, (Chicago: Aldine, 1965), pp. 244–80.

ings" through space and time.[29] Among other things he shows that the spatial character of the communication network is much more complex than the traditional geographer's use of spatial gradients or isocontours would suggest. Thus diffusion of knowledge and practices jumps across intervening spaces with personal communications from one major innovative center to another, and from such a major to its secondary centers, with local tellings and adoptions of practices building up around each of the major and minor nuclei of a quite stable information field. Information fields differ with the kinds of messages or the types of senders and receivers; thus the more highly educated members of a society may exchange information over a much wider geographic area than that characterizing the bulk of a population, and similarly the channels of tellings differ. He also argues that patterns in the diffusion of innovations among individuals and communities ultimately depend upon intensities of face-to-face interactions. Whatever the spread of mass media, their effect depends upon the networks of interpersonal tellings (as evidenced, for example, by migration patterns or patterns of telephone conversations). All these observations apply to the network of communications in the Kentucky mountains and between them and outside urban centers.

Economists have tended to assume the presence of a very dense, undifferentiated network of tellings in their assumptions about perfect knowledge, even though "the economics of information" has recently attracted increasing attention. Meanwhile concern with the economics of education must inevitably lead to more critical analysis of information flow—how this flow affects levels of investment in human resources and how it is affected by the kinds and amount of education embodied in the population. It could be argued with considerable justification that this may be the most critical aspect of the ways in which education contributes to rising productivity and growth in the national income. Sophisticated analysis with this emphasis is just now beginning to appear, and it will unquestionably draw increasing attention among economists in the future.[30]

Until now economists have been most at home in analyzing the resistances in Hägerstrand's model. In conventional economics Hägerstrand's "resistance" becomes degree of potential profitability; if profit prospects are high, the new practice will be adopted, and vice versa.[31] But profitability can also be viewed more broadly to include the profitability of investment in one's self. In this case the geographic diffusion of school continuation rates is "explained" by the profitability of such investments to populations in particular areas, to populations with differential labor-market opportunities (men versus women or white versus nonwhite males), or to persons facing different investment costs (access to funds, for example).

Resistances are not necessarily economic, however. They may also be attitudinal—as in the gap between a traditional culture and the culture in which certain tellings originate. Education can thus appear on either the information field or the resistance side of the model, the economic calculus quite aside. Diffusion of ideas requires men who bridge the gap and serve as intermediaries both to transmit messages and to interpret them.

If an attempt is made to discern the pattern of what Hägerstrand calls the "invisible system of channels and sluices governing the flows of influence,"[32] clearly we cannot confine the study to ecological factors alone, nor is it sufficient to make case studies of individual profiles of communication behavior. Social density may be re-

29. Torsten Hägerstrand, *Innovation Diffusion as a Spatial Process* (Chicago: University of Chicago Press, 1967). This is a translation from the Swedish *Innovationsförloppet ur korologisk synpunkt* (Lund: C. W. Gleerup, 1953).

30. Especially interesting with respect to developing nations is the work of Dharam P. Chaudhri, "Education and Agricultural Productivity in India," (Mimeographed), Delhi School of Economics, 1967. Other studies in which economic models and certain aspects of Hägerstrand's work are fused are being carried out at the Comparative Education Center, University of Chicago.

31. The study of diffusion of hybrid corn, by Zvi Griliches, is one of the most dramatic (and earliest) exemplifications of this approach. See his "Research Costs and Social Returns—Hybrid Corn and Related Innovations," *Journal of Political Economy* 66 (October 1958): 419–31.

32. Hägerstrand, "Quantitative Techniques."

garded as a varying density in networks of tellings, but it can be fully understood only when attention is directed also to the processes by which social institutions intensify and modify the communication networks, and to the strengthening or weakening of resistances to acceptance of one kind of message or another.

The ecological analyses of the regional scientists and cultural geographers are complemented, from the perspective of our interest in modernization, by the empirical study of communication in sociology. Much of the latter stems from the long and well-documented experience of American rural sociologists who have investigated the diffusion of innovations. The rural sociologists were particularly interested in the effectiveness of extension programs (alone or in combination with other channels of communication) in bringing the results of agricultural research to farmers and in influencing them to adopt new practices. The early work centered primarily upon identifying the characteristics of particular individuals in initiating and accelerating the diffusion process. However, as Rogers points out,[33] rural sociologists never integrated their findings into a theory of diffusion. He cites, for example, the important and frequently replicated finding that the cosmopolite who is in touch with a variety of outside sources of information is normally only able to bring to others in his local environment the awareness of an innovation. People who are most strongly identified with a particular locality, rather than mainly with the outside world, can most effectively convince neighbors to accept and use an innovation.

A similar but quite separate development took place in the field of mass communications. That mass communications could and would remake a society, for better or worse, is a theme which has been played upon heavily in both popular and academic writing by a number of sociologists ever since the advent of radio. It was assumed that audiences could be manipulated easily and that attitudes or commercial habits could be changed by merely presenting messages through prestigious mass media. This view, which takes the susceptibility and attentiveness of audiences for granted, has carried over, often in scarcely modified form, into the work of some contemporary social scientists who write about developing societies.[34]

A series of voting studies begun in 1944 and culminating with the publication of *Personal Influence* in 1955,[35] seriously questioned previously held views of how mass media operate. It was shown, for example, that the shifting of political support from one candidate to another during an election campaign could be better explained by interpersonal influences among peers than by individuals' exposure to the mass media, and opinion leaders were found within each social stratum. Lazarsfeld and Katz conclude in *Personal Influence*: "The response of an individual to a campaign cannot be accounted for without references to his social environment and to the character of his interpersonal relations."[36] In fact the notion that the mental set of an individual monitors messages from the mass media and shuts out dissonant elements was one of the first qualifications to the mass-influence theory to be investigated systematically and accepted. These explanations illustrate the importance of the personal element in communication, which is by no means merely a question of the cultural superiority of the influential person or group, and they tend to stress the advantages of the two-way communication system for bringing conviction. This sort of reinforcement seems to be essential, even though the content of the communication may have first reached the influenced person through the mass media or from a person for whom he holds little esteem.[37]

This research led to the hypothesis—new to the "communications" sociologists, though not to the rural sociologists—of the potential ef-

33. Everett Rogers, *The Diffusion of Innovations* (New York: Free Press, 1962), p. 174.

34. For example, in Daniel Lerner, *The Passing of Traditional Society*, pp. 52–54.

35. Paul Lazarsfeld and Elihu Katz, *Personal Influence: the Part Played by People in the Flow of Mass Communications* (New York: Free Press, 1955).

36. Ibid., p. 25.

37. For example, it was found that physicians using new drugs often learned about them from drug company salesmen, but needed some professional support before prescribing them. See James S. Coleman, Elihu Katz and Herbert Menzel, *Medical Innovation: A Diffusion Study* (Indianapolis: Bobbs-Merrill, 1966).

fectiveness of less public messages, circulated through interpersonal channels. The notion of a personalized interaction function is linked to a "trickle-down" conception of communication, or a "multi-step flow,"[38] that corresponds to the commonalities and differentiations of class, status, and power, and other pervasive characteristics of the social structure, such as the type and strength of primary groups in a particular culture or subculture. The networks of habitual communication behavior are thus more significant than the more overt and specialized channels of public communication. This is indeed one of the propositions upon which Hägerstrand's analysis was based, and which his findings support.

Sociopolitical Mobilization in Modernization

Despite the usefulness of Hägerstrand's concept of resistance, there are specifically social and political or cultural interferences with processes of diffusion. (Naturally enough these are barely explicit in Hägerstrand's scheme.) The study of conflict situations and their repercussions upon social and cultural systems has been the domain of the behavioral school of political scientists, and they, more than others, have confronted the problems of mobilization and development of effective social pluralism. In studying the authority systems of societies, the social scientist can adopt a neutral stance. Weber did so, even though he could recognize the expansion of legal or rational authority over traditional and charismatic forms. In the same way one might hypothesize that the pluralizing of authority is becoming a characteristic feature of recent modernization processes.

Beyond this the political scientist gives us a framework for studying the allocation of power in a society and for measuring participation in its public affairs. Included within this framework are the extension of the voting franchise and shifts in evaluations of one another by sociopolitical groups. But even more important, from our point of view, is their concern with the degree of significant involvement by different sectors of the population.[39]

This active dimension of mobilization is particularly worth examining. We refer to the behavior of individuals and groups who pursue their interests according to their own values and definitions of the situation. For most members of a society the possibility of such behavior is excluded where monolithic systems of authority prevail, but it becomes less remote as a pluralistic political structure forms. Kornhauser[40] has characterized the pluralistic society of this type as a mass society in which elites and nonelites have open channels of economic comunication and enforceable sanctions on either side. Unfortunately, with the partial exception of contacts with the younger generation, we have not been able to examine interactions between elites and nonelites of the mountains, or to explore the participative behavior and attitudes of the latter. An account of such relationships and of the informal transmission of information and attitudes within the nonelite segments of the population would have to be taken before one could make a comprehensive assessment of modernization processes in Kentucky or any other area. By serving to provide access to information, ideas, and new social statuses, social organizational changes, including those of formal education, establish connections between groups or strata, between rulers and ruled; and they engender the willingness and capability to participate in the decision-making activities of the society.[41]

The Interstitial Person & the Cultural Bridge Function

Appalachian Kentucky presents a set of problems that includes inadequately developed human resources, low social density, segmented institutions, and sociopolitical conflicts against a

38. Elihu Katz, "The Two-step Flow of Communication: An Up-to-date Report on an Hypothesis," *Public Opinion Quarterly* 21 (Spring 1957): 61–76.

39. A recent attempt to review and assess the relevant research in this latter area is Lester Milbrath, *Political Participation: How and Why Do People Get Involved in Politics?* (Chicago: Rand McNally, 1965).

40. William Kornhauser, *The Politics of Mass Society* (Glencoe, Ill.: Free Press, 1959).

41. The most general relevant evidence upon this matter is presented in Gabriel A. Almond and Sidney Verba, *The Civic Culture* (Princeton: Princeton University Press, 1963). See also Schwarzweller and Brown, "Education as a Cultural Bridge."

background of widely shared cultural values which tend to inhibit modernization in step with processes at work in the larger society. Social scientists have shown that interpersonal communication has an important function in the diffusion of information, attitudes, and behavior relevant to innovation or change. There is consequently an obvious utility to making an operational test of such processes in the Appalachian context.

Whether we speak of government, education, or the functioning of formal and informal groups —within the given area or in the broader social and economic structure—we presuppose communication and the existence of comunication networks. In each case communication has many facets: the transfer of information; the maintenance of channels of contact; the process of acculturation or socialization; the processes by which some people bend others to their will, mutually agree upon a course of action, or agree to differ.[42] Communication requires exposure or contact, social interaction, and the diffusion of information, ideas, and understanding—including the capacity for interpersonal and intergroup empathy.

By the very definition of our interest in modernization we are concerned with both the stabilities and the modifications of information fields as they impede or foster such behavior or attitudes. The extension and alteration of information fields and the increase of cultural receptivity may be fostered, for example, by a statewide educational system or by the involvement of nonlocal persons in localized federal programs or in church or business affairs. Unquestionably social returns to investments in formal education result in increased levels of participation of educated adults in the diffusion of knowledge and ideas, both at work and in volunteer community service activities. Although the diffusion of schooling (with higher retention rates) is in itself a critical component of modernization, we touch on this only indirectly; as it may be reflected, for example, in contacts between school personnel and other educated adults or in judgments concerning local schools. Our focus is upon the position of locally resident elites in local and national information fields—and the messages they are likely to transmit—whether in the course of their regular work or in volunteer activities and leisure time. Whether contacts are strictly part of a job or not, it is the messages carried through the communication channels that are relevant. For example, volunteer social activities are in themselves manifestations of attitudes, and they may differ substantially from "regular" activities and from each other in their effects on how messages are perceived and how people react to them. But all these activities provide means by which development may be either blocked or expanded to reach increasing proportions of both youth and adults.

Plunkett has previously made use of the notion of the cultural-bridge function of intermediaries who served, by their activities and attitudes, to link together or to integrate the local community with the larger society.[43] The central construct around which that analysis was based is that of the interstitial person, who is located, by the nature of his training, work, and/or interests, between two cultural systems, participating to some degree in both. In the situation with which we are primarily concerned here, one of these is the "particularistic" social system of the locality in which he is residing, the other is the "universalistic" culture of the larger society.

Clearly the interstitial person may function as a cultural intermediary not only in the adult world, but also (or alternatively) he may bring local youth into contact with the national culture and economy into which, migrant or not, most of them will have to be absorbed if they are to become self-supporting and successful adults. Indeed it could well be argued that in any but a very short view the most important effect of cultural mediation from adult to adult will be the filtering down of such communications to widen perceptions and opportunities of the youth now in mountain schools. Partly this consideration and partly their unique position in the Kentucky

42. It is argued that social conflict can be understood as a form of social communication. See Lewis A. Coser, *The Functions of Social Conflict* (Glencoe: Free Press, 1956).

43. Plunkett, "The Elementary School Teacher as an Interstitial Person."

hollows led Plunkett to apply the interstitial person construct to an analysis of elementary-school teachers. For this analysis he used an ecological framework that located mountain teachers by degree of isolation and compared them with a control group in Lexington, which is outside of Appalachian Kentucky.

In the most isolated hollows the elementary-school teachers are the most numerous and sometimes the only persons with any exposure to the outside world, though many teachers are almost as local in experience and perceptions as their neighbors. This is especially true of the younger among them, many of whom in fact lack regular professional certificates. On the other hand, the more mature teachers in the isolated hollows, especially the few older men (who were less often natives despite their many years of mountain service), see themselves and are seen not only as carriers of knowledge and ideas to school youth but also as the chief sources of information (and the interpreters of it) among the adults. But while elementary teachers may have wider social contact than most other inhabitants of the most isolated locales back in the remoter hills and hollows, in the more populous of the mountain towns, other groups will stand in key positions as intermediaries between the local and national societies. Indeed they may be more effective than the teachers; for the basic requirements for performance of cultural-bridge functions include not only empathic identification in at least some degree with both inside and outside worlds, but also local acceptance as an influential participant in the local society.

We have concentrated attention upon local social, economic, and cultural elites and semi-elites as the bearers of cultural-bridge potentials. This is not to deny the importance of communications within other strata—for example, as young men who have been in the army bring their impressions back home or as migrants return. A special study of this communication network, which stands quite apart from the information fields in which local elites are direct and active participants, would be very much in in order.[44] That it is important in the Kentucky mountains is indisputable. However, studies of migrants from Appalachia in general and from eastern Kentucky in particular have demonstrated their tendency to remain in cultural islands within the cities to which they go, and those who return to Kentucky are typically those who have the least "psychic mobility."[45] In the past what they have brought back has presumably been limited, but it may not remain that way. Change is certainly in the air, and if the voice of "the poor" of eastern Kentucky has been weak, it is at least beginning to be heard. Attitudes of elites toward participation of the poor in local affairs seem of even greater importance today than when the present research was first projected.

The local elites, on the other hand, are more diverse than returning migrants in both experience and knowledge, and they clearly have a greater potential for understanding the complex characteristics of the national society. How they monitor the messages from outside is one of the important questions with which we will be concerned. While a study confined to the elites cannot provide direct evidence concerning what impact they may have as transmitters of ideas to other members of the population, we can infer some of the potentials and limitations inherent in the kinds of messages the elites give evidence of accepting and in the channels by which they repeat those messages (and to whom). Clearly it is only as messages reach the bulk of the population that regional modernization can effectively occur. Meanwhile forces for economic and social change in the mountains must in any event come to terms with members of the elites, old or new.

44. Research of this kind is now being undertaken and has been partially reported. See Lewis Donohew, "Communication and Readiness for Change in Appalachia," *Journalism Quarterly* 44, 1967.

45. Lerner, *The Passing of Traditional Society*, p. 52.

CHAPTER 2

The Interstitial Persons

Our task is to explore the potential of the Kentucky mountain elites for the performance of cultural-bridge roles in the development of the area and its people. The essentials in carrying out this task are: (1) the identification of groups in which such potential may be found; (2) the collection of evidence indicative of the intensity of exposure within these groups to experiences and influences from outside the mountains; (3) the classification of individuals according to the extent of their involvement with youth and their participation in political or civic community activities; and (4) the measurement of understanding about the local and national society and about mountain problems and prospects. Data on the last three points—on exposure, participation, and attitudes—constitute the basic content of our questionnaires and interviews.

THE STUDY SAMPLE

Elite Occupations

Groups in which potentiality for performance of cultural bridge roles might be found were identified on an a priori basis by their occupational affiliations. We did not assume, however, that membership in those occupations from which we drew samples is equivalent to the exercise of significant influence in a community. On the contrary one of our most interesting sets of questions distributes the persons in each of these groups according to different variables, which are related to how they look at community affairs, how active they are in community life, and how far they reach toward a mediating role in their communities. The alternative approach—that of starting out with sociometric identification of community elites—was dismissed as impossible to carry out over a wide geographical area. We should expect most of the more (along with many less) visible public leaders to be represented among the occupations we sampled.

Beyond the major requirement that members

of the sampled occupations should be spread through the thirty mountain counties included in the survey, the main criteria for inclusion of particular occupations were that they should encompass groups that are commonly well represented in local civic and/or political affairs, groups likely to be involved with youth and schools in a sufficient degree to serve as transmitters of attitudes and knowledge to young people, and groups whose members were likely to have more than an average knowledge of and contacts with people and institutions outside the mountains.

The occupations selected were bankers, lawyers, public officials,[1] clergymen,[2] physicians, and secondary-school teachers. These are supplemented by materials from the study of mountain manufacturers[3] and by questionnaire responses from participants in management seminars conducted at various mountain locations under the auspices of the Agricultural Extension Department and the College of Commerce of the University of Kentucky. Certain significant categories of persons holding key positions in the social structure of the area are omitted. For example, we did not include school superintendents or school board chairmen because of their small total number and the uncertain nature of their social influence. County judges, on the other hand, were included as part of a larger group of elected local officials (city mayors and members of county fiscal courts) who often rotate in office. The inclusion of magistrates reaches down into subordinate roles and much further up in the valleys and hollows, but for this very reason we encountered particularly severe difficulties in contacting this group, and representation of them is undoubtedly biased against the most isolated.[4]

All of the selected occupational groups, with the exception of local manufacturers, are equally considered in this research, but a number of differences in their status and characteristics make it convenient to distinguish a main sample (composed of bankers, lawyers, public officials, clergymen, and physicians) from the auxiliary samples of management-course participants and secondary-school teachers. Unlike the main sample, the management-course participants were self-selected to start with; that is, they cannot be said to represent any group but themselves. They tended to come from relatively bureaucratized businesses, and more were employees (in various white-collar and managerial ranks) than independent businessmen. They were also concentrated in a few counties, mainly those in which the management courses were held, but these counties were well spaced in distinctive subareas. There was, however, no reason to give any special character to our inquiries among this group, and they were given the same questionnaire as the main sample.

Some of the considerations that led to the prior study of elementary teachers as interstitial persons were noted in Chapter 1. That research was very much concentrated on formal education. For this study we decided to survey secondary-school teachers, who seemed in many respects to be more comparable to members of the main sample. We would expect all teachers to exhibit higher levels of educational attainment and wider social contact than most other inhabitants of the mountains and to be key figures in the most rural

1. Of the group sampled from lists of public officials only a minority (43 of the 97 cases) gave their primary occupation as such on the questionnaire. The remainder can be largely classified as involved in business at the managerial level (33 out of 54 cases); others were an assortment of bankers, insurance agents, and lawyers, with a few in other, unclassified occupations. Very few of those persons identifying themselves primarily as public officials gave any secondary occupation in response to our specific inquiry.

2. In the first stages of our analysis the clergy were treated as a single group. However, early results indicated that we were dealing with a heterogeneous group that had relatively little central tendency on many variables. Thereafter the clergy were split into two groups, Baptist and non-Baptist. This proved to be an important distinction.

3. A summary report of that study is presented in Mary Jean Bowman and H. Dudley Plunkett, *Communication and Mountain Development* (Final Report on Project 6--147–66, Economic Development Administration, December 1968). See Part II, "The Study of Entrepreneurs," (pp. 11–98), and Part IV, Selected Comments and Suggestions, pp. 158–72.

4. Coal mine operators, an important group in about a quarter of the mountain counties, were not specifically sampled in this study. However, their central role in the economy and society of the coal counties would have persuaded us to include them if our resources had permitted.

and isolated areas, with other elite groups playing equal or greater roles in countyseat towns and in other population concentrations. Teachers are from five to twenty times more numerous than are members of any other profession in eastern Kentucky, and their ratio climbs much higher for particular localities within some counties. Therefore, even if the input into the adult communication system of the society by the average teacher is small, the cumulative effect could be large.

The special characteristics of teachers' communication roles in mountain society, particularly with respect to youth, could not be surveyed satisfactorily through the main sample questionnaire, and a more appropriate special instrument was developed. One notable feature of the samples is that among all groups except the teachers there were almost no females; this being the case, we have treated female teachers as a separate category in our analysis, but we have not differentiated the very few females from the males in other categories.

The study of mountain manufacturers had a greater economic focus and was primarily concerned with entrepreneurial behavior. However, earlier work with this group has provided us with many clues concerning mountain society, attitudes, and communication behavior. Interviews conducted in 1966 had included a shorter preliminary version of the opinionnaire used in the present research. For comparison with responses of other elites, responses on that prior questionnaire are included in the analyses of some attitude items. Coverage of mountain wood processors employing twenty or more men and of other manufacturers employing ten or more is nearly complete, even though their numbers are small.

Sampling & Survey Procedures

Samples were drawn from lists of the respective occupational groups which we compiled from professional and denominational directories, state government rosters, and an unpublished list of the management-course trainees. Where less than complete coverage was attempted, samples were selected by taking names at fixed intervals from alphabetical lists by name and county for each occupation. Sampling was designed to secure distributions over the total study area in order to ensure that any major ecological effects from the more thinly populated or more isolated areas would come through in the analysis. The total samples, together with the sampling ratios and the returns from questionnaire or interview survey, are shown in Table 2.

No systematic difference was exhibited in the response rate between the groups surveyed by questionnaire and those who were interviewed personally. The low response from enrollees in the management courses did not improve with repeated follow-ups, and it may be partially accounted for by the fact that this sample had been involved, in a short space of time, in two surveys of an exacting nature. In view of the disparate character of this group we did not consider field interviews worthwhile and took the returns for what they were—the voluntary responses of a self-selected element of the business fraternity.

Another observation which should be recorded is that, among the sample populations approached in person, 8 percent had moved out of the area. Given that the sources of the sample lists were in all cases current or very recently compiled registers, we may assume a similar loss from the samples contacted by mail, even though we have no means of knowing the degree of selectivity involved in such loss. Moreover, many intended interviewees were never located by fieldworkers, and this, rather than any lack of cooperation from those contacted, was the major cause of failure in responses. The fact that this problem beset most of the fieldworkers to a similar degree itself speaks to our general emphasis upon the crucial role of communication in mountain development. The isolation of the area from other parts of the nation, as well as the internal isolation evidenced by our special difficulties in contacting the elected county officials, emphasizes the importance of those individuals whose contacts with the outside world are persistent and effective.

The geographical distribution of the respondents had certain features that should be indicated briefly. If we take the two most dissimilar areas—that is, the Kentucky River counties of central eastern Kentucky between the Cumberland escarpment and the coalfields on the one hand, and the southwestern counties of the study area on the other—the ratios of the respondent categories to one another are of considerable interest. In the middle Kentucky River counties, which typically lack even modest population concentrations, public officials are by far the most numerous group in the main sample. Apart from these local public officials and the teachers there is only a thin scattering from the standard occupations, even of full-time clergy. In the southwestern counties the main sample is weighted disproportionately toward physicians; at the same time this locale is the main area of Baptist activity in the mountains. We found, both during fieldwork among entrepreneurs and while establishing our sampling frame for this area, that there was also extensive involvement in the ministry by men who were mainly engaged in some other occupation.[5]

Content of the Inquiry

The format of the questionnaire or interview was identical for all samples excepting teachers and entrepreneurs.[6] In all but the entrepreneurs' questionnaire, however, the main objective was to explore the attributes of interstitial persons as potential resources in efforts to modernize the area; those potentials are viewed in terms of patterns of background experience, social exposure, communication behavior, development-related participative behavior, and attitudes toward the wider national society and current mountain development issues. Individuals characterized as interstitial persons by their background and previous exposure to the broader society may be hypothesized as reflecting that experience in distinctive communication-related disposition and behavior. In general such characteristics are viewed as independent variables, though there are important correlations among some of them—for example, between place of nativity and types of current (not merely past) exposure to the broader society. We may conveniently categorize four sets of items included in the questionnaires: 1. Personal background data: age and nativity, own education and training, parental occupation and education, primary and secondary occupations of respondents, loyalty to, or identification with, the Appalachian area, location within the study area. 2. Exposure to the broader society and communication with it: where educated, work experience outside the state and/or in large cities, military service, recent travel, newspaper reading. 3. Social contact and participation in political and social affairs of the community: political and civic responsibilities, contacts with youth, contacts between school and nonschool personnel. 4. Communication and development-related attitudes: views concerning Appalachian people and institutions, views relating to issues and programs in regional development. The distribution and clustering of traits within Set 1 constitute a backdrop for the analysis of relations among and within the other sets of variables. We therefore begin the empirical presentation with delineation of the Set 1 relationships.

---

5. It should be noted that a series of mishaps, including the temporary isolation of a town following the destruction of a bridge and an intense degree of local political sensitivity, prevented us from obtaining representative main sample respondents from one large county.

6. The questionnaires we used in interview and mail-survey studies are reproduced in Appendixes A and B. The "Economic and Social Leadership Study" (ESLS) questionnaire was administered to the main sample and to the management-course participants. The "Teacher and the Community" (TC) questionnaire, which was administered to secondary-school teachers, is shown without the attitude questions, the majority of which duplicate attitude items on the ESLS questionnaire. Some of the overlap on attitude items was obtained on a second, supplementary mail-out to teachers, however; of the 541 mountain teachers responding to the first mail-out, 377 responded on the second also. These 377 were similar in most respects to the 541, but they were somewhat older. Proportions by age were as follows:

	Age	Original Respondents		Second Respondents	
		Male	Female	Male	Female
	Under 30	38	30	32	25
	30–39	31	14	35	13
	40–49	19	22	19	23
	50 and over	12	34	14	38
Total	Percentage	100	100	100	100
	N	314	226	222	155
	N R on age	1	–	–	–

Background Characteristics of the Elites

Age & Nativity

Age differentiates men by length of experience and by perspectives on what constitutes a short or a long time. Age also marks generations designated by the conditions and societal moods in which men lived their most impressionable years. It is a crucially important factor in the nonvocational roles that men seek or to which they are admitted in community affairs. We expect a rising and ultimately a declining level of activity as we move from younger to older ages. Again, but only on the average, we expect more traditionalism, conservatism, and localism among the older men. Evidently age must be a prime classificatory variable.

A consideration of age structures in terms of replacement rates is also important, if we note that replacement is not only quantitative but may also entail a shift in attitude distributions among future mountain elites. Indeed, once the view of migration as a threat has been dispelled by a more sophisticated recognition that migration is a safety valve but not an answer, an opportunity but also a problem, the importance of these age patterns becomes more evident. Generations will continue to grow up in eastern Kentucky, and American society at large has a stake in the adequate performance of intermediary roles by local leaders. This requires the presence of qualified individuals who are closely in touch with the larger society while living in the mountains and functioning there as links or bridges to bring the outside world in and to support and strengthen those youth of the future who will leave. In this respect it is clear that immigrants into the area from other parts of the country have an important role to play, whether they come to stay a lifetime or only to serve in the mountains for a limited period. This suggests a joint examination of age distributions and place of origin.

The question referring to place of origin, which has been the basis for our tabulations on nativity, asked not where a man was born, but "In what place would you call yourself a native?" The intent was to allow persons who had spent a major part of their lives in places other than those in which they were born to signify their sense of coming from this other place. The distinction between local and nonlocal origin thus classifies as "local" men who called themselves "natives" of the mountains.

The age composition of the various occupational groups is given in detail in Table 3, while Table 4 uses a cruder age-break to analyze the age-nativity-occupation mix. In interpreting these tables it is necessary to compare the age structures of the various occupational (and occupation-nativity) groups in the mountains with age structures for the same occupations in the national population.

The local financial elites and politicians, as well as the lawyers (together the traditional wielders of power), are rarely under forty years of age. We may expect bankers anywhere to be older men, but in eastern Kentucky this is exaggeratedly so, with three-fifths over sixty years of age. The proportions of older men among mountain lawyers are markedly higher than among lawyers in the national population. The public officials, while not quite as old as lawyers, are nevertheless disproportionately over the age of fifty, no doubt a major fact in understanding local social institutions. These three groups are all 90 to 100 percent native to the mountains, with no substantial differences by age (except for a few young lawyers).

Almost equally local in origin are the male secondary-school teachers, but here the age structures are very different. Male teachers are both the most numerous and the youngest group (followed closely by female teachers); this fact sufficiently bespeaks the importance to mountain society of the resource potentials for human development in the teacher corps, not only within the schools but outside of them. It suggests nothing, however, about how far that potential is being developed or utilized, or about the forces that may draw the more alert young teachers out of the mountains instead of fostering their more effective participation in mountain life.

Except for the clergy, physicians are the least local; only two-thirds identify themselves as native to the Kentucky mountains. These native physicians are spread quite evenly among age categories, which makes them older on the average than physicians in the national population. There is, however, a flow of younger replacements.

The clergy are by all odds the most foreign group. Even among the Baptists only a third were mountain-born, though 60 percent were Kentuckians, compared to 45 percent of the non-Baptist clergy. Among the non-Baptists the proportions native to the Kentucky mountains range from only 8 percent among those under age forty to 22 percent among men in their fifties. The age distributions for the clergy, taken together with their nativity by age, witness the importance of rotations and continuing replacements from outside, especially among the non-Baptists. In view of the distinctive orientations of these men and their comparatively high cultural-bridge potential, it is of particular interest to know how far that capacity remains merely latent or how far these men identify themselves with their area and win acceptance in local organizations of a political or civic character.

The management-course participants of our study roughly match the age distributions among the clergy. They are younger than any of the other groups except the teachers, as is perhaps to be expected of men participating in adult educational activities. However, a quarter of these respondents were aged fifty or over, and a substantial proportion were in their forties. These men, like the entrepreneurs, are predominantly eastern Kentuckians.

Education

By the very nature of our selection procedure the men we studied are among the best-educated residents in the mountains today. Nevertheless more than two-fifths of the public officials, a third of the entrepeneurs, and a fifth of the bankers had not completed high school; in fact a tenth of the Baptist clergy eligible for our sample had stopped short of the twelfth grade (Table 5). College graduates were the exception in all the nonprofessional groups, but especially among the public officials and entrepeneurs; most of the latter, it should be noted, were wood processors.

Clearly the younger men in most groups (especially the bankers, Baptist clergy, and entrepreneurs) are better educated than are older men (Table 6)—an education-age pattern we would expect. It is reversed, however, among the public officials: two-fifths of the older, as against only one-fifth of the younger, public officials had gone beyond high school. Education-nativity comparisons (not shown) are significant only for the Baptist clergy and the management-course participants. In both occupations those men from outside the mountains were consistently the better educated, though the contrasts are not startling. If we consider all groups together, those who have migrated into the mountains are by far the better educated, but this reflects the fact that they are largely clergymen and physicians.

Family Background

The educational and career achievements of our respondents cannot have been wholly independent of early family backgrounds and environment, and indeed other aspects of their personalities and attitudes may be more closely related to early socialization than to subsequent experience. In view of the possible importance of such aspects of rearing, we use two indicators of family and early environment: parental education and respondents' attitudes toward living in the mountain area.

The most striking fact about the distribution of parental education (Table 7) is how far men in the higher-status occupations have advanced beyond the levels attained by their parents. Public officials come from the least-educated families. It should be noted that the parental category showing the least education (that is, neither parent completed high school) is the modal one for all occupational and age groups. The proportions of parents who had not completed high school are lower, nevertheless, than for the 1960 resident population of these counties, despite the fact that the fathers of our sample are close to two generations older than the average mountain adult of the present. As of 1960, 85 percent of mountain residents over twenty-five years of age had not completed high school.

The principal occupations of fathers of our

respondents are shown in Table 8. Immediately evident and important to bear in mind are the large percentages of fathers of public officials and of Baptist clergy who were farmers, even among respondents under fifty years of age. Of those who were not farmers, a substantial proportion were in the other primary industry, mining. Physicians, lawyers, and younger bankers show the most prominent inheritance for general type of occupation, if we except the special case of manufacturing entrepreneurs. Teachers were rarely the children of professional men.

The generation shifts in occupations from fathers of the older to those of the younger (under fifty) men are in the directions we should expect, but the magnitude of the shift varies substantially with respondent's occupation. For public officials there was only a slight decline in proportions with farm backgrounds, and the proportions of officials under fifty who were sons of miners substantially exceeded the proportions who were miners' sons among public officials over fifty. The rooting of public officials in the mountain economy and in the life of ordinary mountain men is a phenomenon that should be borne in mind in later chapters, especially when we come to examine their attitudes and opinions. The parental backgrounds of the younger bankers are very different (though the men are equally local, as Table 4 showed); two-fifths of the older bankers were sons of farmers, but only one of the fourteen men in our sample who were under the age of fifty came from a farm home. Although this contrast may be partly a matter of who attains such a position fastest, it is unquestionably a long-term change that will persist. So, of course, is the other most substantial shift, the decline in proportions of male teachers who are sons of farmers. But in this group, as among public officials, we can also see very clearly the reflection of shifts in the mountain economy fifty years ago—the opening of the coalfields and the rapid increase of mining employment during and after World War I.

Identification with the Mountain Area

The identification of eastern Kentuckians with their homeland has often been remarked and is indubitably strong. Our respondents revealed this characteristic in their answers to a question that contributes further to the delineation of local versus nonlocal men, but this time with respect to current place of allegiance (Table 9). For all but the clergy the highest response category is the first, the "most native"; this is overwhelmingly the case among the bankers and public officials. Many of the outsiders checked the second response, indicating an enthusiastic adoption of the mountains as a permanent home. But combining these two categories accounts for barely half of the clergy, who, followed by secondary teachers and entrepreneurs, are most likely to express some reservations about their present place of residence. The fact that so many of the clergy respond in terms of a temporary commitment to the area is clearly indicative of the contemporary tendencies in the style and rotation policies of their profession, especially for the non-Baptists. This might raise some questions about the continuity of development efforts which rely heavily upon this group, and the problem is only partially avoided with institutionalized involvement. But given the strong character and localism of traditional mountain society, some problems of integration into the local life must persist.

Relations between age and the intensity and nature of identification with (or rejection of) mountain life are indicated in Table 10. A third of those under fifty years of age express reservations (or are disaffiliated), as against a fifth of those over fifty. If we exclude the clergy and teachers (who are both younger and less fully identified with the mountains than the other groups), the overall proportion expressing reservations drops sharply, and it drops very decidedly among both the older and the younger men; we do nevertheless find something less than complete commitment to life in the hills among a sixth of the younger (under 50) bankers, lawyers, and businessmen.

Generally there is a positive association between a man's education and his readiness at the very least to qualify his enthusiasm about the mountains as a permanent home. That relationship is substantially modified, however, by occupation and the associated differences in places of origin and in the roles men play in mountain life. Thus the physicians, though they are the most highly educated, occupy only a middle position in the proportions voicing reservations. Moreover, the effects of education show up clearly within some occupations but not at all in others. Thus cross-tabulations not reproduced here showed that among clergy (of whatever denomination), almost all of those with reservations about or objections to the mountains as a place in which to live permanently are men with education to a B.A. degee or more; men with such reservations constituted half of the 125 college graduate clergy, two-fifths (7 of 18) of the clergy with some college education and only 2 of the 14 clergy with high school education or less. By contrast there was no such pattern for bankers, and the management-course participants were quite evenly spread among the three educational categories, both in total numbers and in proportions expressing reservations about living in the mountains.

Summary

Summing up some of the main characteristics of the samples, we find immediately evident the strong association among occupation, age, and nativity. This is important because the special interests of particular occupational groups (either as organized units or as categories of men with common training and roles) may be either reinforced or weakened by age-related interests and aspirations or by differences of origin. In age the comparatively young teachers of both sexes, regular clergy of all denominations, and management-course participants are set off from the older physicians and a secondary cluster of older female teachers (the female teacher age distribution is bimodal); but the female teachers in turn are typically not as old as the bankers and lawyers.

Indeed the coterie of banker, lawyer, and politician might be described as a gerontocracy. This is not to say that younger people are systematically excluded from these groups; it is more likely that local younger persons who might enter those occupations find alternatives outside the mountains more attractive and leave. A more open social system, with less concentration of power in the hands of an older generation, and a shorter apprenticeship before young men could attain positions of importance in local affairs might shift the balance in some of these choices, although it could not be expected to reverse the general trend.

We found it useful in a first approximation to group our respondents in three clusters. The first is the county-seat elite composed of public officials, bankers, and lawyers. This is the local establishment, which is quite diverse in education and can show few persons with advanced formal qualifications. These men are charged with most of the administrative functions of the local community. They were by all odds the oldest men, and the most native, regardless of age. The second cluster is made up of men who are certified to exercise ministering professions; their occupations do not give even near-automatic access to political influence or authority in the community. The members of this group are perhaps best conceived as being at two levels: the free professions, or clergy and physicians; and the teachers. Excepting the physicians (and a small set of older female teachers) these were younger men, though few other than teachers were under thirty. Virtually all of the administrative elites (bankers, lawyers, and public officials) were native to the mountains; the vast majority of the clergy were not. Indeed among the clergy there are varying degrees of nativeness (reflected in Table 4) which are of considerable importance in considering the chains of communication that may be needed to form adequate bridges between mountain people and the national society. In particular, the Baptist clergy tended to come from rural folk backgrounds, whereas the non-Baptists were much more cosmopolitan.

The third broad set in our sample is the businessmen—management-course participants and (where we possess relevant data) entrepreneurs. They are diverse in age, schooling, and degree of community involvement, but are generally accepted from the start as part of the mountain society that is "Us," not "Them."

As a way of summing up some of these key characteristics, we have grouped our respondents into the administrative elites, the professional elites, and the management-course men in Tables 11 and 12, showing how the members of each of these groups are distributed first on the combinations of nativity and area identification, second on combinations of education and area identification. Teachers are excluded from these tables. The main occupational subsamples are weighted to correct for the different sampling ratios used, and all entries in this and in subsequent chapters that refer to "administrative" or to "professional" elites are so weighted.

The extreme localism of the administrative elites, including those who have migrated into the mountains, is unmistakable. The professional elites are in sharp contrast not because of any polarization, but simply because a large minority of them are not natives, and half of the latter have reservations about permanent mountain residence; but even the professional elites on the whole strongly identified themselves with mountain life. The management-course participants fall between the two elites in these respects.

It is of course an oversimplification to treat such heterogeneous groups as are included in our sample as a trichotomy or, concentrating on the administrative "establishment" versus the "professionals," as a dichotomy, and we will of course return again and again to the original occupational categories. But if these two major sets of elites or potential leaders are indeed distinctive in their modal tendencies with respect to age, education, nativity, and local identification, we should expect to find associated differences with respect to their social participation and in their views of local people, institutions, problems, policies, and prospects. In the study of these samples we may also expect to learn about the distribution, availability, and limitations of local human-resource potentials for the communication of knowledge, the bridging of cultures, and the fostering of socioeconomic modernization in the mountains.

CHAPTER 3

The Social Mobilization of Mountain Elites

The cumulative involvement of individuals and sectors of a population in common understandings and in enterprises that transcend primary-group identification or other sectional interests is an important notion for this study, as it is for much of the literature on communication and social change.[1] These processes of involvement can be viewed at both aggregate and individual levels. They begin in childhood with experiences and training that affect the range of roles and of social participation of an individual in adult life. By virtue of our initial selection of occupations to be sampled, and by our delineations of the age, education, and nativity characteristics of respondents, we have already mapped out the more obvious traits that should bear upon potentials in the mobilization of Kentucky mountain elites for cultural-bridge roles. In the present chapter, which examines only overt indicators of mobilization, we consider first what we may think of as *passive* "exposure"[2] to experience outside the mountains. We then go on to examine "participation" or degree of *active* involvement in local mountain affairs. Active participation is broken down into degrees and kinds of involvement with youth on the one hand, political and civic participation on the other.

Social Exposure

Our primary concern in selecting variables to measure social exposure was to obtain indicators of past and current contacts outside the moun-

1. The appositeness of Deutsch's formulation (see his "Social Mobilization and Political Development, *American Political Science Review* 55) for our purposes rests upon a basically similar approach to communication and participation implied in his concept of social mobilization.

2. Cf. the active-passive dimension of political participation suggested by Milbrath in his *Political Participation*, p. 14.

tains, with the wider state or national life. Since we were proceeding to a more detailed treatment of active social participation and of attitudes and opinions, it was important that our measures of the more passive "social exposure" be as simple from the point of view of respondents as possible, to avoid overburdening the questionnaires.

Given the characteristics of mountain culture, particular interest attaches to evidence concerning whether an individual had ever lived outside the region—to study, to hold an ordinary job, to serve in the military—and whether he had had more urban experience than that available to him in Appalachian Kentucky, where the largest town has a population of barely ten-thousand persons. Information upon these matters is summarized in Tables 13 and 14.

It would of course be anticipated that professional persons would more often have received out-of-state college education, simply because they have received more education, but the contrast is impressive. Teachers, who have been to college quite as much as professionals, are much more in line with the non-professional elites in the limited extent of their out-of-state educational experience. Differences between the administrative and professional elites remain even when nativity is held constant; that is, even for the locally born and reared, professional education has led disproportionately to a widening of geographical horizons. The age breaks for professional men show a lower incidence of out-of-state college education among men under fifty than among those over fifty years of age. In part this is attributable to the previously observed decline in proportions of younger as compared with older physicians who are migrants to the mountains; we would expect such migration to be associated with a decline in proportions who have attended college in other states. But the lower incidence of men who had been to college in states other than Kentucky among the younger professional elites reflects also the greater weight of the Baptist clergy among them; the excess of younger over older Baptist clergy with out-of-state college experience is not sufficient to neutralize these other factors.

More interesting, because they can vary independently of educational level, are the data concerning proportions who have worked for a year or more in states other than Kentucky. Again there is a sharp contrast between the professional and administrative elites; but this time the difference is fully accounted for when we control for nativity. Nativity differences cannot explain the very low proportions of bankers relative to public officials who can claim such experience, however. Nor can education (not shown in the table) explain that contrast. Presumably what we are observing is the occupational inheritance already noted in Chapter 2, but shown up here even more sharply, however indirectly. The local bankers are preponderantly men from the upper crust of mountain families, and from the start there has been a favored place for them, along with a family obligation to fill it.

Military service has been most common for lawyers and physicians, and least for the clergy. Apart from the war generation, whose experiences have undoubtedly been of significance for the region (and among all segments of its population), one finds little generation difference in military experience.

Our only direct information on the types of outside environment respondents have known is the size of the largest city in which they have worked for a year or more (ESLS Questionnaire, A. 8). Once again the bankers are notably provincial, and there is a sharp contrast between the combined administrative elites and the professional groups—especially marked if work in a city of 50,000 or more is considered. Age bears little relationship to experience in such cities, though the youngest and oldest members of the administrative elites contrast sharply in proportions who have at least worked in towns bigger than any in the Kentucky mountains (i.e., over 15,000). Moreover, controlling for nativity we see no difference between the administrative elites and the professional elites in proportions who have worked in towns of 15,000 or more; roughly two-fifths of the native eastern Kentuckians and two-thirds of the non-natives have done so in both cases. Teachers of both sexes are limited in their urban experience, but in their experience of city life even the female teachers can match or better the bankers of the Kentucky mountains.

These tables present a clear picture of associations among education, out-of-state schooling or work, and city living, even if the war and demands of the draft have functioned as a leveler in exposing people of Appalachian Kentucky to the world beyond the mountains. The effects of these differences appear to be an impressive gap in experience between the administrative and the professional elites. Teachers and businessmen are close to the level of the administrative group on these measures of social exposure. But remarkable also are the contrasts between the comparatively wide experience of public officials and the extremely limited geographic horizons in the experience of bankers. Paradoxically, this suggests both severe constraints on the vision of members of the local establishment and unexpectedly wide geographic contacts that should contribute significantly to their cultural bridge potentials. Even if out-migration claims large proportions of the more able members of the community, the area still contains substantial numbers of persons among the administrative as well as the professional elites who have spent time away from home, or who have left homes elsewhere to work in the mountains.

Two items that serve as indicators of continuing contacts with the nation's urban society are presented in Table 15. The first of these is proportion reading an urban daily newspaper (ESLS questionnaire, A. 29–34). Those proportions range from 73 percent among the Baptist clergy and 77 percent among the public officials to 93 percent and 96 percent among lawyers and bankers respectively. Reinforcing the localism of the public officials is the fact that (this time with the bankers) they are the group that had traveled least to large urban centers during the past year (ESLS questionnaire, A. 19–28). Indeed, even the lawyers made fewer visits to urban centers than any of those we have categorized as "professional elites," barring teachers; in this as in many other respects there is a strong contrast between the administrative and professional elites. The management-course participants occupy a middle ground, with stronger urban associations than the administrative elites —a fact that should hardly surprise us, given their self-selection for the sample. Among the administrative elites, the oldest respondents (age sixty or more) showed little tendency to travel (only a sixth had visited five major cities or more during the prior year), whereas half of the administrative elites in all other age groups had done so; but there were virtually no age differences among the professional elites.

Education (not shown in the tables) made no difference with respect to travel among the professional elites, but it sorts out the administrative elites very clearly. Among the latter the proportions visiting five major cities or more were a sixth for those with only high school education or less, a third for those with some college, and 55 percent for those who had graduated from college. These figures are the more notable when we consider the fact that the contrasts between natives and non-natives were much less; for the administrative elites the figures were 39 and 46 percent of the natives and non-natives respectively in the "traveled" category, and for the professional elites the corresponding proportions were 58 and 69 percent. Allowing for either nativity or education (or for age), the professional elites are indeed the more traveled, but the importance of education as a factor in direct exposure to a wider geographic horizon among men who hold key positions in the local power structures is a phenomenon to be reckoned with in any evaluation of portents for future modernization in the mountains.

The Elites & the Socialization of Youth

Having reviewed their "passive" exposure and transitional information-seeking behavior, we can now focus upon the more critical "active" aspects of mobilization of our respondents. It is much more difficult to obtain valid and reliable measures of such behavior, and the task has been complicated here by the fact that we are interested in potential resources for the socialization of youth as a crucial variable in long-term social development. Clearly teachers are very directly involved, and we require certain information from these persons who are specially charged by society with the task of "forming" the young. However, the means at their disposal, and the ways in which they most directly act to attain such objectives, differ in some respects from those available to ordinary members of the adult community. On the other hand, the fact that a lawyer, for example, never had a class of pupils in front of him does not mean that he is without influence over the formative life experiences—even school experiences—of the young people in his community. On the contrary, insofar as he takes an active part in affairs of the community, and exercises influence or direct power over its resources and organization, he may be even more directly or more effectively changing the social environment of the young than is the teacher.

We might go further. As data already cited illustrate, in many ways teachers are relatively unexposed to outside influences. This does not mean that they have little of value to contribute, but it does suggest that relatively few of them are equipped to carry a heavy burden, even in the classroom, with respect to preparation of youth for participation in the national society. If the effective socialization of youth and the modernization of the region are tasks requiring the mutually supporting contributions both of teachers and of men occupying other roles in the community, it is important to seek such clues as we can find relating to contacts between and common undertakings of the major sample groupings—the frequencies and nature of teachers' contacts with the other elites on the one hand, and the degrees of involvement of administrative and professional elites with youth or the schools on the other. We will begin, a little obliquely, to look briefly at one or two indicators of the place of teachers in mountain society and their interactions with other adults, direct concerns with youth aside. We then go on to focus directly on evidence from the teachers' and the other questionnaires concerning involvement of members of the various elites in the activities and problems of children and youth.

Teachers & the Adult Community

Chances are better than even that a member of the non-school elites of this study will count one or more close relatives or intimate friends among mountain teachers and administrators. Proportions so reporting ran between 50 and 60 percent for lawyers, Baptist clergy, businessmen, and bankers, between 40 and 47 percent for the non-Baptist clergy, physicians, and public officials (ESLS questionnaire A. 10–11). Such variations among occupational groups as appeared with respect to the incidence of these relationships reflect both differences in proportions of the occupational membership who were native to the area and distinctive aspects of recruitment to and images of certain occupational roles, nativity aside. Thus among the administrative elites, those who had college degrees were especially likely to have close friends or relatives among school personnel—62 percent as against just under half for the less educated of the administrative elites. It is a matter of some importance that many of the members of administrative elites in the mountains lack the sorts of orientation to education that may come either from personal experience or through close personal contacts with friends and relatives in the schools. Among the professional elites the pattern is reversed. It is the men who had not been graduated from college (mainly Baptist clergy) who were the more often linked by blood or close friendships with school teachers and administrators—55 percent reported such associations, as against 47 percent of the college-graduate professional elites. But the differences among these groups should not be overemphasized. In no major grouping of our elites did proportions reporting close ties with school personnel drop below two fifths. The data give evidence of a strong familial or primary-group basis for school-community cooperation, however roles may be defined. The fact that teachers are numerous, and we cannot simply turn these figures around to specify proportions of teachers who had close ties with each of the elites, does not alter this fact—though it is also important to recognize that teacher experiences in community contact and participation are very uneven, even when we confine our attention to the teachers on the secondary school level.

There were two items on the teachers' questionnaires that provide some evidence concerning teacher involvement in community activities, or association with nonschool elites, other than in connection with children and youth. One of these asked for information concerning organizational memberships and activities (TC questionnaire B. 1–6). The findings are summarized by sex in Table 16. The data concerning affiliations with educational organizations are essentially similar for males and females, with higher proportions very active in local than in the national or regional organizations, though men were somewhat more likely than women to remain entirely aloof from the local organizations. Women, as we might expect, were the more often active in organizations sponsored by or affiliated with churches, though even among the men half reported such affiliation (not merely church attendance) and almost a third claimed they played active roles in such organizations. This, indeed, is where we should expect to find the most frequent involvement of school personnel in non-school affairs, especially, perhaps, in communities as small and personalized as those of the Kentucky mountains; such involvement does not necessarily carry over into secular affairs. It is all the more interesting, therefore, to find that a fourth of both the male and the female teachers claim that they take a "very active" part in one or more civic organizations, and a third of both sexes claim "active participation" if we include those who normally attend functions of such organizations as "active" participants. This is a minority of teachers, to be sure, but it is a substantial minority with civic involvements, nevertheless. If we consider all those who claim to be "very active" in any one or more kinds of activity (55 percent of the male and 59 percent of the female teachers), we find that there is considerable overlapping of types of involvement; two-fifths of the very active men and just over two-fifths of the very active women were so classified for two or more kinds of organizations (counting all educational organizations, local or not, as just one "kind"). These data for very active participation are summarized in Table 17.

The other question relating to community involvement of teachers (problems of children and youth programs aside) asked respondents to indicate the frequency with which they had discussed community affairs with persons in each of a specified list of elite groups over the previous year (TC questionnaire B. 38–46). The results indicated once again that teachers of the Kentucky mountains are by no means isolated from the rest of the adult community, although, as we should expect, the male teachers have somewhat more frequent discussions of this sort and with a wider range of persons than do the females. (The only category on which the females match the males is for local doctors.) As Table 18 shows, a slight majority of the male teachers and almost half of the female teachers claimed to have engaged in such conversations with school superintendents; some of them did this frequently. If we had not stipulated for ministers a "church *other than your own*," it may be that the clergy would have taken second place or competed with the school superintendents; even as it is they were included by 34 percent of the male and 29 percent of the female teachers. But more interesting is the fact that among male teachers over half reported discussions of community affairs with local businessmen, and business leaders took a strong second place with female teachers as well. As a comparison of the separate figures for local and nonlocal business leaders with those for all business leaders, regardless of location, shows, virtually all those who talked to businessmen in other counties talked to such men in their own county as well. Communication with bankers, lawyers, journalists, or businessmen in other counties characterized a fifth of the male and a sixth of the female teachers. To be sure, many of these nonlocal persons, defining "local" as the same county, may still have been mountain. Again, those who talk most with one category of the elites tend to talk also with others; this is demonstrated dramatically by the very small proportions talking to businessmen *only* or to school superintendents *only* as compared with the large minorities of women and the majority of male teachers who discussed community affairs with men in each of these categories. Tendencies for men who are active in one sphere to be active in others also have commonly been remarked; what is of interest here is that along with the multiplicity of directions of contact in mountain society among the more active teachers goes such a small percentage of nonparticipants; only a sixth of the male and a fourth of the female teachers returning questionnaires checked none of the categories of persons listed on the questionnaire.

Child-centered Contacts between School Personnel & Nonschool Elites

By centering on children and youth, we can look at the patterns of interaction between school personnel and nonschool elites from the perspective of the teachers and from that of the other elites in our study. This time we look at the teachers' questionnaire first. The teachers were asked (TC questionnaire B. 29–37), "During this school year, have you consulted or been consulted by any of the following concerning particular pupils who were NOT their own children?" The distribution of responses is shown in summary form in Table 19.

As we might expect under mountain conditions, it was the social welfare worker who was specified (checked) more often than anyone else; half of the male teachers and two-fifths of the female teachers reported that social welfare workers had consulted with them concerning pupils (not their own children) during the prior year. Just under two-fifths of the male but only one-fourth of the female teachers reported such consultations with any physicians, clergy, or public officials. Very few reported such consultations with any other nonschool persons, including businessmen. Nevertheless, if we take all A and/or D responses together (regardless of responses on B and C) we come out with two-fifths of the female and somewhat over two-fifths of the male teachers. These are substantial minorities of teachers contacting members of our elite groups in connection with problems of their pupils, even excluding consultations with parents. Nevertheless, there was also a sizable minority of both sexes (30 percent of the male and 37 percent of the female teachers) who reported that *no one* had consulted with them concerning a child other than his own over the previous year. These figures are substantially higher than the 16 percent of male and 24 percent of female teachers who reported no discussions about community affairs with men (or women) in a specified list of occupations, even though the latter list did not leave a place for entry of "other" groups, as did the question concerning consultations about pupils. In other words secondary-school teachers talk to other members of the mountain elites about community affairs more often than the latter consult the teachers about pupil problems at the individual level—though this does not tell us how far they discuss school affairs in general with these teachers.

The question asked of the nonschool elites was broader than that asked of the teachers: "Do you have conversations or consultations with teachers or other school people about programs or problems involving children or youth? (Check any that fit you)." The items to be checked (ESLS questionnaire A. 38–39) referred to frequency of such consultations and to whether they were in connection with the respondent's regular work and/or in connection with other, volunteer community services (some of which were specified). Adding together their contacts both as part of their regular work and as voluntary activities, professionals report considerably more actual discussion with teachers or school people concerning "programs and problems involving children or youth" than the administrative or business groups (Table 20). The difference is largely a reflection of the activities regarded by respondents as part of their regular work, however. If we take the voluntary and voluntary plus regular combined, but exclude "in regular work only" the percentages are 31 for the administrative elites and 30 for the professional elites. Participants in the business management course were the most active on a volunteer basis, with 41 percent in the two voluntary categories.

Nonschool Links of Adults with Children & Youth

Thus far we have considered adult links with youth only as these occur, directly or indirectly, through the schools or the teachers. But respondents were asked about their direct contacts with youth, and their consultations with other adults (outside of the schools) concerning children or young people (ESLS questionnaire B. 36–37 and B. 40–41 respectively). The former question distinguished between those reporting direct nonschool contacts with individual youth only and those who participated in community service activities with youth groups. The latter distinguished, again, between activities that the respondent identified as part of his regular work and those he viewed as outside of or beyond his professional or occupational role. Results of both questions are shown by occupation in Table 21.

Since the responses concerning youth-related contacts with parents and other adults more nearly parallel those concerning consultations with teachers, we look at them first. Clearly, as we might have expected, the proportions of clergymen and physicians who discuss youth problems with parents in the course of their regular work run very high, ranging from 81 percent for the physicians to 92 percent for the non-Baptist clergy. This is well over even the 76 percent (47+12+18) of professional elites (Table 20) reporting consultations with teachers. Looking at volunteer activities (regular work aside), we see that both proportions who reported consultations with teachers and proportions who reported consultations with parents about their children or young people ran consistently at about a third except among the management-course participants.[3] In noting the similarities among the elites so far as volunteer activity is concerned, it is important to remember, nevertheless, that those professionals who consult with parents in the course of their regular work do have special channels of communication. On account of their recognized roles or their presumed expertise they may generally (though by no means always) have easier access to the adults concerned, and they have greater frequency of such contacts. Whether, or to what extent, they have a coordinate level of involvement directly with youth or children is a separate question, however.

That question is partially answered by the last three columns of Table 21, referring to direct contacts with individual youth only or with youth groups (whether or not with individuals). It is immediately evident that the clergy are the most often involved in group activities with youth, as we might expect. They are perhaps the closest to teachers in their role vis-à-vis youth. However, the 25 to 30 percent of administrative elites involved in activities with groups of youth is impressive. This is not far below the 36 percent of male and 28 percent of female teachers who went beyond the call of duty, as it were, to join with nonschool people in the planning of community programs for youth. (See TC questionnaire B. 28.)

The proportions of our elites who claimed to have more than merely casual contacts with individual local youth other than relatives, even when they claimed no involvement in youth groups, ranged from two-fifths to one-half for all except the non-Baptist clergy (and, at 36 percent, the businessmen). Moreover, when we add the third and fourth columns together, to get proportions directly involved with individuals and/or youth groups, it turns out that 75 percent of the administrative elites and 82 percent of the professional elites are included. (For particular occupations the proportions range from 65 percent among the businessmen to 97 percent among the non-Baptist clergy.) In view of the fact that the question excluded contacts with individual youth who were relatives, we may conclude that, at least among members of these elites, the personalism of mountain culture may have a substantial community as well as a primary-group character.

Degrees of Youth Involvement & Their Correlates

We can bring together some of these separate items of information, and at the same time pursue the analysis into finer detail, by the use of a youth-involvement index that combines school and nonschool contacts of the elites (excluding

3. The business management-course participants seem much less inclined to engage in discussions with parents or other nonschool adults about youth or youth programs than to talk about these matters with teachers. Whether this result is spurious, and what it means if not spurious, we are not in a position to say.

teachers). When we constructed this index, the population was first categorized on the teacher contacts variable into (1) those having regular work and voluntary contacts, (2) those having voluntary contacts only, (3) those having regular work contacts only, and (4) those reporting no contacts. These categories were ranked 1 to 4 to represent decreasing active involvement with youth via the teachers. Respondents were then grouped on nonschool direct contacts with youth as (1) has direct contact with both groups and individual (unrelated) young people, (2) has contact with groups only, (3) has contact with individuals only, and (4) no reported contact. The two distributions were then cross-tabulated to form sixteen cells; in practice one cell was empty, and the remaining fifteen cells were split into three groups of five cells each, exhibiting high, medium, or low youth involvement respectively. Using these three degrees of youth involvement we can make some simple summary analyses of how various characteristics of our elites may relate to their mobilization vis-à-vis youth (Tables 22 and 23).

As by now we might expect, professionals are somewhat more likely to be high on youth involvement and much less likely to be low than are the members of the administrative elites. Men of under fifty years of age score higher than men over fifty among both the administrative and the professional groups. Within our samples education has less effect than age, the less-educated professionals appear as an unusually highly motivated group in their concern for youth; but what this really tells us is that the less-educated clergy are no less concerned with youth than are better-educated clergy. (Since physicians are automatically excluded in taking those with under sixteen years of education, all the "professionals" in the under sixteen years category are clergy.) Perhaps the most interesting of all the patterns shown in Table 22 are those for relationships with nativity. Whereas among the administrative elites the local men are low on youth involvement less often than the non-natives, the contrary occurs among the professionals.

The fact of being a nonlocal man cannot be construed as being automatically a quality of experience. The relevant experience is first-hand knowledge of the larger, and especially the urban, society—experience that can broaden identifications and generate a consequent greater potential to perform the cultural-linkage function. It is therefore pertinent to determine whether we can relate social exposure to youth involvement. If the more exposed elites have the more active relationships with youth, that is prima facie evidence that they perform the linkage function. The outstandingly youth-oriented professionals are in fact much the most likely to have enjoyed out-of-state educational experiences (Table 23). But it is among the persons of the administrative elites most concerned with youth that we find the lowest percentages with college experience outside Kentucky (or, for that matter, anywhere). More important among the administrative groups may be the positive associations between at least average youth involvement and the other two exposure indicators of Table 22: prior urban work experience and recent travel to urban centers. What all this adds up to is a very mixed selectivity into youth involvement. The educationally more humble of the administrative elites carry on with localist, familial traditions of the face-to-face society, in parallel with the relatively folksy activities of the Baptist clergy and the equally important, more sophisticated but less intimate, professional involvement of the non-Baptist clergy (whether in regular or in volunteer activities). Overall, however, these figures suggest a slight favorable bias in the degree to which the more rather than the less exposed of the elites have contact with mountain youth.

Political & Civic Participation

How far various elites are mobilized, or mobilize themselves, for active participation in public affairs is obviously an important question in any setting. It takes on special interest in the current eastern Kentucky scene and in the context of recent efforts by state and federal governments to foster Appalachian development. Both wittingly and unwittingly these governmental efforts have tended to bring into active public life men who had previously limited their concerns to their own business or professional affairs. Their social or civic talents lay dormant within the social context of traditional mountain socioeconomic and political structures. Much of the recent socioeconomic history of the mountains is reflected in (and has been affected by) attempts to organize town meetings throughout the region as part of an effort to mozilize the population at large in the area-development and economic-opportunity programs.

It is useful to distinguish two types of activity: formal political activity of the local governmental authority and the voluntary association of community-minded private individuals. We may refer to these activities as political and civic participation respectively, even though political activity in a broad sense is not excluded from the latter category. One pragmatic distinction between these two types of activity is that the political activities involve direct affiliation with the traditional agencies of government and/or political party organizations, whereas the civic activities involve affiliation with organizations and/or ad hoc activities that are, in principle, independent of the conventional political agencies and processes. So far as potential roles in modernization are concerned, we may also distinguish between political and civic participation by an analogy with the concepts of line and staff authority; the line has coercive power and the staff wins its influence through expertise—that is, knowledge, innovation, and adjustment.

In the literature of political science and sociology there is considerable evidence that political and civic (or social) participation are not mutually exclusive. Indeed many writers have demonstrated strong correlations, both at the group and the individual levels, between political participation and general social participation; political participation is then seen merely as a special case of participation in social and community activities.[4] However, in the Appalachian case, with the recent experience of the state and federal programs for area development and economic opportunity and recent attempts to introduce social innovations, we may doubt the applicability of that hypothesis. Local participation in innovative activities may not correlate, at the individual level, with formal political involvement. In fact for the Kentucky mountains we would be surprised to find any tendency for cases to group in the upper left cell of the following diagram of possible participation profiles:

		Political Participation	
		HIGH	LOW
Civic Participation	HIGH	Political-Civic	Civic
	LOW	Political	Inactive

Although to our knowledge no analysis along these lines has been undertaken in Appalachia, the climate of Kentucky political activity and community decision-making has often been described, and such accounts ascribe to the Kentucky politician the say-so on virtually all public matters occurring within his bailiwick. Until recently it could have been asserted confidently that little deliberately-sought or "engineered" socioeconomic change had occurred in the area without the consent of the local political authorities. Virtually the only major exceptions have been partial successes of the UMW in organizing mine workers. For our purposes it is then all the more essential to establish whether those who are the formal authorities are also active in a broader social or civic sense—or, whatever their activities, how far they share in the experience and attitudes of those who are civically active. If the politically and civically active are not the same people, it is clear that the modernizing potential of the civically active will depend to a considerable degree upon the existence of shared goals, and on the prospects for real cooperation that may link the two groups. If civically active men perceive goals or means to their attainment in a way that conflicts with the conceptions of dominant members of the traditional political establishments, they are likely to encounter repeated frustrations and often even to abandon their efforts. Successes will

4. Several studies reporting such findings are cited in Milbrath, *Political Participation*, p. 17.

clearly be more frequent when local power is less monolithic and/or when political leadership is responsive or even committed to change.[5]

Proportions of the various occupational groups who were active participants in political and/or in various civic affairs are shown in Table 24. Since a part of our sample was chosen from among elected public officials, the interest of the first column of this table lies in the rate of office-holding among men in the other occupations. The political activity of lawyers and bankers is very plain, with three-fifths of the former and two-fifths of the latter holding or having held political office, while businessmen take an intermediate position and professionals lag well behind. Among lawyers and bankers most frequently reporting political activities are persons in their fifties, though the proportions who have held office are high for all over age forty (Table 25). Only among the oldest of the professionals had as many as one-fifth been politically active. The low education of many of the public officials (shown earlier in Table 5) accounts for the negative relationship between education and political involvement among the administrative elites.[6] Nativity groups are not distinguished in Table 25. Nonlocals are indeed less likely to have held political office than are men native to the area, but if we control for occupation, nativity makes relatively little difference; there are just very few non-native bankers and lawyers, and very few professionals (even when native) are politically active.

Among the major types of newer civic activities were the county and area development councils, with an essentially physical-resource orientation, and the economic-opportunity committees, with a mandate to carry forward the objectives of the Economic Opportunity Act. In the second and third columns of Table 24 we see the extent of participation of our respondents in these activities. The likelihood of participation to the level of committee membership or office-holding is approximately similar for both types of association, and the rank orders of the occupational groups are almost identical when their participation in area development and in economic opportunity organizations is compared. Along with the public officials it is the clergy who report the greatest activity—especially the non-Baptist clergy, who are the most active group overall.

As a way of summing up the extent of civic participation we constructed a simple index of the number of *different kinds* of civic activities reported by each respondent; we allowed a score of one for an office or offices held in civic clubs such as Lions, Jaycees, etc., one for an office (or offices) in an area development organization, one for such a role in an economic opportunity committee, and one for active roles in other significant community activities (a miscellaneous set included in the last column of Table 24). The maximum possible score is four, no matter how many offices a respondent claimed. The index thus, by intent, distinguishes the persons who participate in a range of community enterprises, and avoids giving too much weight to churches or businessmen's clubs. Taking a score of 2 or more as the cut-off criterion for classification as active in civic affairs, it was still the non-Baptist clergy (40 percent) who were by far the most active, followed by the business management-course group (27 percent). At the bottom were the Baptist clergy and the lawyers (16 and 14 percent respectively). Although there did not seem to be any consistent age pattern for the participation of men within the separate occupational groups, we find that for professionals as a whole (Table 25) there is a negative relationship between age and civic participation, and the oldest men among the administrative elite also have the lowest scores. By contrast such participation was consistently high for all ages above forty among the management-course sample, but was low for the youngest of these men. The nonlocal men were the likeliest of the professionals to be active, but none of the small

5. It has been suggested that a sense of political efficacy is less likely to be developed in the American South than in other parts of the country. This study may give relevant evidence from a border area. See Angus Campbell, Gerald Gurin, and Warren E. Miller, *The Voter Decides* (Evanston, Ill.: Row, Peterson, 1954.

6. Among the professional elites it should be noted that men with less than a college degree are few and that the positive association between education and political activity is of doubtful meaning.

number of non-native public officials was active in "civic" affairs.

The Political & Civic Participation Matrix

It is now possible to fill out the cells of the diagram presented earlier. Table 26 shows the distribution of each of the elite groups across the four cells. (In view of the relatively insignificant nature of some of the civic offices reported, an individual was not considered civically "active" unless, as in Table 25, he had two or more as his score).

Whether we take all the administrative elites together (the first column of Table 26) or look at bankers and lawyers alone, we find little relationship between political and civic activities. On the other hand, among the professional elites and the businessmen there is a definite tendency for those who are active in one of these broad types of service to be active in the other also. Regardless of their degree of political involvement, one-fifth or less of the administrative elites were involved in civic activities, even though we included area development and economic opportunity agencies with "civic"; by contrast, one-fourth of all the professional elite group and the businessmen and over 40 percent of those among them who were politically active were participants in civic affairs. Among the professional elites and the management-course men, the civically active were more than twice as likely to be politically active as were those who were not civically active. However, professionals rarely hold political offices, and two-thirds of them were inactive on both the civic and political fronts.

Age appears to make very little difference to these distributions within elite groups (Table 27). That is, older men do not appear to be more or less active than younger men, nor to make different choices of activities, though they are marginally more likely to be political activists. Less-educated persons are less likely to be active except in political affairs (where we pick up especially the magistrates). Nonlocal lawyers and bankers are more likely to be inactives than their native counterparts; however, it is the non-natives among the professional elites who manifest the higher civic participation, though they virtually never hold political office. A tabulation of the "local identification" variable against political and civic participation (not reproduced) brought out the significant fact that persons who feel reservations about living in the area are no less likely to participate in civic activities than are persons who are content with it—22 percent for all respondents, whether they had reservations or not.

Information on exposure to the larger society may increase our understanding of the significance of these distributions for the diffusion or nondiffusion of modernizing attitudes and behaviors in the mountains. Our interest is not so much in taking political and civic participation as the dependent variable to be explained as in seeing the correlates of these types of activity, with a view to assessing their potential quality. Is the group with the most direct political power made up of men who would appear to have the capacity to act as agents of modernization, in the form of information and ideas diffusing from the larger society, and, conversely, how far do men with such capacities assume positions of political power?

The relationships between the various indicators of exposure and of participation differ substantially between the administrative and the professional elites, and between each of these and the businessmen (Table 28). Experience of education out of the state was very limited among administrative elites or businessmen; but whereas the incidence of such experience was highest for the inactive men in the administrative group, it was lowest for the inactive group among the businessmen. Close to half of the numerically significant inactive professional elites, and three-fifths of those who were involved in civic activities only, had experienced out-of-state schooling, but proportions were much smaller for professionals who were politically active. The proportion who had worked in cities of 15,000 or more varied little with participation category among the administrative elite, but was distinctively lower for the politically active than for other participation categories among the professionals and businessmen. Essentially these same relationships reappear in the last section of Table 28, though here the inactive and exclusively political among the administrative elites share in being the least currently traveled (our best index of continuing contact with urban centers). It is worth noting, however, that even the lowest cell indicates that one-third of the exclusively political among the administrative elites had visited five or more major cities in the past year.

Regardless of occupation the more traveled in the politically and civically active group are clearly important, since here social exposure is combined with formal political power and broad social involvement. Unfortunately such men constitute only 12 percent of the administrative and 5 percent of the professional elite. Taking all those scoring two or more on civic activity, we pick up 18 percent of the administrative and one-fourth of the professional elites. But the largest untapped human resource potential for communication and for modernizing functions would seem still to be among the professional cadres, roughly one-third of whom are both relatively exposed and inactive on our measures of civic and political participation.[7]

The Overall Participation Matrix

We have looked into the participant behavior of mountain elites vis-à-vis youth and in political and civic activities. We have reviewed the correlates of such behavior in the personal characteristics and social exposure of respondents. But we have not yet considered the question of how far civic and/or political activity is associated with degree of involvement with youth. These patterns are delineated in Tables 29 through 31. In addition to showing percentage distributions of participation combinations within youth-involvement categories, we have recorded "ratios to expectancy" for each cell.[8]

Taking the total administrative elites as a group (the first three columns of Table 29), we find the greatest frequencies within each youth-involvement class are where we should expect them: in the low civic, high political cells. The ratios to expectancy display a clear pattern in the extreme corners. Observed frequencies for civic-political activists and high (or medium) youth involvement, and those for the totally inactive, are markedly higher than "expectancy." Low on both civic and political participation with high on youth involvement and vice versa are only half of expectancy. This would seem to confirm the theories we questioned above—that those active in the political sphere tend, by more than chance, to be among those who are active in other spheres as well, and vice versa. However, when those who were among our sample *because* they were political officials (as an occupational group) are excluded (the last three columns of Table 29), the picture is much less clear, and the high-high-high cell even falls below expectancy, though not to a statistically significant degree. Turning to the professional elites (Table 30), there can be no question of the positive relationship between civic activity and high youth involvement, but the politically active professionals who are not also civically active score low or medium on youth involvement.

In Table 31 the bankers, lawyers, clergy, and physicians are treated together: we take the marginal totals from these groups in combination to set up the expectancies for each cell. The most striking result for the lawyers and bankers is what by now we should again expect: ratios well above 1.00 characterize the low civic, high political cells regardless of scores on youth involvement, and low ratios characterize cells involving low political activity (with or without active civic participation). Among clergy and physicians the high ratios to expectancy are in the high

7. Two-thirds of the professionals are inactive, and roughly half of the inactive professionals were high on "exposure."

8. A ratio of 1.00 indicates that the observed numbers match numbers that would be predicted from the marginal totals of a cross-tabulation, assuming no association between political or civic participation and youth involvement. Thus, the Table 29 ratio of 1.00 for low-high on civic-political participation by medium involvement with youth among lawyers and bankers tells us that numbers in this category just match the numbers we would predict merely from a knowledge of the proportions of bankers and lawyers who score low-high on civic-political participation and the proportions who were medium on youth-involvement, without any further clues concerning relationships between the two indexes.

civic, high youth cells, and in the low-low-low cell. Far below expectancy (ratios of .33 or less) are all high political, low civic cells along with that for high civic and political with low youth involvement. Public officials are in some respects intermediate between the distinctive patterns of the lawyers and bankers on the one hand, the professional elites on the other.

Summary

Evidence on personal characteristics presented in Chapter 2, which leads to the identification of administrative, professional, and business clusters among our respondents, is to some degree confirmed when, as in this chapter, we turn our attention to "exposure" and to the patterns of participation in civic, political, and youth affairs. The most consistent differences are those between the administrative and professional elites. We noted, first, the experience gap that characterized their exposure to the larger society, through education, urban living, and other indicators. Teachers were less exposed than professionals and were more like the administrative elites in their responses.

Secondary-school teachers, it was seen, report a considerable degree of contact with other elites, at least at the level of discussions of community affairs, and especially with businessmen (over half of the male and 37 percent of the female teachers). Though their involvement in organizations and in organized activities outside of the schools and educational associations tends to be preponderantly through the churches, a considerable minority also reported active involvement in civic organizations as well. Mountain teachers, even female teachers, do not appear on the whole to be an isolated group, although this research did not probe beyond the surface to determine the intensities of their contacts. Moreover it may be significant that (talking to parents about their own children aside) larger minorities of teachers reported a complete lack of contact with nonschool people on matters relating to problems or programs for children and youth than reported lack of participation in discussions of community affairs with members of the nonschool elites. And one-third of the teachers (both male and female) stated that there was no PTA in their school. A substantial minority of teachers reported involvement with nonschool people in the planning of community programs for youth, to be sure, but on balance it may be that mountain teachers are integrated into the community more as individuals, and on other people's terms, than by virtue of their occupational concerns.

Turning the examination of contacts with youth and the schools around, to see it from the point of view of the nonschool elites, essentially the same patterns emerge, but to these we now add the direct involvements of these elites with mountain children and youth. Proportions who count teachers or school administrators among their close friends and relatives are impressive. Even among professionals, with their high nonnative proportions, two-fifths or more claimed relatives or close friends among school personnel. To repeat, sizable minorities (around 30 percent) report consultations with teachers about problems and programs for youth (strictly professional contacts aside). But more striking is the extent to which respondents claimed frequent direct contacts with youth. Three-fourths to over 90 percent of the administrative and professional elites claimed such associations with individuals who were not relatives (with or without involvement in youth group activities). Professionals were of course more likely to have direct contacts with youth through their work than were the other elites, and the clergy were the most often involved with youth groups. This we should expect. But despite the extent of youth involvement associated directly with their work, the professionals were no less likely than others to be involved also in various forms of volunteer youth-focused activity. Overall the representation of mountain elites in contacts with youth was remarkably broad, and with only slight biases toward the clergy and more generally toward men with more than average exposure to outside experiences. Those involved to at least a medium degree with mountain youth ranged from the traditionalist of an older but continuing face-to-face culture, whose contacts were almost wholly on an individual basis, to the less homespun but no less committed youth involvement of the most sophisticated of the non-Baptist clergy. From our data, of course, it is not possible to show how these influences operate among the children of the area.

The distinction that we suggested between political and civic modes of participation in wider community activities, youth aside, did appear to have heuristic value. We found that the Kentucky data did not altogether fit the generally held expectations of political scientists to the effect that political participation is a special case of more general social and community participation. Although there is a weak association between these two types of behavior, in our sample political and civic activists are to a large extent different people with widely differing characteristics. The pattern with respect to political activities is particularly clear; the order is plain, with the administrative elites (even excluding the public officials for this purpose), the business elites, and the professional elites respectively showing a decreasing probability of political participation. Professional elites were the most likely to be involved in civic activities. They are also the elite group that had the highest proportion of members inactive in both the political and the civic spheres, even though by a number of indicators the inactive professionals were considerably more exposed than were any of the subcategories of the administrative elites. We found high youth involvement to be associated with political activity among the administrative elites and with civic activity among the professionals.

It will be remembered that a large proportion of those who were picked up in our sample by virtue of their political offices in fact described themselves as businessmen. At the same time the largest proportion of any sampled group with really low schooling was among the public officials. Public officials are a heterogeneous group of men, but one thing, at least, that they have in common is that in one way or another they exercise a critical influence on the operation of local communication facilities, whether for the mobilization of disparate elite groups and the general populace in the planning and carrying out of development programs and the modernization of local communities and their people or in blocking such endeavors and obstructing communication channels. This operation might almost be taken as a definition of the roles of local mountain politicians. In any case, be it the public officials, the other administrative elites, the professional elites (and teachers), or the local businessmen, if we are to have some clue as to what is communicated, from whom and to whom, by those who are more and less involved in civic, political, and youth affairs, we must look into the attitudes that these elites express on matters relevant to mountain modernization.

CHAPTER 4

Attitudes toward Tradition & Change

The preceding two chapters might be viewed as presenting a crude map of "information fields" through which mountain elites, as interstitial persons, could receive and transmit attitudes and influences conducive to change. But these intermediaries could also communicate antichange influences. The measures of exposure of elites to information and ideas from "outside," the extent and kinds of activities that connect them to mountain youth, and their involvement in community discussions and activities are the components of the communication nexus that has been portrayed. But to infer the nature and direction of the influences they exert from information about exposure and participation would be both inadequate and misleading. One of the most important gaps, indeed, cannot be filled by the present research: we have no direct clues as to the impact of ideas and attitudes the elites may transmit upon those at the local receiving ends of the communications.

What we can do is to identify the sorts of messages that are most likely to be transmitted. A major part of our research had exactly this purpose—to look into elite attitudes and opinions as they are related to the modernization process and the performance (or nonperformance) of cultural bridge functions. What pertinent messages have they received and what messages are these elites likely to feed into the system? How far, for example, does the mountain culture as mirrored in views of the local elites appear to be inherently compatible or incompatible with modernization or progressive integration of the local into the larger national economy and society? How do these elites view mountain prospects and policies pertaining to development of the area and its people? What roles do they see for themselves or others as participants in the communication of ideas and the implementation of change?

In this chapter we will examine such questions

in the light of evidence from the responses of the elite samples to attitude inventories included in our survey questionnaires.[1] The propositions built into the opinion section of the questionnaires embraced problems that have been raised by various writers on Appalachian affairs and by individuals with different areas of working experience and responsibility in the mountains. We developed this set of questions (opinionnaires) out of a concern with matters of continuing topical controversy—not in order to delineate personality types or fundamental values that characterized our respondents. In terms of our interest in modernization of the region, this strategy seemed the valid one. It means furthermore that the responses to each item will have intrinsic interest for readers with corresponding firsthand experiences (in mountain organizations, antipoverty programs, compensatory education, etc.). Exchange of views upon such matters is, of course, ceaseless "in the field," but a survey of the kind we have carried out serves to extend systematic questioning to representative groups of mountain society.[2]

For these reasons we will in this chapter give detailed attention to the background and implications of most of the opinionnaire items. Our discussion is organized around an a priori grouping of items that stems from the broad lines of our research design. A rough summary of the overall responses is provided in the accompanying tables, which give for each occupation the proportions who agree to each proposition (whether the response was "agree strongly" or "agree mildly"). Chapter 5 will take the analysis further, using more elaborate statistical methods to study attitudinal clusters and their correlates in background traits, exposure, and activity characteristics of respondents. Thus these two chapters, by building in data on the resistances side of Hägerstrand's scheme, complement our earlier focus upon information fields in an attempt to highlight the potentials of mountain elites for the exercise of cultural-bridge roles.

In terms of their content the items in the opinionnaire may be divided roughly into two sets. The first consists of propositions concerned with local culture—with how respondents perceive the rest of the local population, with how they view outsiders, and with the communication of information and attitudes between the mountain people and the rest of the nation (Tables 32A, 32B, and 32C). The second consists of more particularized propositions concerning the prospects and policies of mountain development (Tables 34A, 34B, and 34C). Each of these groupings is too diverse to describe adequately under a single label, but for convenience we may call the first "Mountain Culture and the Outsider"; the second we call "Prospects and Policies for Modernization."

Mountain Culture & the Outsider

Two basic questions must be central in this selective preview of responses pertaining to local culture and the outsider. First, how far are key attributes of local culture as reflected in responses to our questionnaires compatible, how far incompatible, with modernization? Second, how extensively do mountain elites manifest attitudes that can undergird both ends of a cultural bridge between the local (or "inside") and the national (or "outside") sociocultural systems?

Yesterday's People[3]

The predominant values in a culture can be seen as the assumptions by which a participant in that culture lives out his daily life. Traditionally the major aspects of mountain life and culture have been an ethic of rugged individualism, though tempered by strong family sentiment; deeply per-

1. See the ESLS and TC questionnaires. We employed a Likert-type method to establish the degree of agreement-disagreement with a series of opinion statements. A preliminary version of this opinionnaire was used in interviews with mountain manufacturers—research whose purpose only partially overlapped with that of the present study. However, data on entrepreneurs' attitudes will be presented where available.

2. As it happens, more than a quarter of the respondents and nearly half of the professional elites wrote comments in some detail on their questionnaires that we were able to code as relevant. An analysis of these comments, many of them elaborated and outspoken, was of considerable interest to us, and we have given a brief account of it in Chapter 6.

3. This evocative phrase is of course the title of the book by Jack Weller.

sonal and loyal human relations; and attachment to very localized and segmented religious and community institutions that were characterized by an ethos of grassroots democracy or egalitarianism. These values, all of them features of small community life of the nineteenth century, run counter to the complex organizations, interdependencies, and depersonalization of modern urban society.

Insofar as these older values survive in the mountains today they take their meaning from the local setting, reinforcing the identification of mountain people with their homeland, and their unquestioning and passionate loyalties to mountain institutions. Without taking account of the strength and coherence of these traditional values, neither the full potentiality nor the complexities of the cultural-bridge role could be appreciated. Interpreted most sensitively by such writers as Caudill, Weller, and Brown, the Appalachian understanding of man as an individual and as a member of an extended family community (or a closely knit primary group) must be seen as limiting the diffusion of modernizing influences and as inhibiting what the political scientists have termed psychic mobility.

How far the ideologies of either rugged individualism or grass-roots democracy persist among Appalachian elites is a question on which we can present some fairly direct evidence. Though we have no similar evidence with respect to the strength of familism and its associated traits, their persistence has been amply documented by other investigators.

Rugged Individualism: The most striking characteristic of the mountain manufacturers was their strong manifestation of an individualistic ethic in almost nineteenth century purity. In this they were by no means unique. This view was pervasive among all but the non-Baptist clergymen, as exemplified by virtually universal agreement on item 1: "If a young man really has ambition, he can make a success of his life no matter how poor or ignorant his family may have been." But if this attitude taken as a precept for living was once the bedrock of a sound economy, economic growth, and intergenerational economic mobility, it is also an expression of implied intolerance vis-à-vis those who are less successful and a denial of structural malfunctioning of the economy.

The intolerance that is the reverse side of the ambition ethic is more directly expressed in the strong support for item 2: "Public assistance has made people into lazy loafers, and they won't work even when a job is offered them." Here again agreement was virtually overwhelming among the businessmen, the bankers, and the Baptist clergy. Among the non-Baptist clergy, lawyers, and public officials large minorities disagreed. In parallel with the prevalent intolerance for men on relief, we found very firm support for the quality of mountain workers. Virtually all of the manufacturers and 90 percent of the other categories of respondents agreed that "mountain men are good workers if you understand how to get along with them" (item 3). On the other hand (but part of the same individualistic syndrome), three- to four-fifths in all occupational groups subscribed to the view that "labor strife has kept a lot of business out of East Kentucky" (item 4). It may be noted that it is the clergy and the public officials who are the most supportive of mountain labor. In rallying to the defense of mountain men, the common strain remains, quite unambiguously, the individualism of the Protestant ethic. Evidence for a softening of this theme, expressed primarily in at least indirect support of labor unions, appears only among minorities of clergy and politicians. Meanwhile a majority of the clergy and sizable minorities of all the other occupations perceive a negative version of individualism, the "suspicious" attitudes of mountain people (item 5), as a serious problem.

Grassroots Democracy and Maximum Feasible Participation: Local government in remote settings such as these in America has been infused with deep feelings about the preservation of individual rights and the acceptance of political contest with no small amount of infighting as an integral part of community life. Yesterday, as today, any widely based program of general community welfare and development has presupposed legitimate conflicts of interest and the recognition of the role of any interested party as both beneficiary and contributor. Perhaps the major difficulty encountered in the recent development efforts within Appalachia, though not peculiar to it, has been in reestablishing the "town meeting" or self-help concept after a lengthy period in which any social progress was associated with a mixture of benevolent provision by haves for have-nots and of paternalism by outsiders.

The process by which the resources of individuals and of primary groups become available and then actively involved in the seeking of wider community goals (the process of social mobilization) depends in the first instance upon the development of positive intergroup attitudes. But the ways in which this occurs, and how far it is carried, will be quite different in a small egalitarian, self-sufficient community than in a community with a complex urban social structure, characterized by sharp vertical as well as horizontal differentiations among its subpopulations. One of the most important dimensions of contemporary attitudes and behavior is clearly the extent to which elites welcome or resist active involvement of wider categories of the population in community planning and its implementation: the poor, the young, and other subelite or nonelite groups. Items 6 through 9 of Table 32A are directed to these questions, but before we comment on the responses, a few remarks are needed concerning historical grassroots democracy in Appalachia versus the "maximum feasible participation" of the antipoverty program.

Even if a tradition of social and economic egalitarianism has largely been eroded—as it has been, most emphatically, in the coal areas—precepts passed down from the simpler society of yesterday may carry over into the values that men profess today. But this does not mean that old-fashioned grassroots democracy and new-fashioned involvement of the poor, or of the young, amount to the same thing. The combination of self-reliance and mutual assistance that once characterized the local communities of Appalachia gave an egalitarian flavor to their government that emerged naturally and inevitably out of the conditions of pioneer life. Conflict and suspicion were there, to be sure; they are well documented in the history of clan warfare in the area.[4] But this was a horizontal kind of conflict, virtually devoid of communication gaps between social classes, or between the better-off and the poor. The war against poverty was every man's war.

Recently, by contrast, "maximum feasible participation" and its sequels have been urged upon local policy-makers, not chosen by them. And instead of being a part of every man's life, as in an earlier day, the war against poverty comes now to an Appalachia in which (as elsewhere) "the poor" have become increasingly recipients of a paternalistic and bureaucratic public assistance, various forms of voluntary but often depersonalized "caretaking," and a growing measure of scorn.

Apart, therefore, from the contribution of the new politics from outside the region, we may expect to find mountain traditions working both for and against acceptance of widely diffused mass participation in local public or community decisions. There would seem to be three ways in which the men included in our study may align themselves on questions concerning participation in community planning.

(1) First, there are those economic elites, most conspicuous in the coal areas, who retain an individualistic rationale, but who oppose active involvement of the poor (or the young) in affairs they have come to regard as their particular preserve, or who have a very low opinion generally of the competence of the less-favored members of the local society. Bankers, physicians, and participants in the business-management courses all fit into this first category, with roughly half agreeing with statement 6, that having representatives of the poor on planning committees would retard development; and these men (with lawyers) are decidedly the

4. A remarkable early article begins, "Kentucky has an unenviable reputation as a state of feuds and private fights. Christmas day, 1900, thirty deaths occurred in the state from violent causes." See S. S. MacClintock, "The Kentucky Mountains and their Feuds," *American Journal of Sociology* 7 (July 1901): 1–28. (This article is continued into the next number of the journal.)

least supportive of representation of the poor in matters concerning the poor (item 7). These are not yesterday's people in the oldest and most traditional variant of mountain culture, but they are strongly rooted in a less-distant yesterday, nevertheless.

(2) Some, who are most numerous in the poorer noncoal counties and whose lives and local settings are closest to the older traditional scene, express their faith in and their experience of grassroots democracy by strong support for giving a voice to the poor, whether or not to the young. So far as the occupations we surveyed are concerned, we may expect men of type 2 to be most numerous among the minor public officials; this is unquestionably at least a partial explanation of the ranking of public officials on items 6 and 7, politicians' protestations of undifferentiated democracy aside. Had we included them, the nonregular and often self-proclaimed mountain preachers and many of the elementary teachers up the hollows might have responded with yet more emphatic support, in the old tradition, for participation of everyone—and hence of the poor, who are no different from other folk. A few of the regular clergy are among this category of traditional grassroots respondents, but it is impossible to separate them from the third group.

(3) Finally support for wider participation comes from those who bring to the mountains attitudes that arise from the contemporary national scene elsewhere or that blend strong elements of humanism (rather than old-style individualism) with their democratic precepts. Thus we can hardly be surprised to find especially strong support for participation of the poor among the clergy, many of whom are not native to the area and who take their position on universalistic arguments, quite independent of local traditions (though not, obviously, of contemporary mountain conditions).

Responses with respect to participation of youth are on a somewhat different ground. Young men will grow older, and wide diffusion of participation among social classes, poor or not, does not necessarily imply giving youth a major voice. Indeed proportions agreeing with the position (item 8) that young people are not given a sufficient chance to participate actively in community affairs were generally lower than those on the questions relating to participation of the poor. That contrast was particularly striking among teachers, both male and female; although they ranked first in support of an active role for the poor, teachers dropped to the median among occupations in the extent to which they favored a greater role for the young.

Local Loyalties: Inside versus Outside

The pervasiveness of identification with the mountains, even among those who were nonlocal or who did not expect to remain there all their lives, came out very clearly in responses to the question concerning feelings about the area, discussed in Chapter 2. To recapitulate, among our respondents public officials and bankers (predominantly both native to the area and older) were the most fully committed to their local habitat. But lawyers, management-course participants, and physicians fell in very close behind. The relatively mobile clergy stood out in contrast in that only half of them (Baptist or non-Baptist) considered themselves as permanently settled in their localities. There was a substantial group among the clergy who considered their present residence in the mountains as a rewarding experience provided that it did not last too long; these temporarily resident clergymen are generally more, not less, involved in community human-development programs than are men with greater permanent commitment to the locality.

The degree of local identification expressed by teachers is of special import in view of their comparative youth, their large numbers, and their occupational contacts with mountain young people. Among teachers under fifty roughly one-fifth to one-fourth (of males and females respectively) expressed reservations about living permanently in the mountains; this was a larger proportion than in any other category except clergy, but far below the percentages of clergy.

Identification with the local area to a degree that entails some empathy with local people and culture is probably essential to effective performance of a cultural-bridge role, and in fact only a tiny minority checked "I definitely do not like living here." Given the overwhelming majority who identified strongly with their mountain localities there can be no question of the existence of a very solid attachment at the local end so far as potential cultural bridge roles are concerned. The national, or outside, end of the bridge is less secure. This is evident both in defensive manifestations of local loyalties and in resentments of outsiders among large fractions of the local elites. These attitudes are clearly evident in responses to the opinionnaire.

Confronted with the proposition (item 10, Table 32B) that "mountain people are proud and they don't like outsiders coming in and trying to change the way they do things," proportions agreeing ranged from roughly half of the male teachers to three-quarters of the physicians and non-Baptist clergy. But this is of course a judgment about how "other people" see things, not a statement of one's own attitudes. A direct and clear-cut expression of this mountain pride, which reverses the position of physicians and non-Baptist clergy, is given by item 11: "Our local schools are doing a good job." This is both of intrinsic interest in a policy context (in which we will return to it) and as an indicator of the ecology of local loyalties where the wider awareness is lacking. In fact, if we exclude the manufacturers, we find that this statement received strongest support in the more inaccessible areas of the mountains, precisely the areas in which the objective evidence of inadequacies in the schools is typically most striking.

Along with defense of local institutions goes a pervasive resentment of national institutions and of peripatetic outsiders who come to look, advise, or help, but rarely to learn or to share. Three-quarters or more of the respondents in most occupational categories agree that "one of the biggest problems in trying to plan and coordinate local development efforts is that the Feds don't understand the situation here" (item 12). But among the most frequently articulated resentments has been that against journalists who have given unwanted publicity to mountain affairs. In part this has been a resentment of sensationalism or of the exploitation of distress, but the ill feelings seem to have been directed not only at the outside television and newspaper commentators with their local color stories. As a reading of local newspapers will reveal, the sense of injury is evoked by anyone who challenges mountain practices and institutions, no matter how constructively. What we observe is clearly a compound of personal feelings of injury (whether on one's own behalf or that of others) and the quite different notion that somehow the mountains would be able to attract substantially more industry if they were not given such a poor image. The latter would seem to account for the fact that the management-course participants were particularly emphatic in their agreement with the proposition (item 13) that "the journalists who have been publicizing mountain problems in the national press do a lot of harm." In general, it will be noted, sizable majorities of each of the occupational groups agree with the statement.

Two further items elicited evaluations of other categories of persons for whom there has been widely reported local criticism. Half of the respondents agreed with item 14 that "it would be better if the young volunteers who come in to help were all local; outsiders don't belong and mountain people often resent their interference." As we might expect, a more tolerant attitude appears among the non-Baptist clergy.[5] To many readers it may come as a surprise that it is the entrepreneurs, the bankers, and the management-course participants (in that order) who are the least inclined to take the position (item 15) that "East Kentucky has been exploited by outside capitalists," though even among these groups roughly half complain of such exploitation; among all the nonbusiness elites substantial majorities accuse "outside capitalists."

Taken together, responses on items 10–15 (subset 1.b) suggest a configuration of localist loyalties; cosmopolitan perspectives are minority attitudes among mountain elites. Complement-

5. The responses of the manufacturers on this item should be interpreted in light of the fact that "young volunteers" had not, in 1966 when the manufacturer interviews were conducted, had the impact on the mountain scene that they were to have later.

ing this localism, the responses to items 1–9 (set [1.a], Yesterday's People) indicate support among most of the sampled group for a traditional culture and way of life. Under these circumstances it is plausible to suggest both that participation of the mountain elites in national information fields is constrained by local attitude structures and that considerable resistance (in Hägerstrand's terminology) may be expected both with respect to hearing or listening to messages or "tellings" that come out of the national culture and, when those messages are heard, to the actual diffusion of modernization and social innovation. Despite the rising pace of interaction between mountain elites and the rest of the nation, the social climate of Appalachian mountain communities still resists importation of new ideas in education, local development, or other institutional adaptations to the needs of human communites participating in advanced industrial societies. Successful adaptation of the regional culture and social structure must depend very heavily on the persistence and persuasiveness of a minority of local men who are motivated and equipped to perform cultural-bridge roles.

Interstitial Persons & the Cultural-Bridge Role

Some evidence, schematic though it may be at this stage of the analysis, has been presented as indicating the existence of a considerable gulf between the values and the evaluations of institutions among the mountain elites, on the one hand, and what might be supposed to be the attitudes of the nation's modern elites in industry and government.

That mountain elites are defensive of their culture and resist alien intrusions is not in itself particularly distinctive; indeed ethnocentrism characterizes all human societies. The important point here is the strength of identification with a distinctive traditionalist subculture and the extent to which that culture may inhibit the kinds of change that would expand social and economic opportunity for members of the mountain population at large, whether they continue to live in the mountains or migrate. Clearly such an enlargement of opportunity entails also, as both cause and effect, an enlargement of horizons. Critical in the processes by which these changes may come about (or fail to eventuate) are the interstitial persons, who constitute the main human potential for the building and activation of the "inside-outside" communication network.

By virtue of their occupations, and/or their formal education, we are able to define our respondents as interstitial persons. This means that we recognize them as occupying positions in the social structure that could more easily than others be exploited to link the local and the broader societies or to bridge the traditional and modern outlooks. However, the interstitial person does not necessarily perform a cultural-bridge role. Several items on the opinionnaires were intended, therefore, to identify more directly how respondents perceive themselves and others with respect to performance of public services that contribute in one way or another to the relating of mountain people and society to the larger national environment.

It is of general interest to note that there are very few respondents who are opposed to widespread dissemination of information or to discussion with respect to local development. However actual power may be distributed in the mountains, majorities of all occupational categories agree with item 16: "Some of the money now spent by the federal government on new projects would be better spent in bringing greater understanding of programs and policies to the community as a whole." But apart from this favoring of investment in information, there is also a very high degree of support for the idea (item 17) that "establishment of a development discussion or planning group is *in itself* an important step toward community betterment." Even when interpreted in the light of our findings about the personalism of mountain life, this should not be ignored. In the mountains there is time for talk; the bankers and the clergy are closer to seeing eye to eye on this than on many substantive matters.

The difficulties of getting agreement about the specifics of peoples' roles and responsibilities in mountain society are illustrated by the remainder of the items grouped under (1. c) concerning interstitial persons and the cultural bridge role.

A modest majority of all except the non-Baptist clergy believe that business and professional people "serve the common welfare best by concentrating their efforts on developing as fully as possible their own firm or practice." This, however, does not necessarily preclude the idea of other services to the society. In fact proportions ranging around nine-tenths of all respondents subscribe to the idea (item 19) that "men with my educational background should actively encourage programs that will help bring mountain people into closer contact with ideas and events outside the mountains." The agreement on this latter item may have very little meaning when it is only mild, however, since it may be nothing more than lip-service to a generally "good" proposition. Table 33 presents the proportions who strongly agree on both items 18 and 19 of Table 32, along with the differences (the item 19 minus item 18 proportions). Responses now spread out more widely on both items. Generally we might expect a negative relationship between the responses on the two items, and if we look at the extremes of the bankers and the non-Baptist clergy this would seem to be the case. The public officials are quite different, however. Next to the bankers they are the most emphatic in their insistence that businessmen and professionals would contribute most by following their occupations; but they also ranked first in proportions who strongly agreed that men like themselves should actively engage in performing a cultural bridge role, i.e., to "help bring mountain people into closer contact with ideas and events outside the mountains." If they see themselves as either "business" or "professional" people, their responses on items 18 and 19 may be reconciled, however. To correct for effects of such occupational roles we may look at the differences shown in the third column of Table 33. By eliminating the strictly occupational roles, we can gauge the influence of the "invisible hand" view of public prosperity that may be used to rationalize civic apathy. The differences in percentages shown constitute a rough index of broadly based attitudes concerning voluntary services to the community beyond what would be inherent to the occupation. A very strong contrast appears between the non-Baptist clergy, on the one hand, with their commitment to social responsibilities, and the bankers and businessmen, on the other.

Since we find that the clergy are most ready to accept the responsibility of serving as cultural mediators, it is interesting to review the responses to item 20: "An educated preacher can contribute more than anyone else to help mountain people bridge the gap between mountain life and the outside world." Clergymen themselves, along with entrepreneurs and bankers, rate their profession highly as to its mediating function; lawyers and teachers are the most skeptical. It is not at all clear, however, what images of the preacher have evoked these responses; it is possible that the genuine variance among the clergy makes any general assessment impossible. At the same time the responses do show that for many in the mountains the preacher is not now seen primarily as a locally identified man with traditional moral concerns, but rather as an individual with outside experience that can be brought to benefit local people.

Occupational differences in responses to items 20 and 21 make possible further interesting comparisons. The teachers were relatively skeptical about the cultural-bridge role of the preacher. Despite the small differences it is the clergy who are least likely to agree that "An out-of-state teacher is more of a problem than an asset to most local elementary schools." Secondary teachers were not less inclined than other occupational groups to agree with this proposition about their colleagues in the elementary schools, a proposition which reflects, though indirectly, their own role. However, it is clear that it is only the extreme localists, more likely to be found among bankers than in other groups, who object to bringing teachers from outside. It must be added that there is evidence that this tolerance of the teachers may mean that they are interfering very little if at all in the settled ways of the local culture.

We saw that there was general agreement that mountain people do not like outsiders who try to change local ways. One category of outsiders who have attempted, often in a quite uncompromising manner, to do just that is the young volunteer. Majorities of many of the occupational groups agree that "it would be better if the young volunteers who come in to help were all local; outsiders don't belong and mountain people often resent their interference" (item 14). The volunteer does not have the reputation of fitting in with local arrangements, and a number of conflicts have arisen in the region within the last few years in which volunteers, without any deference to local authorities or institutions, have sought to innovate or to instigate social change in community organizations, in education, and even in labor-employer relations. In the sense that the volunteers do not have any substantial local links to mountain society they are not yet truly interstitial. But neither are those local elites who most strongly oppose them. Only the non-Baptist clergy, some of whom are tarred with the same brush from the local standpoint, evidence a predominantly favorable opinion of outside volunteers.

Two final items of set (1. c) concern bankers, the representatives of whom among our samples are predominantly older men who have been shown to include more than a fair proportion of extreme localists. It is interesting to find that while the bankers' image of themselves is typically more favorable than the view of bankers in most other groups, a fairly sizable minority are self-critical, which may point to an important edge of change. Thus 40 to 50 percent of most occupational groups agreed with item 22, that "local bankers know only the traditional kinds of local enterprise; they won't back a man with new ideas"; one-fourth of the bankers joined in this critical view. Only the entrepreneurs approximated the low critical proportions among the bankers, and here it must be said that many of the manufacturing respondents are survivors from a traditional economy. In fact the contrast of the manufacturers' attitudes with the management-course participants' much more critical evaluation of bankers' localism and conservatism is of particular interest. On the other hand, the manufacturers join the management-course participants in their comparative skepticism with respect to the proposition (item 23) that "local bankers know people as individuals and can serve local businessmen better than the impersonal city bankers." Only half of the entrepreneurs agreed on this, as against 88 percent of the bankers. The strong localism of the Baptist clergy is illustrated by their support of this proposition.

In general it seems fair to infer from these responses that a large proportion of the elites envisage the cultural-bridge function as served better by people who come from or strongly identify with the local society, rather than by free-floating and culturally distant individuals. Unless an individual is closely linked to, or can get himself adopted by, mountain society, as a cultural mediator he has one hand tied. There is also the difficulty of finding men who are not only acceptable in the mountains, but who are also linked to, and to some extent identify with, a national cultural system. In fact such men are rare everywhere, and the cultural-bridge function is likely to be performed by a chain of interstitial persons, not by a single one. Development agencies and programs must inevitably encounter difficulties in this complex and indirect communication framework. These agencies also constitute in themselves a massive innovation, injecting ideas and issues into the local setting and bringing a new dimension to the mountain communication nexus by providing additional channels of communication both among mountain people and communities and between them and other parts of the nation.

Prospects & Policies for Modernization

Area development has been a focus of concern in eastern Kentucky for over a decade. Active intercounty local involvement received a particularly powerful boost from the 1957 flood disasters, the flood rehabilitation study of that year, and the ensuing creation of state and local development agencies concentrating on the problems of the mountains and on policies that might ameliorate conditions. The first relatively comprehensive and systematic statement of the economic problems of the area and the magnitude of those problems was the Eastern Kentucky Development Commission's *Program '60*, prepared under the leadership of John Whisman. Ideas and pressures coming from Kentuckians were important in bringing about the 1963 Appalachian regional development legislation. The initial emphasis was almost entirely upon physical resources and infrastructure, however. Human resource problems and social development received short shrift and least political support exactly where such programs were most needed. Thus national legislation directed to the problems of human-resource formation and rehabilitation among backward populations has had little active support in the Kentucky mountains. Nevertheless, since the passage of the four major pieces of national legislation (the Area Redevelopment Act, the Appalachian Development Act, the Economic Opportunity Act, and the Elementary and Secondary Education Act), a variety of new programs and agencies have begun to operate in the area. In our view this development of social infrastructure and opportunity brings to the region a radically new potential for modernization. The extent to which such a potential is realized will of course depend upon responses by the local population. We can begin an assessment of their response by examining the views of mountain elites about regional prospects, policies, and problems as a decade of ferment, determination, frustrations, and readjustments was approaching its close.

Economic Prospects & Priorities

Several items were introduced into the opinionnaire to help delineate how the elites see prospects for the mountains and how they evaluate recent and current policies and programs. The issues posed are, first, to what extent does a special Appalachian situation exist with respect to the rest of the nation that justifies a deliberate regional development program? Second, to what extent can there be solutions in regional adaptation without extensive migration? Third, is the physical investment priority that characterizes the most established programs well advised?

One of the questions asked respondents, but not as part of the opinionnaire, was: "Do most businessmen you know feel encouraged in their long-run business prospects by the new national interest in Appalachian development?" (This phrasing of the question is out of date, but in 1966 it was meaningful to the respondents.) Favorable responses fluctuated around three-fifths, with public officials and bankers the most sanguine, lawyers and Baptist clergy the least. Item 24 of the opinionnaire turned this question around to ask for reactions (this time direct) to the statement: "Rising national prosperity would do more for the mountains right now than all the special programs for their economic development." There is no inherent contradiction in giving a response that agrees with this statement, as an indicator of the relative importance of overall prosperity and of area development programs, while at the same time agreeing that businessmen felt encouraged by local programs. In fact the majority of bankers and public officials agreed with item 24, even as they also had been the most inclined to consider businessmen to be encouraged by recent (at that time) national interest in regional problems. A majority of the manufacturers took the same view, looking upon national prosperity as the basic medicine for local ailments. In all other occupational categories (including the management-course participants) substantial majorities rejected this proposition, however.

A set of items that specifies some of the actual and proposed regional development strategies or programs indicates that these are generally assessed favorably by our respondents. Though peripheral to the main thrust of this study, the question concerning control of strip-mining and requirements of land rehabilitation is of interest in its own right. To our surprise a very large majority in all occupational categories rejected the statement (item 25) arguing that effective controls would put mountain men out of jobs. There may be more support for effective action on this front than is usually believed, though it must be remembered that we did not include in our sample the relevant interest group (and power centers) on this matter—the coal operators—and over one-fourth of the administrative elites displayed a timorous or reactionary view.

Responses to the statements concerning highways were very similar across various occupations. Minorities of only a tenth to a fifth agreed that development highways would "move people out of the mountains more than bring business or industry in" (item 26). And there was virtual unanimity in agreement with the statement (item 27) that "development highways are essential and it's about time the back country got its share." An extraordinary faith in the potentials of tourism is evidence in responses to item 28: "A well-planned program to foster tourism could put the mountain economy back on its feet," though a third of the clergy are less sanguine in this respect. (Bankers are the most enthusiastic, with 91 percent agreeing.) Indeed the strain of naive optimism running through these responses turns to complacency when we consider the reponses to item 29: "Technological progress is going to hurt more than help the futures of children now in mountain schools." Proportions agreeing with this statement vary around one-fifth of most groups and a little over one-quarter of the clergy and politicians. This general lack of concern about the effects of technological change upon the coming generation is consistent with the large majority who defended the quality of local schools (item 11).

In the first chapter we contrasted the view of development that focuses upon aggregate income growth with other criteria. We presented the definition that seemed to us both the soundest philosophically and the most hopeful as a guide to a clearer (and perhaps refreshing) view of potentialities and policies: development is the cumulative diffusion of enlarged actual and perceived opportunities, both among the people who will remain in an area and among those who will leave it to live elsewhere. Attitudes toward out-migration may be very different according to which of these views of development—an aggregate-income or an opportunity-diffusion view—is closer to a man's interests and/or values. Nevertheless adherents of both of these views (or of some other) can join in recognizing the problems that out-migration creates, both for those who leave and for the morale and viability of the communities they leave behind. There can be no doubt that the familism and personalism of mountain life, together with its internal geographic segmentation, have contributed not only to strong ties with the local area but also to feelings of insecurity once a man ventures beyond the familiar valleys. Under these circumstances migration can be a painful alternative even for individuals who are otherwise equipped to compete in urban labor markets.

These mountain attitudes have been reflected in the preservation of pockets of mountain migrants in urban ghettos, and in the impassioned resentments evoked in mountain leaders of the late 1950s and early 1960s by any suggestion that out-migration must be part of new adjustments of the mountain economy to a changing national scene. It is our impression that a softening has taken place in local attitudes concerning migration, however. Migration is not nearly so bad a word as it was, probably because a more realistic view of local development prospects is spreading and the first dramatic out-migrations from the coalfields are past. The rate of out-migration has slowed or come to be accepted, however regretfully, as part of an inexorable readjustment. But this shift in opinion, which has been notable in recent public discussions in the area, is not yet so great that all would reject item 30: "Too many young people have been emigrating from East Kentucky without adequate reason." Not surprisingly the bankers are most divided, with almost half agreeing with the statement.[6] The teachers, both male and female, are the most likely to reject this viewpoint. The other statement relating to migration (item 31) ran: "It is unfair to ask a man who has grown up in the mountains to leave his friends and kinfolk in order to get a job." Again only a minority in each group agreed, running from roughly one-fourth in the professional categories (including teachers) to just under two-fifths for each of the administrative elites. But these are substantial minorities, and there is a substantial hard core among the administrative elites who still propound this prescription for what would amount in fact to persistent and pervasive demoralization of a proud people.[7] In general, holders of such

6. The entrepreneurs' questionnaire omitted the words "without adequate reason," and so their 87 percent agreement, while interesting in its own right, is not comparable and was not entered in Table 32.

7. The designation as a "proud" people has long

views among the elites are also men whose interests would be best served by pursuing a regional goal of maximizing aggregate income, rather than more people-centered goals. The communication of better understanding and more constructive goals to some of the local elites themselves is evidently still going to be a necessary and a difficult task; it is a task that must be carried out mainly by men who identify closely with mountain people and their ways of life.

Actual policies for development are matters of value in the first instance. There can be little doubt that now (as earlier) a majority of local people, and certainly most of the key decision-makers, give strong support to physical-resource development programs, ranking them ahead of human-resource development (item 32). Majorities of all but the female teachers favor the proposition that "the next million dollars for Appalachian programs would be better put into water, sewage, access roads, etc. than into efforts to develop the economic potential of the working population." Particularly strong in support of this view are all the administrative elites. If this is a correct indicator of where they stand, and if the bias in favor of physical over human-resource development programs is a strong one, then this could be a situation with serious implications for the modernization of the mountain region as we have understood that process. But public choices, like private, are conditioned by many external facts, and such a preference may mean less in action than we might suppose. Moreover, in their views of mountain prospects and policies, mountain elites make few clear choices. A much more detailed examination of attitudes toward human resource development programs considered in their own right is in order.

Human-Resource Development Policies & Programs

The human-resource development policies of a modern society find their major expression in a formal school system, but there is also a growing public sponsorship of multiple agencies of education supplementing the schools, and a vast complex of learning and training agencies and activities, formal and informal, in the private economy—including simple learning-by-doing on-the-job. The questions on our opinionnaire touch the more informal types of training and learning only peripherally. They are concentrated on the formal agencies of education and training, and in particular on the schools and on recent training programs that have been (and still are) widely discussed.

Attitudes Relating to the Functions and Performance of the Schools: Schools perform many functions, and their objectives may be seen in diverse perspectives. But if the schools are seen as helping the young to prepare for living in tomorrow's society—certainly their central function—then policies relating to schools should reflect the social, economic, and political factors that are shaping that future society. In the Appalachian context the extent to which the schools can serve a cultural-bridge function will depend upon the teachers and upon the communities that employ them. It would appear that a majority of elite respondents are not yet really ready to see the local schools serving as bridges to the wider society, not so much because they deliberately resist this idea as because of the limitations of their own information and horizons. In general most of the mountain elite have little appreciation of the extent to which even the new generations of mountain men are at a disadvantage when competing in national labor markets. But partially countering this is the fact that despite their general defensiveness of mountain schools just over half of the public officials, the non-Baptist clergy, the physicians, and the manufacturers agreed (item 33) that "the education given young people in mountain schools does not prepare them for life elsewhere." Those least inclined to agree were the Baptist clergy and the teachers. The defensiveness of the teachers is understandable here, especially when we remember that they gave the most support to out-migration. In these patterns of response we are encountering not only the particular situation of

been standard political terminology in reference to the people of the Kentucky mountains. It sums up both the inheritance of the nineteenth-century ethic of individualism and the pervasive identification of inside versus outside among members of a long-isolated and remarkably self-contained subculture.

the Kentucky mountains, but also a tendency that is very widespread—both to defend one's schools and at the same time to ask the impossible of them. Another item about the schools pointed to their relevance or irrelevance to mountain life but in this case with reference to vocational schools in particular (item 34): "Local vocational schools don't put enough emphasis on training for work in the mountains." There was a large minority giving no response on this question, but among those who did respond we again find a mixture of attitudes toward schools and toward the mountains versus the outside world. Thus two-thirds of the public officials and the lawyers agreed with the localist position that the schools were not preparing students adequately for jobs in the mountains. Even among the teachers, two-fifths took this position. A related statement, one that was less directly critical of the schools, evoked almost universal agreement (item 36): "There would be less welfarism in the mountains if the proportion of time the schools devoted to vocational courses were greater." Here vocational bias is compounded with the individualist ethic in mountain culture. Finally one other item was related to performance of schools and preparation of youth for participation in the labor force (item 35): "The main deficiencies in mountain labor are attributable more to lack of opportunity to acquire know-how on the job than to inadequate school learning." On this four-fifths of all of the administrative elites were in agreement—more, we may suspect, because of their pragmatic leanings than as a defense of local schools. Indeed those least inclined to attribute deficiencies in mountain labor to lack of opportunities to learn on the job (rather than to deficiencies in schooling) were the non-Baptist clergy, the physicians, and the female school teachers.

These questions relating to human-resource development raise complex issues, and no simple interpretation of responses is justified. Clear, however, are (1) a pervasive ambivalence with respect to the schools (by no means unique to the Kentucky mountains), (2) a localist bias, (3) a differentiation of attitudes associated with occupational roles that parallels relative positions we should expect to find elsewhere, (4) a substantial, resistant hard-core minority of traditional, extremely localist, pragmatist, anti-education men among the administrative elites, and (5) a widespread vocational bias that is blind to the effects of economic and technical change on the *general* education requirements for effective jobholding, the acquisition of technical skills, and the avoidance of obsolescence. The obtuseness of this last attitude pattern is, again, by no means unique to the mountains, but it appears to be exaggerated there.

Concerning Human Development outside the Schools: Some of the major recent programs in human-resource development in the Appalachian region have been outside the range of normal school programs. Furthermore some of these nonschool programs have attracted wide attention and support. Though we do not have the data to determine whether local elites are coming to consider their physical-investment priorities, there is some evidence that greater support is available when the people-centered programs are presented without linkage to the governmental machinery that instigated them. Thus three- to four-fifths in most groups (even more of the non-Baptist clergy) agree (item 37), that "Kentucky school systems need more of programs like Head Start for the preschool-age child." The proposition (item 38) that "the inclusion of classes for unemployed fathers is a major advance over old relief programs" is a reference to the Work Experience and Training Program, which was experimentally initiated in Kentucky and which made its welfare payments to the unemployed fathers of families conditional upon their attendance at classes leading to grade, high school, and vocational diplomas. This item finds support among roughly three-quarters of all groups. Least favorable to classes for unemployed fathers were the male teachers, a noteworthy exception since it is the teachers in the local school system who have been called in to staff such adult-education programs. Fewer respondents were ready to agree with item 39, that "the Job Corps camp program will do a lot for East Kentucky youth," perhaps because this similar though more developed program of compensatory education was not sufficiently well known among our respondents at that time. Some of them would have known of the existence of two camps in eastern Kentucky itself, but this can hardly explain the marked contrast between public officials, almost three-fourths of whom approved the statement (and the program) as against half or less approving among those in other occupational categories. On this, as on several other items, the public officials are not consistently localist, as the bankers tend to be. The politicians, indeed, give virtually indiscriminate approval to all programs that would increase federal disbursements in the area, but that is not the whole story either; for example, they were among the majority agreeing on item 33. Finally responses on item 40 indicate that there is remarkably strong support for basic elementary schooling for adults, with around 70 percent agreeing that "the kind of adult education that could accomplish most in the mountains would be long programs (a year or more) in basic reading, writing, and arithmetic." The bias toward vocational education for today's youth, and the limited awareness of deficiencies in the general education of mountain youth, do not preclude awareness of and concern about the functional illiteracy of adults. It is interesting, at the same time, to note that male teachers were only half as likely as members of other groups to agree on the adult basic education statement, possibly once again because of their personal experience with the difficulties in making such courses effective.

It is one thing to support a program when it carries no price tag and is not compared with alternatives. It is another to choose between alternatives. We must therefore emphasize, once again, that the degree to which these attitudes generally supportive of preschool, youth, and adult compensatory education would be maintained in any tussle for resources with programs of physical investment remains problematic. Undoubtedly much would depend upon the presentation and handling of human-resource development programs by sponsoring agencies and particularly by the federal government.

Local Development & the Federal Government

A very important aspect of development policies, especially in an environment such as that of Appalachian Kentucky, centers around who does what—which brings us full circle to the inside-outside theme, but with a difference because we now look at institutions and agencies, rather than individual outsiders. Thus there is a marked difference between responses to the statement that "the Feds don't understand" (item 12) and responses to item 41: "Recent national education bills will bring too much federal intervention in local schools." In no occupation group did agreement with the latter statement characterize more than a small majority, and it was distinctly a minority view among teachers, public officials, and, above all, the non-Baptist clergy. Especially interesting are the public officials, who are almost as inclined as are the bankers to view "the Feds" as not understanding local affairs, but who are not nearly so fearful of federal intervention in local schools. However, the occupational patterns shift in statements unrelated to schooling, such as items 42 and 43, where the concern is with area development and community action types of program in which the federal government has been directly involved. Public officials are again the least opposed to federal funding on its present terms, but the professionals showed much disapproval of the preempting of local initiative, taking up perhaps the ideas that local involvement in development programs is in itself a contributor to human development, and that development is for people, not vice versa.

Given the fears and the ambivalent attitudes of many, it becomes interesting to refer back to item 16, which was concerned with whether the elites believe there is an adequate effort on the part of the federal government to bring information about programs and policies to the local people. Most (80 percent) of the politicians agree as to the need for more information, and two-thirds of the teachers concur, as do smaller majorities of all other groups. There is thus the suggestion that we may be identifying a need that is well recognized and perhaps even felt by the respondents themselves. With the multiplication of legislation and the programs and agencies that have descended upon the mountains, only a few even among the better informed of the elites are able to keep track of the operations and their objectives—let alone to make strategic decisions among priorities in regional development. This much is clear from the responses to the second part of our opinionnaire on prospects and policies for modernization. Given the further difficulty of major differences in the basic presuppositions of men with inside and outside cultural roots, who must get together to implement programs, it should not surprise us to find that communication often breaks down, or that conflicts arise, or that locally unpopular or unappreciated programs (and goals) are simply bypassed.

As a whole the responses reviewed in the second main part of this chapter, relating to mountain prospects and development policies, must raise considerable doubt as to whether the most influential members of the local elites really attach much importance to the kind of social values that underlie the human-resource development programs. In essence most of the programs are coordinated with development goals and are designed to compensate for initial disadvantages by enlarging human horizons, potentials, skills, and thereby opportunities. But despite their personalism and individualism, or even in part because of it, we find among the local elites widespread and tenacious adherence to narrow economic goals and physical (nonhuman) means. There is also the insistence that what a man accomplishes depends on his own efforts. These two themes are mirrored in beliefs that the mountains have been unfairly treated or exploited, on the one hand, and that handouts are destroying the moral fiber of the people on the other. Solutions to human-resource development problems, such as lack of the skills demanded by the labor market, or lack of initiative to find remedies for an impoverished background or environment, are implicitly envisaged in terms of individual adjustments. The structural characteristics of development, especially of social modernization, are ignored. There is a strong defensiveness that blocks constructive reappraisal of local institutions and allows only a limited, because too narrowly vocational, conception of a human-resource development process. As a result the modal approach to educational questions is a half-hearted and undiscriminating approval of a string of remedies—acceptable only so long as local institutions can remain securely undisturbed.

The traditionalism of the mountain elites is broadly apparent from the data presented in the first part of this chapter. Not only is there overwhelming support for a series of affirmations of a personalist and individualist philosophy for living, but there is a pervasive strongly localist sentiment and resistance to acculturation into the larger society. It is these cultural traits, together with the severe limitations of the mountain economy in other respects, that give a distinctive meaning to the responses of mountain elites concerning prospects and development policies for the area.

In sum the elites view change primarily as growth in yield from natural resources and from the development of physical infrastructures. There is only limited support for programs concentrated on development of human beings or for the components of modernization that we have called social mobilization—at least in their structural and redistributional aspects. Limited awareness of the pace and the implications of change in the nation as a whole acts to restrict the development of more active communication with the outer society, and an unjustified complacency about local schools except in very narrowly perceived vocational terms undergirds the passive resistance to increasing nonelite opportunities through education and training. Such constraints upon the development of human beings suggest that modification of the relatively widespread stereotypes of the "welfare" population, of "the poor," of the "proud," the "resentful," and the "suspicious," will be difficult. It would be unwise at this juncture, however, to extend interpretation of these responses solely on the basis of the evidence concerning frequencies with which particular attitudes are held among those in the various occupations sampled, without consideration of the ways in which particular attitudes are related or of the associations of one or another attitude pattern with participant behavior. It is to the examination of such relationships that we turn in the next chapter.

CHAPTER 5

Mountain Elites: Resources for Modernization?

Modernization may be viewed as a process involving an interplay of values, experiential knowledge, and socially mobilized behavior. Evidently that process will move most smoothly and rapidly when the men who are best informed and most experienced and who carry attitudes most conducive to modernization are also active participants in political, civic, and youth affairs of the local society. Turning this around: if those who have most influence in the public affairs of mountain society and who are most closely involved with local youth have narrow horizons and attitudes that resist change (or adjustment to the ongoing national life), the forces making for modernization will be blocked or distorted. But the pattern of resistances is much more complex than that. There are distinctive kinds of participation, and the degrees to which various elite groups seek or are drawn into one sphere of activity as against another may be quite different. This could have important associated implications for the effective diffusion of attitudes and information, since information fields may be established and to a greater or lesser extent reinforced or bounded by patterns of sociopolitical activity.

Participation and attitude variables have been explored separately in considerable detail in preceding pages. We have talked of who (by occupation, age, experience, etc.) was most likely to be active, and to what degree, in political, civic, or youth affairs singly or in combination. We have also delineated attitude styles and related them to the occupations of our respondents. In this chapter we extend the assessment of mountain elites as resources for modernization by studying clusters of viewpoints and associated activity profiles. A first question is simply how far are there clearly identifiable, distinctive attitude configurations, and do the attitude clusters appear meaningful in terms of the framework and focal interests of the present study? Once such configurations are identified, the major question we ask of our data is whether there are typical attitude configurations characterizing those holding positions of formal political power or of informal civic influence in mountain society, and how far in each case there may be substantial contrasting minority attitude clusters among the more active and influential men. Corollary questions are concerned with discovering what predispositions characterize the unmobilized members of the mountain elites, and with identifying categories of men who may represent, on the one hand, wealth in human resources or, on the other hand, barriers to the modernization of mountain society as a whole.

The Components Analysis & Attitude Clusters

A discussion of responses on particular attitude items grouped informally, as in Chapter 4, by a priori classifications provided a useful if impressionistic overview of how the various mountain elites view themselves and others, and of how they look at mountain prospects and some programs related thereto. However, it is all too easy to misinterpret responses on single items, projecting meanings that were not in respondents' thinking, or assuming associations in attitudes that are not prevalent in fact. Components analysis of the inventory of attitudes provides a check on the validity of interpretations of particular measures, and it serves to identify dimensions (or clusters) of attitudes that may not have been anticipated but that challenge us to fresh thinking.

All those opinion items in the questionnaires and the interviews for mountain respondents that were common to the teachers and other occupational groups (except manufacturers) were subjected to a components analysis with varimax rotations. Eight factors were obtained, all of which appeared to be significant. Table 35 lists the factors, giving them interpretive titles and recording the highest-loading items (with their loadings) on each factor.[1] It shows also the distributions of responses on those items, including proportions N.R.; the percentages total to 100 in each row. To allow easy cross-reference, we have identified the items by the same numbers as in Table 32 (which is not, of course, the order of their appearance on the questionnaires). It should be remembered that components analysis is designed to explain variance, and we should not expect it to highlight items that express the most universal attitudes of mountain elites. Indeed we are doing this in order to identify distinctive clusters of attitudes. The weighting of the factors yielded by this procedure tends to bring out the reverse of some of the points emphasized in Chapter 4 for precisely this reason —after the first factor the analysis increasingly picks out attitude clusters that constitute distinctive minority views.

In addition to identifying distinctive attitude clusters (factors), components analysis can also provide the basis for further study of relationships between where individuals stand on a particular attitude cluster and their other attributes —whether by direct use of factor scores or by use of an index suggested by loadings in the components analysis. We report in Appendix C on some multiple regressions in which we use factor scores as dependent variables. However, use of factor scores has a number of disadvantages. In the first place, they tell us nothing about position on an absolute scale but only state a relative position. For example, an individual may have a high factor score (relative position) on Factor 3 (critical view of local schools), yet he may be more defensive than critical; he is just less defensive than the average man. If a cluster of attitudes can be conceptualized in quasi-absolute terms, it may be quite as important to locate individuals or groups in those terms as to assess the significance of differences between them. Second, inevitably one interprets factors in terms of the variables that have high scores; it is from those

1. Since the agree-disagree scoring ran from one for strongly agree to five for strongly disagree, a negative sign on the factor-loading for an item indicates that strong agreement with the statement would contribute to a high factor score, strong disagreement to a low (negative) score. The distribution of overall responses is included in this table as a guide to interpretation.

variables that the factor takes its meaning. But all the variables included in a statistical program affect both the factor scores and loadings of variables on a factor. One of the best uses of components analysis is sorting out sets of variables with high loadings on the same factor; this having been done, the raw data on the variables of each cluster can be used to form an index freed from the extraneous effects of low-loading variables. We constructed such indexes from each factor in the components analysis, giving equal weight to each variable shown under each factor in Table 35. The indexes carry the same numbers as the factors to which they are related.

The first factor (with which Index 1 is associated) relates quite closely to our prior grouping of items in Chapter 4 under the headings "Human Resource Development Policies and Programs" and "Local Development and the Federal Government." The most interesting feature of this factor is the clarity with which it distinguishes those who both support compensatory education programs (a modest majority) and who also are least concerned that federal activities of this or any other kind would bring too much federal intervention in local affairs or sap local initiative. All items that could definitely be placed in one or the other of these two categories are included among the highest-loading items on Factor 1, but other responses concerning education and those on questions relating directly to outsiders are not.

Most of the remaining items that were classified in Chapter 4 as concerned with "Prospects and Policies for Modernization" carried high loadings on either Factor 7 or Factor 8. Factor 7, which we have labeled the "Anti-migration Syndrome," was discussed in its essentials in Chapter 4, even though not precisely as it appears in the components analysis; we will have frequent occasion to come back to consideration of this factor and its associated index. Factor 8 turns around the majority support for physical-development priorities, to pick up the minority who express skepticism or a less intense conviction that the mountains have been exploited or neglected in these respects.

Factor 3, which stands apart, pulls out, as a distinctive cluster, three items pertaining to the quality of mountain schools and the competence of their teachers (items 9, 11, and 33 of Table 32); it is pointed to the critical view of mountain schools. The fact that these responses form a cluster independent of responses relating to vocational training and on-the-job learning should surprise no one who is familiar with the worldwide arguments about educational and manpower planning; there is an inherent (even when unconscious) logic in these differential patternings of attitudes. But it is interesting to observe that there was indeed discriminative reaction to statements in the opinionnaire that related in diverse ways to human resources and at the same time, in varying degrees, to localism of outlook. A comparison of the high-loading variables in Factor 3 with those in Factors 5 and 7 reinforces our earlier intuitive interpretations (in Chapter 4) of the mix of responses relating to the schools.

Factors 2, 4, 5, and 6 draw almost entirely on the items we grouped under "Mountain Culture and the Outsider," in the first half of Chapter 4. The ethic of rugged individualism, which we identified most strongly in the initial interviews with manufacturers, is less conspicuous in this components analysis for at least two related reasons: the basic optimism about what can be accomplished by a youth with ambition (item 1 of Table 32) is too pervasive to contribute much to variance, and the other key items on which we drew empirically for our sketch of individualism in attitudes (items 2 and 3 of Table 32) were not asked of teachers, and thus they were not included in the components analysis. However, Factor 5 turns the individualistic ethic around to gather in the distinctive minority who view ordinary mountain folk with at least some measure of sympathy and in national perspective—as victims of a poverty of experience and background that is more serious than their lack of income. The grounding of this attitude cluster in national rather than local perspectives is obvious. More explicitly related to the "inside-outside" theme is the attitude cluster picked up in Factor 6, which is oriented (as our title for it indicates) toward "Receptivity to Outsiders." It is important in interpreting this factor to remember that it is double-edged; the receptivity refers both to a respondent's own attitudes and to his evaluations of how *other* people feel. For most respondents these perspectives will be very much the same, since men project their own views onto others; however, for some, especially among the non-Baptist clergy who are not natives, respondents' perceptions of how other people feel and expressions of their own attitudes may contrast sharply.[2]

We found it convenient for our discussion to group Factors 3, 5, and 6 together in presenting mean values of indexes for one or another subpopulation. These three indexes in their positive sense indicate low cultural resistance to social change. All three reflect the application of external criteria with respect to mountain people and institutions. Only those persons who are capable at least in some degree of bridging the gaps between the mountains and national life are likely to perceive the limitations of the local schools or of the local environment in preparing oncoming generations for fuller participation in the wider society. And only those who are reasonably receptive to outsiders are likely to facilitate the diffusion of knowledge and ideas from the more dynamic outside nodes of development back into the mountain communities. That Indexes 3, 5, and 6 all measure attitudes conducive to development seems hardly open to debate; but Index 7, already mentioned, carries an opposing meaning. If high scores on Indexes 3, 5, and 6 are preponderantly favorable to development and modernization, high scores on Index 7, the antimigration syndrome, are as unambiguously unfavorable. The fact of the matter is that high scores on Index 7 reflect extreme localism in perceptions and orientations, given the objective situation and economic disadvantages of most of the mountain area.

Factor 4 picks up clearly and unambiguously one of the themes stressed in Chapter 4 in connection with mountain culture. In this factor and its associated index we have a clustering of positive views (affirmatively expressed) favoring broad democratic participation in community affairs, whether in the traditional grassroots or the "maximum-feasible participation" sense. We were somewhat surprised, however, at the way in which items were split between Factors 2 and 4, which are closely related in some respects. Factor 2 is broader in perspective (as may be expected given its ordering among the factors yielded by the components analysis). Moreover, in all instances high scores on Factor 2 go with disagreement, which is one of the reasons why we give it the abbreviated label "Defense of Ordinary Folk." It is indeed more the defensive, as against the active or positive variant of the populism it shares with Factor 4. Turning Indexes 2 and 4 around, we might interpret extremely low ratings as indicative of relatively wide gaps in empathy and in person-to-person tellings across strata within mountain society.

Attitude Patterns among Mountain Elites

In the remainder of this chapter we will make use of attitude indexes to analyze relationships between various characteristics of our respondents and the ways they look at things. Before we proceed to do this a word is in order concerning construction of the indexes and interpretation of their values. Each individual response on each of the high-loading items on a factor was first given a value from 1 through 5 for answers from strongly agree through undecided to strongly disagree when for that item disagreement was the appropriate sign for the factor (i.e., the loadings in Table 35 carried positive signs). The values ran conversely when the direction of response indicated by the factor was agreement with an item (factor loadings were negative). In our averaging of these responses, the scale was calibrated to run from zero (the opposite of the attitude described by the factor) to 100 (the fullest possible expression of the attitude cluster). Thus, if an individual or group of individuals gave the most extreme possible answers on all the items included in an index in the direc-

2. This among other things creates some discrepancies between index values and factor scores for factor (index) 6 that highlight very general methodological problems in the interpretation of factor analysis and the use of factor scores. A brief discussion is given in Appendix C.

tion pointed by that index, the score would be 100; at the other extreme it would be zero. An index value of 50 is the equivalent of an average item value of 3, or the point of indifference between responses in the direction of the factor and against it.

Table 36 provides an overview of mountain attitude patterns that could be regarded as one way of summing up the content of Chapter 4. Looking first down column (2) we see that the highest values are on Index 4 (Fostering of Grassroots Participation), where the balance is decidedly in favor of the attitudes indicated by the index (and factor) title. No other index claimed support significantly above the halfway mark. At the other extreme there were few respondents who perceived the general run of local children to be disadvantaged in their future prospects by their environment (Index 5); a score of 20 implies a mean value between disagree and strongly disagree with the cluster of attitudes picked up in Factor 5 and its index. (Even the non-Baptist clergy, with a score 10 points higher than the median, reached only 30 on this index.) There were also relatively few who took the position suggested by Index 8; on the whole the belief in physical investment is strong among the mountain elites. But the rankings in mean scores among the three indexes implying external criteria are also interesting, moving as they do from scores most nearly approaching neutrality on Index 6 (Receptivity to Outsiders), where there is no direct challenge to local life and institutions, to Index 5, with its serious and penetrating challenge. Cumulative movement from Index 6 through Index 3 (a critical view of local schools) to Index 5 could be viewed as stages of awareness through which we might expect alert mountain leaders to move as strong communication chains are formed and as inside-outside information fields become progressively denser.

Some Occupational Contrasts

Most of Table 36 is of course an analysis of variations among occupational categories in mean values on each of the attitude indexes. Entries under each occupational designation give the mean index value for members of that occupation minus the median of the occupational means. In computing the median values of column (1), in contrast to the means in column (2), we included male teachers, female teachers, and management-course participants. (The distinction between businessmen and public officials as opposed to pure politicians, set out in the last two columns of the table, was not used in arriving at the median occupation scores.) On the whole the medians of column (1) run very close to the means for the main sample, the most important exception being the lower value of the median on Index 7.

Turning now to particular occupations we demonstrate the distinctive position of the non-Baptist clergy: theirs are definitely the highest scores on the attitude indexes that call for application of external criteria (Indexes 3, 5, 6) and also in support of local-federal cooperation and of compensatory education (Index 1). Also, it is only the teachers and the physicians who score lower than the non-Baptist clergy on the anti-migration syndrome (Index 7). The bankers, public officials, and Baptist clergy, by contrast, are relatively low in their ratings on Indexes 3, 5, and 6, and decidedly high in the localist anti-migration syndrome. The businessman politicians deviate, however; we will come back to this point.

There is a relative polarization of occupation groups on Index 4 (Grassroots Involvement), with public officials (and teachers) at one extreme; the bankers, lawyers, physicians, and management-course participants are together at the other extreme. It will be noticed that the management-course men have near-median scores on all indexes other than those which refer to support of ordinary people, where they tend to approximate the distribution for bankers. In view of the fact that the non-Baptist clergy and the public officials differ in their responses on most items, their convergence on Index 1 may appear paradoxical. But given that these groups were also at opposite extremes in their holding of local positions of formal power, the competition for new or informal types of authority would be likely to heighten their interest in local-federal involvements and in the human-development activities suggested by Index 1.

Attitude profiles for public officials reflect both the internal diversity of this group and their common ground in the dictates of local political life—a generic species over most of the nation, but with its particular mountain variants. If we look only at the summary column for public officials, they may seem to go right down the middle so far as the first three indexes are concerned. However, there is in fact a sharp split on Index 3 between the pure politicians and the businessmen holding public office. The former match the Baptists in their defense of local schools, whereas the businessmen-politicians more often qualify their assessments. Both categories of public officials commonly share in the antimigration syndrome (and in optimism about mountain employment prospects) so often expressed by bankers and lawyers, but it is the pure politicians who take decidedly the most extreme position on Index 7. On the other hand, regardless of whether they are "pure" politicians or not, public officials were quite unlike bankers both in their strongly held enthusiasm for local-federal cooperation in compensatory education and in their support of grassroots participation in community affairs.

It is clear that the heterogeneity among public officials is by no means unbounded, and if we may find among them both conservatives and progressives in the mountain scene, they rarely reject the tough individualism of mountain culture. Indeed, "pure" or not, public officials typically manifest both the strongly defensive loyalties and resentments that go along with the antimigration syndrome (in which they are joined by bankers) and a relatively high professed commitment to action for human betterment (in which they are most likely to be aligned with the non-Baptist clergy). Along with these characteristics the quite numerous businessmen-officials display more modern and outwardly oriented attitudes than do the pure politicians. This view is most striking in relation to the schools, which is a favorable omen for the prospects of communication and human development in the mountains.

Views Associated with Age, Education, & Exposure

It is interesting to contrast attitude patterns among subcategories of our respondents considering other than occupational differences. A number of personal characteristics of respondents —especially age, level of education, local or nonlocal nativity, and prior experience of living in an urban environment—are indicative of exposure to wider experiences and ideas and may be expected, therefore, to separate members of the elite with respect to attitudes. An analysis of several differences in attitude profiles as related to these characteristics is presented in Table 37. Each column refers to a difference in mean scores for the subpopulations indicated, and in each case the comparisons have been set up so that a plus value should be expected if the attitude was oriented toward national (rather than local) values and toward modernization. Thus, for example, we subtract mean scores of older from those of younger men, or less from more educated respondents, and so on.

In every case the differences are uniformly positive for Index 3 (critical view of local schools), for Index 5 (disadvantaged environment of mountain children), and for Index 6 (receptivity to outsiders). Such views are relatively more prevalent among non-natives, young men, those who are most educated, those who have worked in a city of 50,000 or more and, especially, those who visited five major cities or more during the previous year. It should be stressed, nevertheless, that even the young, the non-native, the educated, and the traveled were on balance *not* particularly critical of local schools; none of these groups averaged scores even of 50, at the breaking point between critical and uncritical. (The young and the best educated did just move up to or cross that line with respect to receptivity to outsiders.) Mountain men who can make a critical assessment of mountain institutions or take a cosmopolitan viewpoint are the exception even when they were born elsewhere. On balance the antimigration syndrome was clearly rejected by non-natives, the young, the better educated, and those with experience of urban life elsewhere, although it was not rejected without qualification.

That Indexes 2 and 4 are indeed picking up different value clusters (as statistically they must, going back to the components analysis) is clearly revealed in the quite different patterns displayed on the indexes in Table 37. Perhaps few readers would be surprised to see that the young and the better educated are more inclined to stand up for the ordinary man when the form of a statement may be interpreted as an attack on him; the differences on Index 2 put the young and the educated on balance in the "democratic" camp in contrast to the leaning toward the other side among the older, the less educated, and the less widely experienced members of the mountain elites. However, the patterns on Index 4, "Fostering Grassroots Participation," might well occasion some surprise. All the items included in this index, it may be remembered, express the desirability of actively involving more of the poor and of the young and show the importance of a more effective diffusion of information about what is going on. Differences on Index 4 are all negative, but slight, excepting the positive figure on age, and the difference here is only two points. The best educated are the least inclined to support active grassroots participation, while the real commitment to this value comes from the most isolated and backward groups, more as a survival of the past than a herald of the future.

In Index 1 there are seemingly contrary effects of youth and "foreign" nativity on the one hand and education on the other. No simple explanation can be offered since, in the mountain setting, the responses seem to be compounded of judgments concerning the seriousness of social needs, priorities for attending to them, how well compensatory programs have actually been operating, and how far they have been perverted to serve sectional political interests or have preempted local initiatives. In other words similarity of response on this index is no assurance of similarity in profile of personal background or of choices of commitment in sociopolitical activities. Index 1 scores demand more study.

Age-related Views within Occupations

Among the personal characteristics of our respondents (occupation aside) that best predict both attitudes and behavior has been the simple fact of age. That age contrasts in attitudes were not attributable solely or even mainly to underlying correlates with occupation is demonstrated in Table 38, which suggests also how far age differences may be important within one or another occupational group. Because of the marked contrasts between occupations, two sets of comparisons are used: those persons under 40 are compared with those aged 50–59 and those aged 40–49 are compared with those aged 60 and over. The reader can easily identify which is the most informative comparison in a particular case by referring to the sample numbers shown at the top of the table.

In general the positive association between relative youthfulness and relatively high scores on the three indexes entailing application of external criteria or receptivity to outsiders is repeated within all occupational groups for each of the age comparisons. Out of fifty-four comparisons there are only six reversals of the relationship, and the only noteworthy negative difference is in the first comparison for public officials (on Index 6), which involved only eight men in the younger age category.[3]

Age differences carry negative signs on the antimigration syndrome (Index 7) without exception among the administrative and professional elites, and the age effects here generally run quite large. Especially marked is the decline in the antimigration syndrome among bankers, lawyers, and Baptist clergy under forty as compared with colleagues in their fifties. Scores are slightly erratic for management-course participants and for teachers, where numbers in the older groups are small. However, the large group of young male teachers (under forty) do score distinctly lower than either their older confreres or most other subcategories of the mountain elites; these teachers are unquestionably closer to the young people who are and have been migrat-

3. They display similarly inverted scoring on Indexes 8 and 1.

ing, both in their own experience and perceptions of alternatives and in their communication behavior (as receivers as well as conveyors of messages).

The general tendency for younger men to score higher than older ones in "Defense of Ordinary Folk" (Index 2) is repeated consistently within each occupational category for both age comparisons, if we except the teachers. The age relationships are less systematic with respect to Index 4 (Grassroots Participation) for the comparison between men under forty and those in their fifties. However, within each occupation (except lawyers and male teachers) the men in their forties showed less enthusiasm for involvement of the young and the poor in community affairs than was displayed by men in their sixties. These figures are picking up, once again, the importance of the traditional element in positive commitments to grassroots involvement in local affairs.

On the important Index 1 (and also Index 8), age effects are erratic both between and within occupations. This is especially notable for public officials and bankers, and interpretation would be hazardous. Age differences appear to be nonexistent among the Baptist clergy, but the non-Baptists, the lawyers, and the physicians show consistent and unmistakable patterns in the two sets of comparisons; older men in these occupations give less support to the newer, federally assisted development programs. Indeed, as we study mountain profiles on Index 1 in relation to the personal characteristics reviewed here, the attitude on local-federal relationships comes to look more and more like an indicator of orientation to action. Taking into account its human-resource focus, this attitude would seem to be clearly allied with development or modernization, but carried into practice it does not necessarily operate that way.

On this and on several other indexes associations of scores with actual occupational or participational roles call for careful scrutiny. Some respondents—and obviously the public officials by definition—have occupied positions of formal authority in the political structure. Others (most notably the non-Baptist clergy, who were the least likely to have held such positions) may or may not have access to informal or less established types of social power. These different experiences of power in the community can be expected to affect perceptions of social structure and of the processes of social change. We will therefore go on to examine the attitude profiles of participants and nonparticipants in informal or associative activities, as well as in the formal authority structures, as clues to the significance of the opinion differences we have noted.

Social Mobilization & Attitude Patterns

In Chapter 3 we presented two indexes of social mobilization: (a) involvement with youth and (b) political and civic participation. These were the most comprehensive measures we could devise from our data of the extent to which elites were mobilized within mountain society. However, we can know whether to weight such activity positively or negatively with respect to modernization only if we have correlative information about the values held by the respondents. In the next series of tables the attitude patterns of mountain elites with greater or lesser degrees of social mobilization are broadly summarized.

Attitudes & Youth Involvement

It will be immediately apparent, from Table 39, that although three of the attitude indexes (3, 4, and 5) included items directly concerned with mountain youth, no large differences in the mean attitude scores were associated with differences in degree of youth involvement. The biggest difference in scores, still only very moderate, was on Index 3, "Critical view of local schools"; persons who have the most contact with local youth were the most critical of local schools, while those rating low on youth involvement were least critical.

Excepting Index 3 none of the differences in mean scores seems noteworthy; variation within each of the youth-involvement categories is far greater than variations between them. It seems clear that, in their out-of-school experience with members of mountain elites, youth come in contact with men whose attitudes are quite representative. That is, the more cosmopolitan persons among mountain elites are neither more nor less distant socially from youth than are their localist counterparts. Within the schools, messages that are oriented more adequately to the wider society than are attitudes among the general run of mountain elites will come from the male, not the female, teachers; female teachers whose attitudes promise effective performance of cultural-bridge roles are a smaller minority.

Attitude Correlates of Political & Civic Activities

The relationships summarized in preceding pages should in themselves lead us to anticipate a fairly close association between levels of participation in political-civic affairs and several of the attitude clusters. Table 40 indicates that the sharpest distinctions are again on Index 3; those who were civically but not politically active are set apart from others in their more critical judgments of the schools, though on the average even they balance out just under the 50 mark, leaning slightly to the uncritical side. In general it is clear that the more cosmopolitan attitudes (Indexes 3, 5, and 6) are associated with civic activities. In the cases of Indexes 6 and 7 (concerning inside-outside relations and the antimigration syndrome) interpretation of the distribution of scores is aided by the hypothesis that political involvement increases localism; i.e., the inactives are more cosmopolitan than the politically active on both of these indexes. Political activity, with or without civic activity, was distinguished by the lowest scores on Index 5, as we should expect; this is the most sensitive of the indexes in its challenge to locally rooted loyalties.

The civically active—this time whether or not they are also politically active—give the most support to local-federal cooperation and to compensatory education. The public officials, who were rated highest among the occupational groups on Index 1, were not of sufficient weight among those who were politically active alone to neutralize the low scores of bankers; those public officials who in fact scored highest on this index were usually both civically and politically active.

In Table 41 information concerning activity on social participation and on youth involvement is combined in the classifications for the analysis of attitude differentials. By taking those who were high and those who were low on youth involvement and then comparing the mean attitudes across the civic and political participation categories within each of these youth-involvement classes, we sharpened a number of contrasts, with the greatest differences appearing sometimes within the high, sometimes within the low youth-involvement sets. Thus in receptivity to outsiders (Index 6) the greatest contrasts are within the low youth-involvement set, where the politically active only are distinguished by their very low score. Contrasts on Indexes 7 and 4 were also greatest among those with low youth involvement; political activity is seen here to be associated with a sharp rise in antimigration attitudes (Index 7), while support for grassroots participation (Index 4) differentiates the low scores of the civically active who are not involved with youth. It is also interesting to note the high score on Index 4 of those who were closely involved with youth but who had otherwise no political or civic involvements.

Most striking is the sharp contrast with respect to their evaluations of local schools (Index 3) between political and civic activists within the high category on youth involvement. The former (politically active), as we might expect, are decidedly defensive of the local schools, a position in which they are approximated by men who are inactive in every respect. On the other hand, men who are high in both civic activity and youth involvement are the one category whose attitudes toward local schools are predominantly critical. While these patterns should not surprise us, they show very clearly why school reform involves so much conflict, and they indicate why efforts to improve mountain schools have encountered many difficulties.

Profiles & Prospects

Despite the complexity of many of the relationships that have been examined in this study, certain distinct patterns emerge that are very illuminating with respect to problems and prospects for mountain modernization. In the last two sections of this chapter we sum up these salient points in terms of three attitude dimensions: (1) The first dimension derives overall "modernization scores" as the sum of scores on Indexes 3, 5, and 6 minus the score on Index 7. We might equally well have labeled the result "predisposition to function as a cultural bridge"; that is, we are in effect defining as modern those attitudes and perceptions of the mountain elites that reflect their adoption of standards from the wider society or display attitudes of receptivity to people and ideas from that outside world. (2) The second dimension is simply Index 1, scores on which indicate the degree of support that may be expected in federally sponsored or encouraged human-development programs for the mountains. (3) The third dimension is Index 4, which is indicative of how much support may be expected for efforts to involve wider sectors of the population in community planning and development activities. Position on this third dimension is significant especially as it may bolster (or dampen) the diffusion of knowledge and responsibility among the younger age cohorts (whatever their social status) and among the poor and the most disadvantaged sectors of the local population.

Mountain Elites Today

These attitudes are diagrammed in relation to present (1966) occupation, activity patterns, nativity, and feelings about the area in Figures 4 through 6. The vertical scale on all three charts is modernization score.

Figure 5 distinguishes among the various occupation groups for degrees of "modernization" (or cultural-bridge inclination) versus localist orientations, plotted against mean scores on Indexes 1 and 4. As previous tables have shown, respondents fall into three groupings: (a) at the top, and distinct from all others, are the non-Baptist clergy; (b) in the middle are the physicians, male teachers, participants in the management course, female teachers, and lawyers, in that order; (c) distinctly low are the other administrative elites and the Baptist clergy. On the horizontal scale, those of our respondents who were most supportive of federal-local cooperation in compensatory education are the non-Baptist clergy, who are the most cosmopolitan (with high modernization scores) and the public officials, who are close to the localist extreme. This position of the public officials should warn of difficulties that must arise in the carrying out of such programs. All the other groups hover in the vicinity of 50 on Index 1, a position of net indifference. With the exception of the public officials none of the administrative elites displays enthusiasm for social mobilization at the grassroots. After the public officials this democratic value finds its strongest support among teachers and clergy, who are the furthest removed from the established local centers of power and influence over public action. Furthermore, the "pure" public officials of our sample are only a fraction of the politically active (who include, especially, bankers and lawyers).

In Figure 6 the administrative and professional elites are classified by activity type and by whether or not they are native to the mountains. The size and shading of the square symbols used in Figure 6 for the plotting of modernization score against score on Index 1 distinguish nativity-activity categories that are most frequent, moderately frequent, and rare. The non-native civically active who are not politically active stand out with high modernization scores and with the highest score on Index 1; they are exceeded in their position on the grassroots participation index only by the smaller set of men who are both politically and civically active. (The non-native civically active are predominantly the non-Baptist clergy once again, though there are some other professional men among them—from the ranks of physicians, Baptist clergy, and lawyers.)

There is a clear gap on the modernization scale between the subcategories civically active/non-native, civically active/native, inactive/non-native, and all others. One of the contrasts which is particularly interesting is that between the native and the non-native inactives. Outsiders have emphatic and positive views, while natives, though more numerous, are usually indifferent

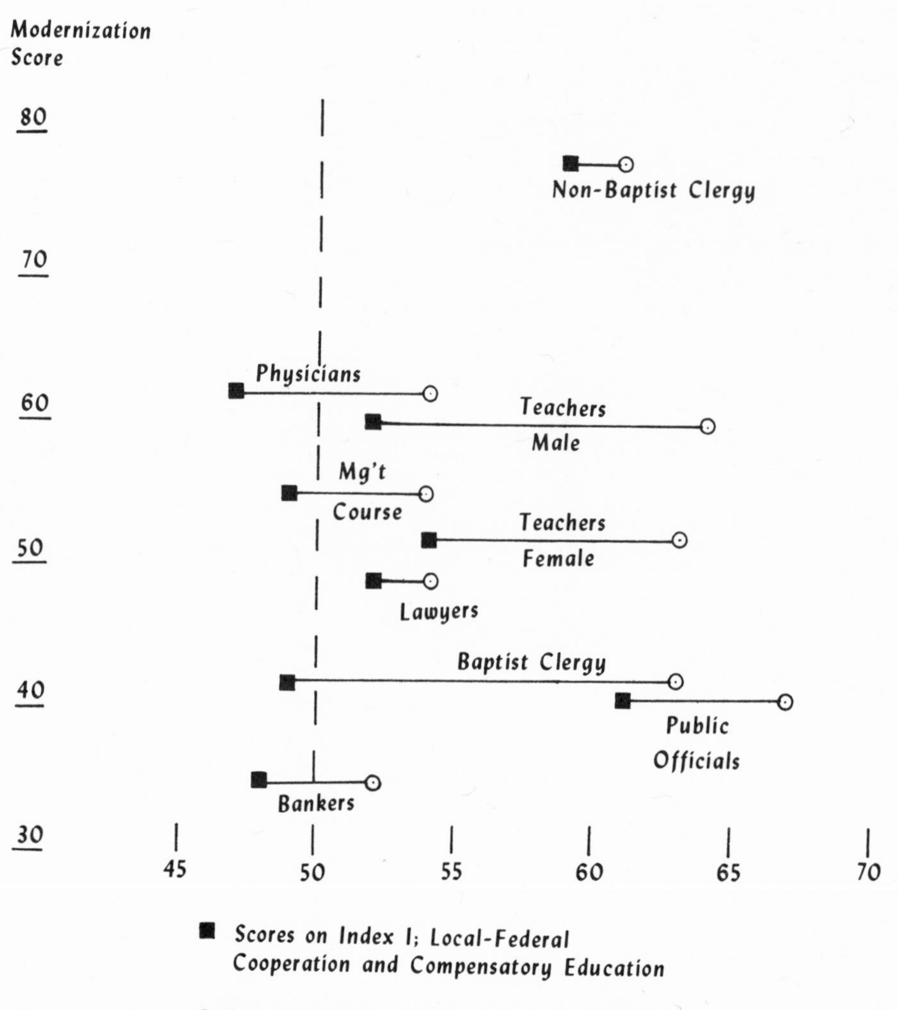

FIGURE 5.
Selected Attitude-Occupation Profiles

to modernization. Non-natives who have taken an active place in local political life (whether or not with civic activities as well), and the natives who were active both politically and civically, are all low on modernization scores, but next to the civically active/non-natives they are the most favorably inclined toward local-federal cooperation (Index 1); taken together, however, they constitute less than 10 percent of our weighted sample. Apart from the civically active/non-native, no other quantitatively major activity/nativity group stands high on Index 1: in fact the remaining big categories (the inactive/native, inactive/non-native, and politically active/native) have the lowest Index 1 scores. The contrast between the politically active mountain natives and the other three categories of politically active men distinguished in Figure 6 is the

FIGURE 6.
Nativity-Activity Classes & Attitude Patterns

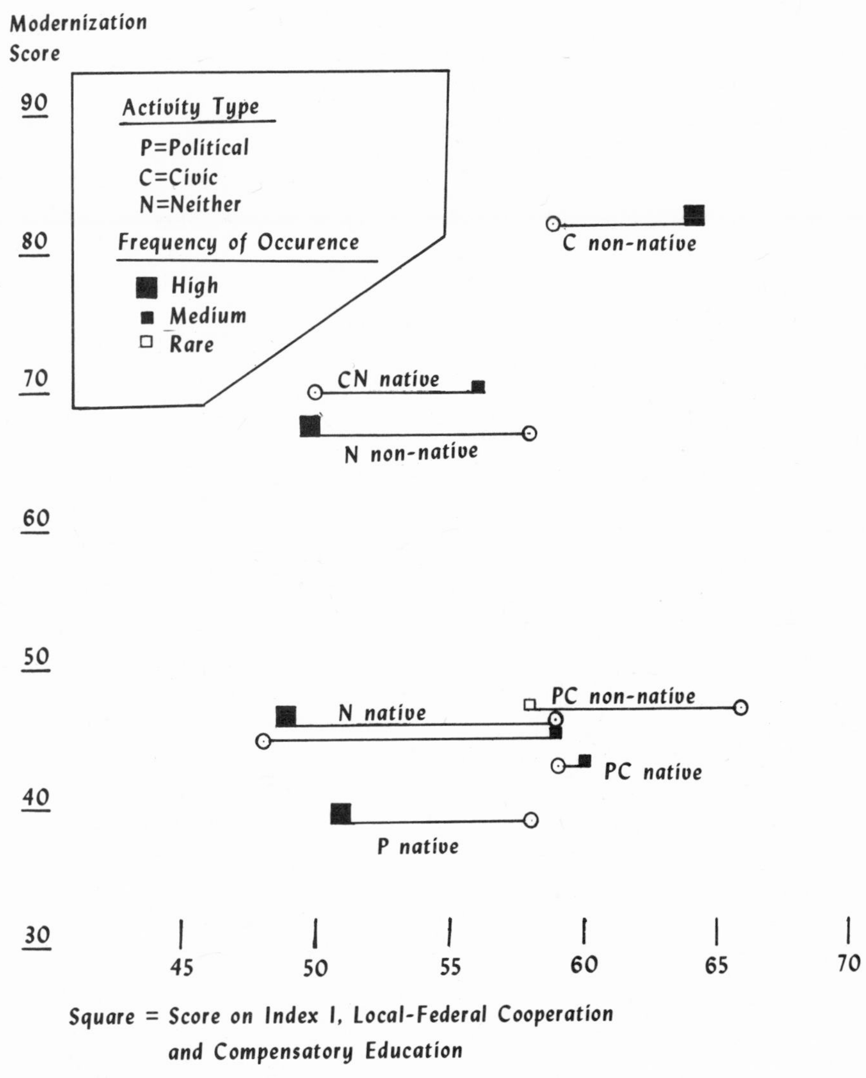

more striking in view of their similarly low scores on "modernization."

In their attitudes with respect to grassroots participation, mean ratings for most of the activity/nativity categories were within a narrow range around scores of 58 to 59. The only exception exceeding that level was the very small group of non-native men who were active both politically and civically. Two groups with moderate numbers scored distinctively below the rest in their support of effective involvement of the poor and the young in community development planning: the civically active natives and the politically (but *not* civically) active non-natives.

In Figure 7 we have attempted to relate the patterning of modernization to Index 1 attitudes by combined activity/age and activity/youth-involvement categories. All the categories included in the figure had frequencies in our sample of 30 or more with the exception of two with frequencies between 16 and 20: they are the PC_h and PC_m cells (active in both political and civic affairs and with high or medium youth involvement respectively). The highest frequency is for N_m, men who are not active in political or civic affairs, but who have moderate contact with youth and school personnel, usually (though not always) as a facet of the respondent's regular work. Next to this group the highest frequency is for men who are inactive in all respects. Civically active men rarely had less than a medium degree of youth involvement, though politically active men commonly rated low in contacts with youth.

The broken lines of Figure 7 encircle the four activity groups; the solid lines connect age categories within those groups. Immediately evident, once again, are the high modernization scores of men who are civically but not politically active, along with their relatively strong commitment to local-federal cooperation and to compensatory education. In the opposite corner are men who were politically but not civically active and who were over age fifty and/or scored high in youth-involvement, along with the oldest of the inactive respondents. In fact the importance of the age factor is repeated in each case; men over fifty rate decidedly lower on modernization attitudes than younger men in the same activity category. This is especially striking for the civic-only group, where the gap between men over fifty and those under fifty years of age is truly dramatic; here we are picking up an occupational distinction as well, for the older men in activity type "civic only" are bankers, lawyers, and physicians. Nevertheless the oldest of the civically active score almost as high on promodernization attitudes as the highest of the subgroups (of any age) within the activity type politically but not civically active.[4] The older men who were politically and civically active, along with the overlapping category PC_m with average youth involvement, occupy the lowest right-hand corner of the diagram. They are low on modernization but high in their support of local-federal cooperation and compensatory education. Men in category PC_4 rate higher on modernization (as do those who are civically and politically active and at the same time high in youth involvement). This should hardly surprise anyone. But it is more difficult to explain the fact that they rate considerably lower than the PC_5 or PC_m men in their support of compensatory programs. Given the comparatively low freguencies in all the PC categories, we must be extremely cautious in interpreting their attitude profiles. At the same time all the respondents who were both politically and civically active, along with those who were politically active with high youth involvement, command special attention because of their key positions at the communication centers of the local societies.

The part of Figure 7 within which we find all the subcategories who were active neither politically nor civically displays a systematic patterning that has not been so readily observed before. These men generally have higher modernization scores than comparable age or youth-involvement groups who are active politically, whether or not active also in civic affairs, but they score below men who are civically and not politically active. As might be expected, relative to their modernization scores they score low on Index 1; but it is significant that nevertheless the younger among them and those with high youth involvement approximate the politically active men in their forties (and younger) in degree of support of compensatory human-development programs. This suggests the presence of a substantial potential for such programs among men in the thirties and forties who stand at a midpoint in their local-national frames of references vis-à-vis the rest of the mountain population and who are not necessarily averse to taking part in local development efforts. However, these inactive younger moderates are disproportionately non-

4. This statement would still hold had we included the low-frequency cell for P_3; the youngest of the politically active scored below those aged 40–49 in modernization—the only instance among the four activity groups in which this was the case.

FIGURE 7.
Selected Attitude-Activity Profiles

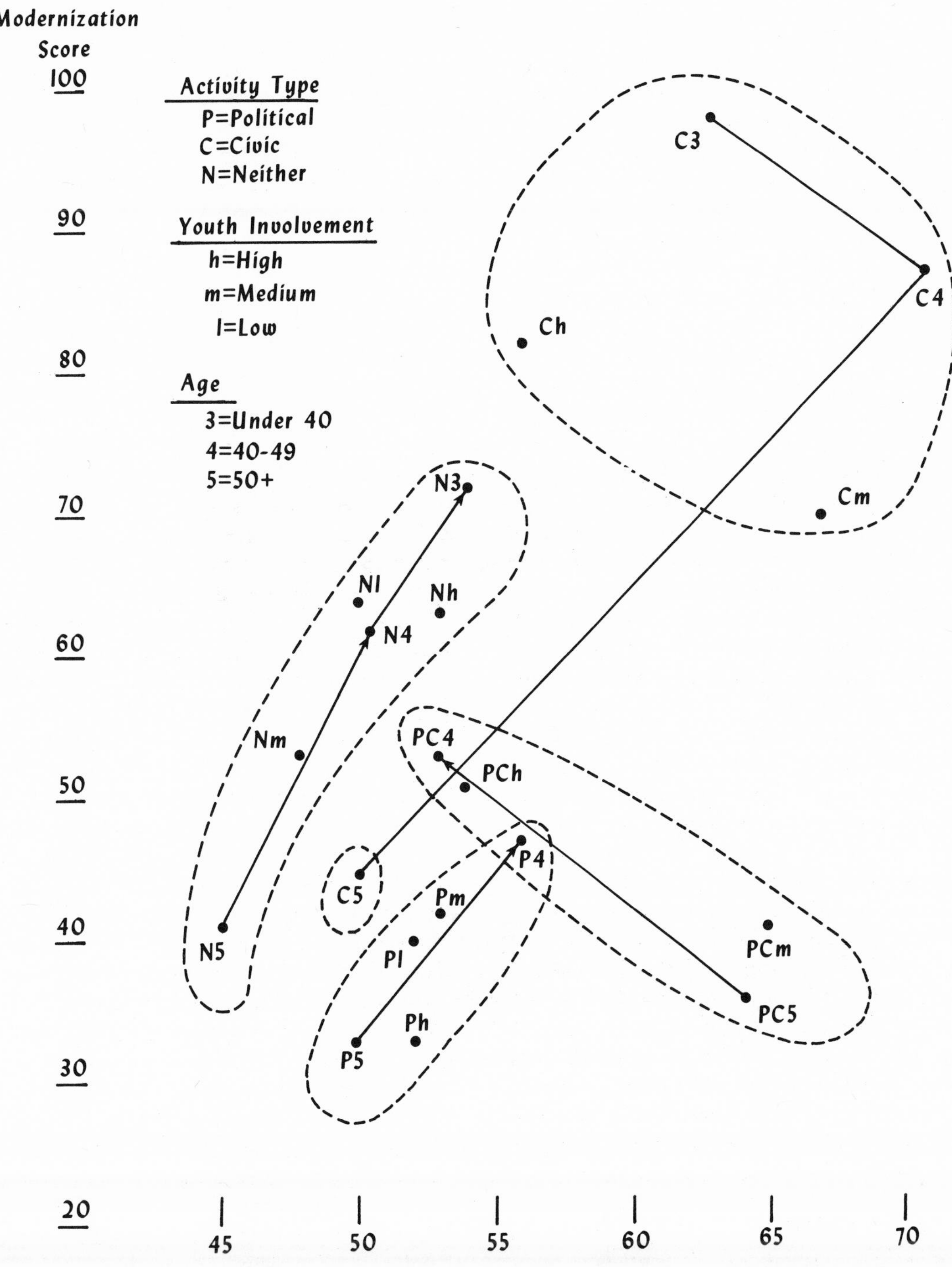

native, and their very moderation with respect to localism of orientation could make them doubly suspect to the established native residents. As the relationships depicted in Figure 5 indicate, even the natives among the civically active undoubtedly experience frustrations on this account, although there is no reason to assume that most of them would wish to be more active politically—or that their contributions to mountain development would be strengthened rather than diluted by diversion of energies in that direction. Given the generally low modernization scores among politically active men, the uncharacteristic persons among them are all the more important.

It was suggested in Chapter 1 that the social mobilization of the population in the affairs and decision-making of the community could be regarded as one dimension of modernization (a dimension that is distinct, however, from that measured by the modernization scores by which we summarized ratings on Indexes 3, 5, 6, and 7). We also put forward in Chapter 4 a scheme or typology of possible orientations to grassroots participation that range from traditionalist to decidedly contemporary. These variants showed up in some degree in the analysis of age differences controlling for occupation (see the previous discussion of Table 38). The mix of elements entering into response patterns relating to Index 4 is such that score means for the various activity/age categories show extremely little variation, ranging only from 54 (the civically active under forty years of age) to 62 (men in their forties who were active both politically and civically). Nor is there any systematic association between variation of Index 4 mean scores within the narrow observed range and any of the other mean attitude scores for the various activity/age groups. This being the case, we have not charted relationships between modernization scores and scores on Index 4 for the activity/age subsets of the mountain elites; such a chart would tell us no more than what is already shown in other figures with respect to modernization scores.

Tentative Projections of Attitude Change

In view of the persistent age differentials in modernization scores that have been observed within each occupational and activity category, we may gain insight into future prospects by reexamining those differentials. What might we expect as the younger cohorts among the native and the non-native permanent resident population progressively displace the older generation in community affairs? In thus speculating, we return to occupational categories as the most convenient way of inventorying the human-resource potentials. This procedure has the advantage also that it enables us to include teachers again.

Undoubtedly the very process of growing older, with all the associated changes in roles and responsibilities, alters some of the ways in which men typically behave or view themselves and others. With respect to opinions and activities that relate to regional modernization it is to be expected that as men age they acquire an interest in keeping things as they are; change may be expected to benefit those least bound to the established values and customs of traditional culture. Two sets of factors may affect this simple accommodation. Traditionalism may be reinforced by the outmigration of individuals predisposed for a variety of idiosyncratic or social reasons to challenge the prevailing order. On the other hand conservatism may be subverted from the outside by intrusion of a new climate of political and cultural values—as, for example, through the momentum of anti-poverty or civil-rights programs. Given the variety of factors operating, predictions are hazardous. If, however, we make projections assuming the stability of an individual's viewpoints over time, the fact that many "modern" opinions correlate negatively with age would mean that the projections should be biased in the "modernizing" direction.

We started with this assumption of individual attitude stability, together with an unchanging age composition of each occupational group, in constructing the estimates of 1976 modernization scores by occupation. Because the numbers of bankers and of public officials under forty years of age and the numbers of clergy and teachers over sixty are so few, we made ten-year attitude-change estimates after excluding these small cells. For bankers in particular this was the more important in that we should expect those

FIGURE 8.
Modernization Scores & 1966 Feelings about the Area, by Occupation

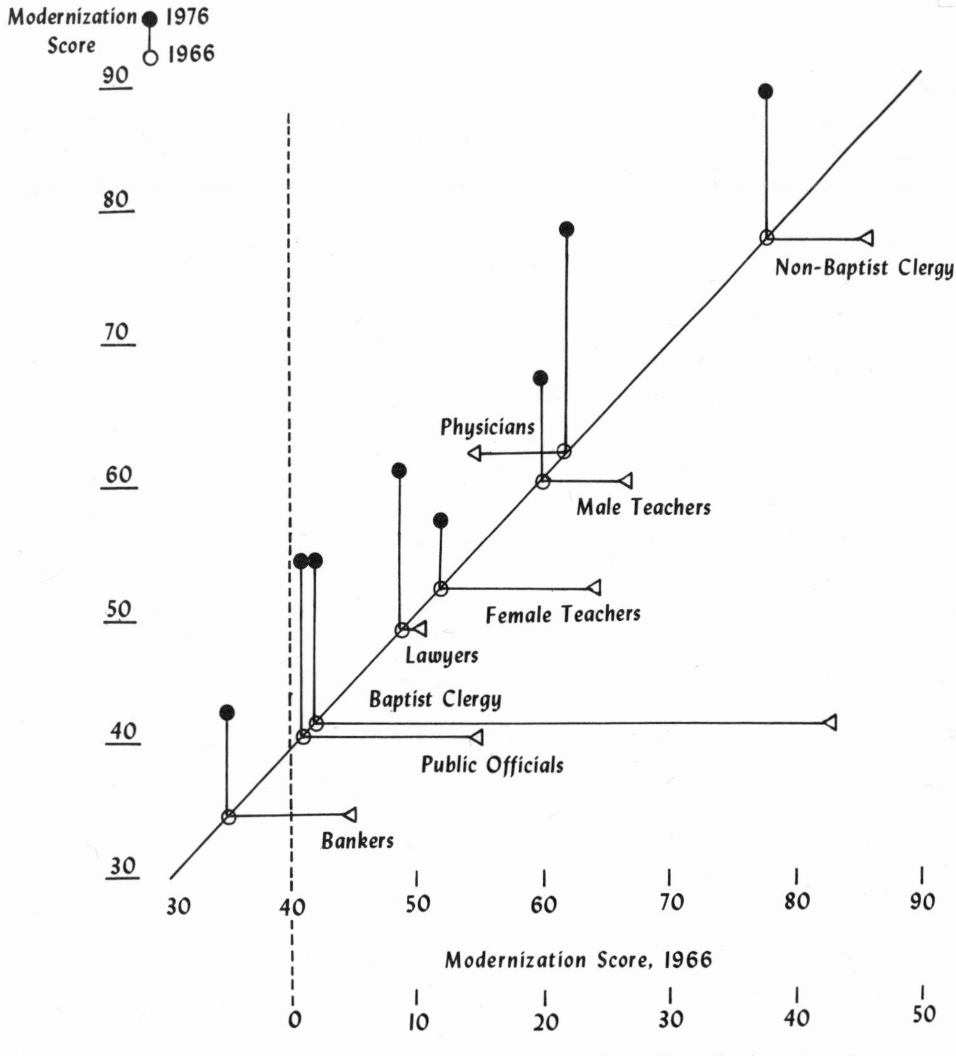

men who attain a position that would qualify them for inclusion in the banker category before reaching the age of forty would be highly exceptional; the bankers who are in their forties in 1976 will have come not only from the cohorts of younger bankers of 1966 but from men in less elevated ranks as of 1966. The procedure in arriving at the 1976 estimates was to find the *average* ten-year differentials in attitude scores within each occupation using the remaining age categories (imposing an age linearity adjustment that modifies the initial cohort-stability assumption). These mean ten-year differentials were then added to the 1966 scores of each age category to derive the projected 1976 scores diagrammed in Figure 8. The younger replacements to the population of 1976 were assumed to have views similar to their 1966 young predecessors, which may introduce a slight conservative bias in the projections as against the bias already noted in the other direction. We have added to Figure 8 the proportions of each occupational group who (as of 1966) expressed reservations of any kind about permanent residence in the mountains.

Modernization Scores: The projections for 1976 modernization scores do not shift the ranks among the occupations except that lawyers overtake female teachers. If the simple hypothesis on which these projections are based were valid, we would anticipate a progressively more favorable climate for modernization among all the administrative elites and among Baptist clergy (relatively the bankers would lag even further behind than in 1966, however). Female teachers would drop back in relative position to a place very close to the Baptist clergy and public officials (who lead the administrative elites). Next to the female teachers, the male teachers would make the smallest advance. Physicians, on the other hand, would move farthest in the modernization direction; already above any of the other predominantly native elites in their 1966 modernization scores, they would pull still farther ahead toward the non-Baptist clergy and in fact overtake the 1966 position of the latter.

The slippage in relative position of the teachers is especially worthy of comment; unless policies with respect to teacher recruitment and training change (along with an increase in readiness of other groups to evaluate local schools objectively), these estimates for teachers are probably optimistic. Teacher training is very localized, and recent in-service training policies in the state have exaggerated rather than modified this tendency. Only a minority of the mountain teachers, even in the high schools, feel secure to dwell and work in any other setting. Those of the younger teachers who have the most "modern" views are among the educated specialists in the mountains whose numbers are most likely to be depleted by migration. Under these circumstances, the capability of the nonmigrant, permanent teachers to perform effective cultural-bridge functions with mountain youth are limited because of their tenuous linkages with outer (or national) communication fields, whatever the strengths and weaknesses of their grounding in the local communities.

Grassroots Participation: It is not at all clear that support of grassroots participation will increase with the progressive shift among local leaders toward more national awareness suggested by the projected modernization scores. In fact when we applied to Index 4 the same methods used in projecting the modernization scores we found that only the lawyers and the female teachers would score higher in 1976 than in 1966; clergy and physicians would change very little; public officials and bankers would score lower in 1976. But the adjustment to impose age-linearity on the relationships is least justified in projections for attitudes toward grassroots participation, given the mixture of elements affecting this attitude cluster and its meaning that we have noted many times before. Small-community democracy is also everywhere in retreat before the bureaucratization of local government. Genuine grassroots participation for a new and more complex era has yet to be realized in the modern world outside the mountains, and there is no model that the nation could bring to the mountains in this respect. How far and in what ways mountain communities will find viable solutions to this problem (or whether they will find them) will depend upon local political and economic conditions and associated social structures. Grassroots participation is a phrase that changes its meaning in diverse mountain settings and varies through the political and semantic battles fought over the "maximum feasible participation" stipulation of the Economic Opportunity Act; this process of definition is a continuing one. It is also one of the reasons that it is so difficult to interpret publicly and privately expressed attitudes concerning local-federal cooperation and compensatory education.

Human Development Programs: The inherent value of human-development programs, the ways they have in fact been conducted, and who has

FIGURE 9.
Scores on Attitude Index 1;
1966 & Projected 1976 Values, by Occupation

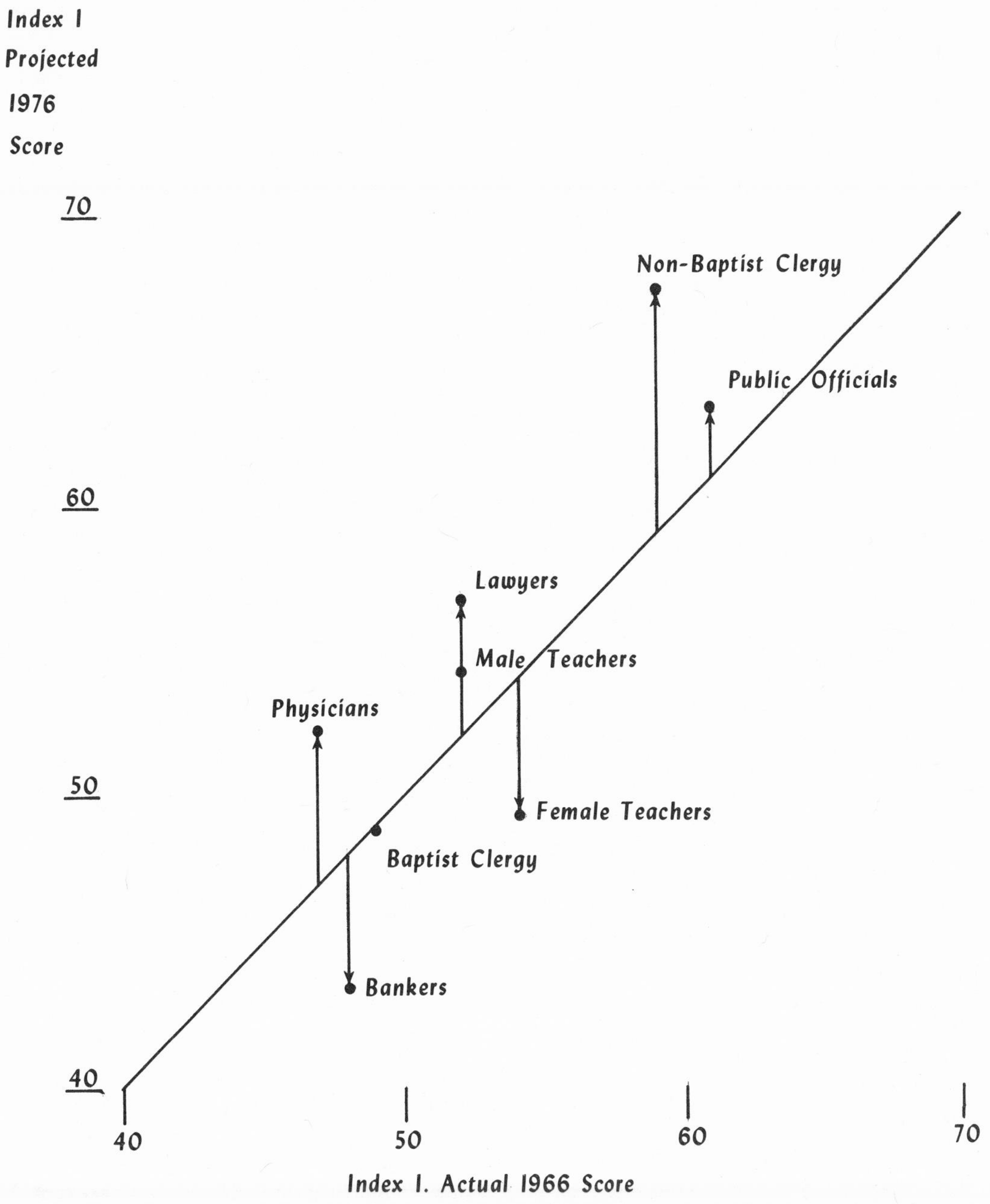

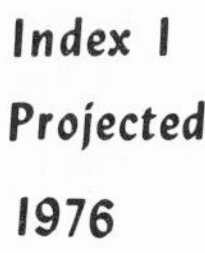

been doing what, often become entangled in the very particularized and personal modes of local social perceptions and intergroup relationships. Under these circumstances projections into the future based on age patterns in attitudes of the present is a particularly vulnerable procedure. Nevertheless the changes indicated in the Index 1 projections (Figure 9) are of considerable interest. The mean index value for bankers slips even further down, the Baptist clergy remain fixed just below the break-even or 50 mark, and female teachers drop back to a score of 50. Physicians, on the other hand, move up to join male teachers in a position of moderate support. The Index 1 score for lawyers rises remarkably; younger mountain lawyers are a distinct breed. Indeed this shift in the younger cohorts among the mountain legal profession is such as to inspire considerable faith in the validity of the projections for lawyers at least. And the projected change is of special importance in view of the firm position of the legal profession within the administrative elites, together with their fairly extensive exposure to experiences and ideas outside the mountains.

It is all too easy in a study such as this to (1) start with the observation that generally there is no lack of strong identification with and firm roots in the mountain area among the men who live there, (2) go on to seek groups whose attitudes and exposure to outside experience suggest a capacity to communicate from the "outside" end of the bridge, and then (3) conclude that it is men with high modernization scores who can most effectively serve cultural-bridge functions. But this reasoning overlooks how attitudes, activities, perceptions, and identification with the mountains combine in individuals and in the roles they play. It overlooks the importance of the information fields in which the various elites participate, the messages they convey to each other, and the resistances that may be encountered by a group who rate high on modernization. Those resistances will depend on how far the modern-minded men may also have roots in, be accepted by, or be alienated from the mainstream of the local society. It is probably a safe generalization that in most areas public officials will express more local attachment (and possibly more resentment of outsiders), while professional men will be more nationally oriented or more cosmopolitan. The problem is that in eastern Kentucky there has been so wide a gap between the region and the world outside. But there is also much cross-cutting of attitudes and diversity within occupational and even political-civic activity groups;[5] we have seen, furthermore, that the degree of respondents' involvement with mountain youth had very little correlation with their ratings on any of our attitude measures.

Among the most discouraging findings, given the severe and recurring mountain needs, is the persisting localism of teachers (especially among the women) and the continuing unawareness of most of the local leaders with respect to the deficiencies of local schools and the magnitude of the area's human-development gap vis-à-vis the rest of the nation. This problem has a distinctive and persisting ecological pattern in the mountains (despite one or two notable exceptions) that damps the pace of diffusion of enlarged opportunities among the rising generations. On the other hand we have noted the existence of substantial numbers of elite individuals who are inactive on our political and civic participation index and yet who express cosmopolitan and progressive attitudes. It is clear that most of these persons have not been co-opted into the local development and antipoverty programs (our measures of participation aside), and they are more inclined than most other groups to express themselves critically with respect to local-federal development efforts (Index 1). Nevertheless, some of these men (and women) may perform other highly important cultural-bridge roles; many have the potential to do so. Another hope-

5. In an analysis of this kind one has in fact very limited information about the closeness of the relationships observed. It was in an attempt to compensate such deficiencies that we undertook the multiple regression analysis reported in Appendix C. What that analysis showed more clearly than any of the tabular presentations of this chapter is the relatively small amount of total variance in attitudes that we are able to explain. Even allowing for the advantages of our indexes, which are better measures of attitudes for our purposes than were the factor scores we used in the regressions, one should be wary of ignoring what we have *not* explained.

ful sign is the finding of a loosening up and modernization of orientations and affiliations among the lawyers.

Before we started this study, one of the ablest mountain politicians stated that "the preachers are our biggest asset, they do more for the mountain communities than all the rest together." (He was referring to a non-Baptist area.) Whatever the truth or falsity of his assessment, it is interesting that non-Baptist clergy matched public officials in their enthusiasm for local-federal cooperation and for compensatory education, but were very different in their "inside-outside" perspectives; and they differed also (though less emphatically) in their positions with respect to active grassroots participation. The presence of commonalities in the views and civic activity patterns of these groups (clergy and politicians) may be interpreted as one of the more promising features of mountain culture and society in a modernization prespective; but it is also one of the complexities that must challenge the powers of empathy and diplomacy among extra-regional individuals and agencies seeking to share in mountain efforts toward modernization.

CHAPTER 6

The Market of Ideas

Our survey project unexpectedly became something of a market of ideas as a result of the relatively abundant comments that the mountain respondents wrote, at only slight prompting, on a final blank page of the questionnaire. This bonus of some 37,000 words of information about our respondents and their communities we have transcribed and analyzed in some considerable detail. The principal features of this analysis are reported here for the interesting light that it throws upon other interpretations of mountain culture and change, including the more objective findings of the research reported elsewhere in this volume.

Overall more than a quarter of the survey respondents provided at least one codable comment, a remark that was relevant to the general themes of our research. Of the different groups in our samples the teachers and the management-course participants most closely matched this overall average, along with the lawyers. Other administrative elites, however, commented less frequently (bankers 15 percent; public officials 20 percent) and, at the other extreme, two-fifths of the professionals (clergy and physicians) made written comments.

The great preponderance of these comments concerned the character of the agencies and the means that could bring at least partial solutions to recognized mountain problems. The major tenor was one of constructive criticism, as indeed might be expected as these respondents were taking the trouble to write their views at the end of a substantial questionnaire. The regional flavor of the themes and topics that attracted major attention was clear enough and these could be categorized into (a) general cultural and environmental characteristics of mountain society, (b) local administrative processes, and (c) the theme of outsiders with particular reference to federal personnel and agencies. The other principal way in which we could characterize the comments made was in terms of the solutions they offered to mountain problems. Comments and proposals on these lines could be categorized as being mainly related to either (a) welfare provision, (b) the development of physical resources, or (c) the development of human resources, largely through educational agencies.

The Mountain Scene

General Cultural & Environmental Characteristics

Over and over again respondents reiterated moral assertions of personal responsibility. In a score of cases disintegration of the ethic of rugged individualism was seen as *the* mountain problem.

> Cure-all programs are poor substitutes for natural intelligence and determination. Many young have those qualities and succeed on their own.
>
> Get all the education possible, work hard and enjoy work. Shun charity and handouts but give generously to others where real and honest need exists, but never when it creates parasites. Live and practice the Golden Rule.
>
> No source of planning or help can change the personal responsibility that belongs to each individual. We owe no man a living, but we owe every man a chance to make a living.

Another twenty general comments went further, deploring the abnegation of personal responsibility. For example:

> There is a social class in the mountains which believe that the government will provide for them and they in turn should not have to work for what they receive.
>
> Mountain people are selfish, ignorant, anti-social; "hillbillies" have lost their pride. . . .
>
> I do not agree with the "something for nothing" programs. Such a program destroys pride and self-sufficiency, and in many instances makes vagrants out of men who were formerly self-respecting.

Much rarer were the comments that suggested that mountain life and culture, rather than the moral failings of individuals, were or could be seen as impediments to development or change.

> Appalachia is a way of living. It will only be changed by the growth of a new generation and then only in part. The people may not want change.

Or the moral and cultural elements are mixed:

> The people have lost their self-discipline. They have been brain-washed by religion and consequently spend money on little used churches instead of libraries, hospitals, community centers, etc. Poor community planning.

A more nuanced view of the function of religion in mountain culture was contributed by a clergyman:

> Our isolation, ignorance, superstition, and indolence are largely a result of our theology. Much of the personal resignation to indifference in the past has been due to a religious animosity toward education and science. Likewise, the lack of personal ambition and initiative are due to a fatalistic philosophy of life that is largely due to a deterministic theology.

If the observations of another respondent are valid, and indeed the idea is commonplace, other related handicaps result from the interaction of character and the mountain environment:

> Many people in the mountains who are unemployed know little of travel and the knack of getting a job away from home. The older and middle aged especially have been raised in their local environment and when they "get away from home" they are homesick and frightened.

But the "people may not want change" theme is often stated more positively, as, for example, in the view that "mountain people value human relations over vocational advancement."

Local Administrative Processes

Some respondents wrote of mountain politics as a pervasive and distinct mode of conduct of local public affairs. Twenty-six comments were thus coded, though these were only a small proportion of the total comments about mountain people, entities, and programs in which disparaging references were made to politics or to politicians. Many of these comments were quite vague:

> Make programs non-political.
>
> Federal projects are controlled by local politicians for their own benefit.
>
> Mountain politics hamper welfare, industry, etc.

Though these comments lack specificity, they are not necessarily trivial or irresponsible. The same position is expressed with care and precision, totally without rancor, by one of the clergymen:

I feel that Politics or the ideas of the small town politicians misuse the intention of the Federal assistance for personal gain, and often detour the thinking officials to the wrong slant for the Politicians' own area. The best for people is often deferred, or hindered for personal gain.

But there were many much stronger statements in which there may or may not have been elements of personal vindictiveness. These included many allegations of corruption, vote-buying, and political oppression. Whatever the facts may be, such comments evidence the strength of bitter feeling that the subject of mountain politics arouses.

Apart from the comments so far referred to, there were twenty-one further observations that alleged the politicization of the public welfare programs. Certainly a number of these were trivial, but in many instances they referred to the Work Experience and Training Program for unemployed fathers, often in terms of ridicule or indeed obvious ignorance of the nature of the program.

Happy Pappy programs should be taken out of the school system and directed by non-political administrators.

The self-employed father program is used as a political football.

But other respondents claim closer knowledge.

As an advisor on a local welfare committee I have often observed how people in real need are reduced to a state disgracefully close to slavery to get and keep welfare aid. The new programs also appear to have this goal in mind. While ostensibly aimed at training men, they are set up so as to discourage "graduation" from the program. I believe the various aid field workers would do a great, lasting service if they were free from political manipulation. Mountain people make loyal, honest, hard-working employees and most only want a decent job. Unless they can somehow be freed from political oppression, they may never make it.

We look below at some of the assessments made of welfare programs viewed from other angles, but it is clear that there is fairly widespread, if often vague suspicion that their administration is characterized by inequities and political manipulation. At the very least it has to be said that their public image, at the time of our survey, was seriously compromising their declared objectives.

A similar number (twenty-three) of the respondents commented on political abuses in the school systems. Opinions centered upon the undesirable powers of patronage of school superintendents and the frequency with which educational purposes were subordinated to objectives of personal power. Again comments were often vague, for example that, "local school-systems are tied up by local politics"; but some of the charges made by teachers and others would be serious indeed if they were sustained: "A teacher should have greater freedom in voicing his opinion in civil affairs; most are afraid to do so for fear of losing their jobs." One teacher claims to be able to prove his statements that:

There is no problem, social economic or otherwise, that this section has that could not be solved by the people themselves if the politicians and some of the businessmen did not want to keep it exactly as it is. Politics is so entwined in education in Kentucky that if it were not for a minority of tenacious, aggressive, self-sacrificing classroom teachers the whole system would collapse.

Clearly there are teachers who gain security in mediocrity from the existence of small county and independent school systems. In contrast one respondent proposes: "Rotate mountain teachers in order to stimulate new ideas and break up kinship and friendship school systems."

The comments made upon the politicization of the school systems do not, on the whole, have the same kind of sting about them that the observations about welfare programs or about the general mountain political climate have. And in any case the subject of education occasioned more optimism than pessimism among our respondents. What perhaps was remarkable was that so few respondents spoke of the administration of mountain institutions and their personnel in other than these political aspects. A few of the comments referred, nevertheless, to inadequacies or ineptitute of personnel rather than political manipulations. Two examples will suffice:

Those that are in positions of leadership of public education often have little education or are from isolated backgrounds, which affects the type of education offered to children.

Once enthusiastic, many of us are losing patience with projects that had real constructive possibilities for good that through very poor local supervision the program is reverting to a near hand-out proposition again, with the recipient being required little or no responsibility and experiencing nothing that will help him be prepared for a regular job in the future.

Perhaps the main conclusion to be drawn from the incidence of comments upon the administration of the institutions of local government is that a widespread image of its politicized nature clouds assessment in other terms.

Outsiders

Mountain culture breeds a heightened awareness of outsiders, so that the very word often betokens antagonism.

Eastern Kentuckians do not like to be told how backward they are. A person from their own locality can discuss problems with them in their language and on their level. A local worker knows the people in the community that can and will help. An outsider more often disregards the advice of local people. . . . They stir up more resentment than they do good.

Even where a need of outsiders is acknowledged, their frequent failings are noted: "Outside ideas and people are needed. But sometimes outsiders fail to comprehend, and misunderstand mountain life. Urban standards are not always best for Appalachia." A major problem to the Appalachian is the impatience of these outsiders: "In our county, we have had considerable problems with young people who have come in from the outside with no knowledge of local situations or people and have tried to change total life patterns overnight." And the young are here the worst offenders, as numerous references to the volunteer programs attest:

Volunteers should be local.

Vista workers and social planners do more harm than good.

One was bold and unkind to tell a community teacher that it was a well known fact that a college student could do a better job teaching than she.

The local populace does resent this type of "outsider" [VISTA workers] because we feel they can and do influence our own youth toward moral digression.

The clergyman who made this last comment added that he knew of notable exceptions.

The most visible outsiders are those connected directly with programs of the federal government and who are seen as officials. Federal "control" is strongly resented, but many expressions of this view sound more like axioms of the mountain culture than specific criticisms:

Too many programs are worked out of Washington.

Too much federal control in schools, relief, and public works.

"Most people" in the area resent the trend toward Federal control in social and economic development.

In a few cases (not more than a dozen), the point was put that the federal government should foster more local involvement and get local advice. However, there is not enough material here to indicate whether these respondents think federal programs should be taken over by local government, or that local people should be recruited to man the federal programs at the local level.

Far the most frequent type of comment on the present position of the federal government in regional programs was to the effect that there was substantial financial waste involved. Forty-two comments of this type were coded. Some of these were utterly condemnatory, as for example: "Never has there been a program that tolerates and encourages waste as does the anti-poverty program. If the program should stop today, tomorrow there would be nothing to show for the money that has been spent." Other comments refer to waste and inefficiency, while implicitly approving the programs:

Most Federal programs are fraught with waste and inefficiency.

Poor management of Federal programs causes discontent among taxpayers.

Among the colorful examples of wastefulness that were provided was an account of the $75 cost of washing a school bus with Neighborhood Youth Corps help. In these and other examples given, there is little suggestion that it is outsiders who are being directly wasteful; they are examples of poor control rather than of too much control. The main shortcomings on the federal side are seen to be in the failure to maintain adequate standards of administration and in the proliferation of ineffective regulations.

The Federal government is sometimes so wound up in red tape, it defeats its own purpose.

But, for as long as the poor can lay in bed or the shade and make more money than our teachers can . . . we are in a sorry government-made mess, and to everyone, every single one I talk to, they feel the same.

The range of these comments on the outsider and particularly on the federal government points to an ambivalence arising from the combination of a strongly felt resentment of the stranger (which is a part of Appalachia's culture) and recognition of the need for even greater controls by outsiders, actually called "policing" by one respondent, to ensure both equity and efficiency in mountain welfare and development programs.

Strategies for Change in the Mountains

Welfare Provision

Clearly the whole concept of welfare provision and its place in social and economic development in the mountains is seriously in question among many of the respondents to our surveys. In fact no fewer than eighty-eight separate comments were coded as critical of welfare programs as such—that is, apart from the views already referred to concerning their excessive politicization. These comments were overwhelmingly concerned to stress the unproductiveness and even the positive harm that the various welfare provisions had introduced into mountain life. For some persons this harm extends through the generations with parents leading their children into perpetual pauperism:

There is a third and fourth generation of people refusing to work in favor of getting a government handout.

People on relief are encouraged to stay on relief and pass this feeling to their children.

No one I know knows of anyone in the so-called mountains who ever went hungry or lacked for clothing that would work. . . . There are too many give-away programs. . . . Give away programs are making vagrants of people. . . .

More often concerns of this kind were implicit, as when the need for a public welfare system was assumed but particular aspects of a program were condemned. Thus in the words of a public official: "The 'Unemployed Fathers' program will not accomplish the intended goals because: 1. The idea of 'no work with good pay' is permitted. 2. County supervision is 'nil' and there are no sound provisions for the discharge of the unworthy. 3. No apparent 'screening' of applicants. 4. More authority should be given to 'local' supervisors." This respondent's first point is by far the most common refrain, but there are many others. Some feel that the programs fail precisely where they are theoretically strongest—that is, in their educational provisions. It is widely believed that class attendance on the Work Experience and Training Program is bought with the welfare check but that the education itself is ill designed or unsuccessful.

I am not opposed to teaching reading, writing, and math to the dependent fathers. I am opposed to the way it is taught. It is absurd to teach a 60-year-old man from pre-primers and primer books.

How much good would you say these poor unemployed fathers will get from this education when they take the attitude "Why should I learn to read? I make more money than you do." This was a comment made to one of the teachers of an adult education class. . . . Let them learn to read, write, and do arithmetic, but it should be because they want to learn, not because they are paid for sitting so many hours in the classroom each week.

There is in fact a very widespread doubt in the minds of our respondents that the welfare programs are getting anywhere, either because of fallacies in their conception or inadequacies in their operation. At the time of the survey the Work Experience and Training Program had become such a talking point in the mountains that it preempted reference to a wider range of familiar provisions, such as food stamps and aid for mothers with dependent children. Where these were mentioned, and especially in the latter case, there was most often the same demand for the stiffening and the enforcement of conditions for aid.

Provide no ADC money after child no. 2.

Many people "up the hollows" let good garden plots lie idle in weeds while they scrounge food-stamps and watch television.

The Development of Physical Resources

Against the background of skepticism with respect to the potential of welfare and job-retraining programs to make any significant positive contribution to social and economic development in the mountains, there appeared on the questionnaires a flood of suggestions about the need and advisability of investment in physical resources, and it was frequently suggested that money now spent on welfare should be diverted to these purposes. In all, 138 comments and proposals relating to physical resources were coded. The vast majority were brief references to, or lists of, desired amenities or facilities: roads, industrial plants, jobs, water supply, etc. There were also a number of proposals relating to the attracting of industrial firms to the region, but only in a small minority of such instances was there any mention of how this might be done. The most frequent reference was to the need for roads. But other comments included the suggestions that the government should subsidize industry to create jobs, that there should be tax policies designed to encourage industry, land rehabilitation from strip-mining, better sewage systems and reservoirs, and that a better climate for industrialization should be created. The difficulties of small businesses are particularly noted: "The government seems to discourage small business. Too much red tape laws, rules; too many people looking down the small man's collar. He can't keep up with all the records, taxes, labor laws, regulations, and government representatives are so hard, harsh with small business they get discouraged, scared and ofttimes run him out of business."

Very few of the contributions develop any lines of thought that are original or, if they are original, practical. One detailed set of proposals involving tax concessions, accelerated depreciation schedules, federal defense investment, competitive road systems, and the building up of a revivified free enterprise economy is tied to the suggestion that it be financed by the monies now wastefully "filtering through the poverty program."

The Development of Human Resources

The largest general category of proposals for approaches to development in the mountains, however, was that of education, broadly defined. There were 178 comments containing some significant reference to education. Apart from the bankers, only three of whom referred to education, from 10 to 20 percent of each occupational category did so. These remarks covered a wide range of topics: general curriculum, vocational and compensatory education, problems of attendance and dropout, the role of the federal government, the facilities and organization of local schools. Many of these were elaborate and reasoned statements or at least agendas for fuller debate. Among other comments one teacher wrote:

The basic problems of Eastern Kentucky are rooted in the lack of education. There are many reasons for this lack of education. Some reasons are:

1. Inadequate or outdated school plants.
2. Use of inefficient teaching methods and techniques.
3. Insufficient materials and instructional supplies.
4. Inadequate curricula.
5. Non-enforcement of school attendance laws.
6. Local political decisions affect adversely educational personnel and policies. (Rather than what is best for the students, it is too often what is the political influence and strength of personnel involved.)
7. Lack of follow-up on good and well-inten-

tioned rules and regulations ("this is what they said last year and nothing happened"). Note: Some of the items mentioned above are in the process of being corrected. Yet, immediate "check-up or follow-up" on *new programs including Federal* would help break down the traditional "we'll get around to it later attitude."

Many of the more articulate and concerned of the respondents expressed the view that it is first and foremost in education that hope for the future of the region lies:

Education and training along with an opportunity to work with a living wage is the only hope for our mountain people.

The "living only for today" attitude of the majority of the mountain people who need help is going to have to be changed by education. Only then will all the relief and development programs be effective.

Frankly I see no solution except through the schools. . . . Seems to me as if our only solution is to start with dedicated, well trained teachers and ministers.

I worked with the Head Start program during the past summer—this is undoubtedly one of the best programs the government has put out.

These remarks were all written by businessmen, but for other groups the pattern is similar, except that the teachers are far more specific.

The rural schools do not offer the courses to broaden the students' horizons.

I don't believe multiplying vocational schools is the answer—on the job training and enrichment or progressive training can best be handled by industry.

The government programs are taking some of the best teachers for supervision, thus leaving poorer ones in the schools.

Too many of our Kentucky high schools are doing little to meet the needs of those students in the lower quartile of the school population . . . our middle class teachers do not understand the lower (working) class students. This lack of acceptance (understanding) is a big factor in the high dropout rate in Kentucky.

The people of the hills are gaining a broader outlook on life and an increasing interest in outside political affairs. The resistance to change in educational affairs is small.

One of the greatest exports of Kentucky is our teachers.

One question does puzzle me. As a vocational instructor hired by the school system, should I try to train for skills needed locally or should I try to equip my students with skills required further north?

Perhaps the main message of such comments is the evidence that there is interest and inspiration that could be tapped among teachers and others in the mountains who are concerned with education. Set against the range of comments about the political manipulation of the schools and their personnel, such concern and professional commitment among the alert and sizable minority is impressive.

It is undoubtedly true that the vast majority of the comments written upon the questionnaires by our respondents were critical of some aspects of mountain life and institutions. Disillusionment resulting from past failures to adapt to change, dislocations caused by the persistence of individuals and institutions in old ways, particularly in struggles for power and influence, the inequities or injustices suffered by individuals or groups represented among our respondents, and the discouragement or even despair that is seen to characterize mountain welfare recipients, whether or not this is seen as morally reprehensible—all these are impressions sustained from the writings we have analyzed.

It is equally clear that mountain communities are not without leadership or leadership potentials in planning and working for the future. Dignity, humanity, and dedication characterize the free comments of a large enough minority to offer real promise. In such a context modernization must meet strong opposition, and conflict is to be expected—both among interest groups and in encounters between mountain and nonmountain cultures. Undoubtedly the most important problem in the longer run lies in resolution of the more fundamental conflicts in cultural values, and in how far that resolution may prove to be a two-way creative process rather than a process of progressive domination and retreat or disintegration.

CHAPTER 7

The Social Dynamics of Modernization
The Appalachian Kentucky Case

The approach to the study of modernization that we have followed has entailed an analytical framework in which convergent approaches to resource development, communication and cultural diffusion, and social mobilization are built into the concepts of the "interstitial person" and the "cultural-bridge function." In reviewing here the principal empirical findings of the research, we will be assessing also the heuristic value of the analytical constructs we have proposed. Even where the research interest is highly particularized, as indeed is much discussion of Appalachian problems, this need not obscure wider pragmatic and theoretical implications. The fate of the millions of people who live and who will live in (or come from) Appalachia, with their lack of economic and educational opportunities, is undeniably a matter for wider (and not merely ethical) concern. In addition, a case study in the social dynamics of modernization is also a contribution to the clarification of conceptual and methodological problems.[1]

Appalachian Kentucky: The Problem of Modernization

Interstitial Persons in the Mountain Context

One view of Appalachia that emerges from many studies emphasizes its isolation from the remainder of contemporary society. We have indeed noted the segmented character of Appalachian Kentucky's human ecology, culture, and social structure, both internally and with respect to its larger physical and social environment. And we

1. From this point of view the fact that the eastern Kentucky case could be viewed as an exaggeration of certain features of highland Appalachia can be as much an advantage as a limitation.

have had frequent occasion to remark, and to build some of our analysis around, the "inside-outside" mental construct. But this is a stereotyped image, and to expound it once more is no part of our intention. Instead our focus is upon social communication, the obverse of the isolation that has usually been the theme of writers about Appalachian culture and society. We seek to identify and to explore the potentials among regional elites for communication of the information and values that can contribute to increased social mobilization for all sectors of the population and to the wider diffusion of social and economic opportunities. There is a gulf between region and nation to be bridged, and the bridging of it—through the diffusion of information, of new cultural patterns, and of opportunities for a more humane, abundant, and democratic existence—is central to our concept of modernization.

Understanding the responses of persons, both as individuals and in their patterned roles, is of crucial importance insofar as those responses represent reinforcement for tradition or for change. An overly functionalist view of society, or a deterministic one, may blind us to evidence of the presence of dynamic social relationships that convey and strengthen new values, even as there are always also conservative resistances to change. In order to explore change potentials in terms of communication in some depth, we have conducted our inquiry at the level of the individual, rather than using the more aggregative types of data (and of analytical models) that have characterized much of the sociological research on diffusion. To begin with, this required that we draw samples of presumptively "interstitial persons" of the Kentucky mountains, and by studying them attempt to identify the catalytic potentials for change—how far which sorts of interstitial persons were qualified to bridge cultures, and how far, in the particular mountain context, each might effectively perform significant cultural-bridge roles. The "interstitial person" was defined simply as one who, by virtue of his position and status in the local structure and his past experiences and contacts (or his professional affiliations), has access to both the local and national societies. This definition allowed us to avoid the morass of attempts to identify leaders and to deal instead directly with selected occupational groups whose members could be regarded a priori as interstitial in the context of our study, whatever their characteristics otherwise.

For a person to contribute in significant degree to cross-cultural communication, and to exercise a coordinate influence (direct or indirect) upon individual behavior or public policy, requires considerably more than merely to be placed in some respect at the interstices of subsocieties or cultures. Both the incidence of men capable of performing cultural-bridge functions and the realization of those potentials in a particular society will depend upon a number of analytically distinguishable, though deeply intertwined, factors. Broadly speaking, these factors are: first, the extent to which the society equips individuals in their youth to move between the local and national societies; second, whether the local social environment is sufficiently hospitable to more cosmopolitan values to encourage men who might act as agents of modernization to remain in the area, or at least not to penalize their continuance there (whatever the economic alternatives may be); and, third, the extent to which local institutions offered an active role to individuals capable of genuine intercultural communication, be they native or non-native men. In practice, of course, much of this comes down to the question: How ready is the local society to listen to and to accept the active involvement in local affairs of men with some knowledge and normally with at least some degree of empathic identification with the more cosmopolitan culture beyond the limits of the mountain community? The man with the fullest knowledge of, or identification with, the national culture and society will not necessarily be the most effective in performing cultural-bridge functions. He must possess genuine empathy with mountain people as well. But men who can fully bridge the gap between the localistic mountain and the cosmopolitan national cultures are extremely rare. What we observe here—and what, indeed, we might expect in a wide range of situations of subcultural lag—is a diversity of positions and roles in intercultural communication that, by their interlocking, relate the inside to the outside very tenuously.

That there is indeed a strong sense of belonging among mountain people—and a strong identification with what is believed to be a distinctive way of life—is evident enough. This cultural loyalty of the people of the eastern Kentucky mountains has been often documented, and it came through very strongly once again in our study. This in itself is not evidence of isolation from contact with or participation in the wider national society. Two sorts of data were directed toward delineation of variations in communication with the world beyond the mountains among the elites of our study. (1) We had data concerning family backgrounds and what we called exposure to the outside (as evidenced by experience of living or traveling in other areas and the reading of urban newspapers). (2) We also obtained data concerning attitudes and opinions relating to the local culture and local people and to outsiders and the wider national culture. Other attitude data, more concerned with sociopolitical structures within the mountains, with mountain prospects, and especially with human-development policies, also contributed to the identification of shared values and to distinguishing inside-outside communication systems. Here we take only a summary overview of what appear to us to be the most significant findings.

If we look at the majority of the administrative elites (public officials, bankers, and lawyers), the image of a population confined within the bounds of mountain experience will not be challenged by data on work experience elsewhere. But one of the most interesting aspects of these figures, which is surprising to many people, is the sizable minorities of all (except bankers) who had experience in urban living. If we take a population of 15,000 (which is greater than that of any eastern Kentucky town) as our cut-off for an "urban place," we find that only a fifth of the bankers can claim to have worked for a year or more in an urban location. Two-fifths of the lawyers and public officials and over half of each of the professional groups (Baptist clergy, non-Baptist clergy, and physicians) had such experience. A third of the lawyers and of the public officials (and also of the management-course participants) had worked for a year or more in a city of 50,000 or over, as had almost half of the clergy and the physicians. In other words the men we sampled as in "interstitial" positions between mountain society and the rest of the country did include sizable minorities who could bring a direct experience of urban life to bear on their roles both as facilitators of communication between the mountains and the nation outside and as participants in shaping the life of local mountain communities. That substantial proportions of even the administrative elites continue to have direct contacts with urban America is indicated, further, by the fact that even among bankers and public officials, three-tenths had visited five or more major cities during the preceding year; half the lawyers (and the participants in business-management courses) had done so, as had large majorities of each of the professional elites.

The important questions, then, are how far experience of life outside the mountains is reflected in perceptions and attitudes, and how far the mountain residents who participate most in the national society may exercise leadership or, contrariwise, be alienated from the less cosmopolitan of the area's elites. Social mobilization is a topic we will defer to the end of this chapter, however; for the moment we confine our remarks to some very summary comments concerning attitude profiles on the inside-outside dimension and a few of their correlates. In doing this we omit comment on methodology in the attitude analysis, referring to clusters or attitude factors or indexes without further elaboration.

Because of the interactions among variables (age, education, occupation, and experience of life elsewhere), associations between attitude patterns and other characteristics of our elites are of course statistically complex, and only huge samples (for some groups much greater numbers than exist in the sampled universe) would permit decisive isolation of particular effects or analysis of their interactive impact. But if this introduces empirical complexities and problems of identification, it does not complicate the basically simple theoretical-analytical framework with respect to the place of exposure and communications in attitude modification. To say this is, of course, to set aside idiosyncratic variability in attitudes. Indeed, on some matters, variations in individual attitudes occurring within any of the most refined subclassifications our data would permit were as impressive as variations between categories. This individuality is an important feature of mountain society which affects the potentials of and processes through which change occurs. But there were important systematic differences among various subcategories of elites against and within which the place of individual deviation must be seen.

In a final attitude analysis we included modernization scores, which summed up attitude clusters expressing a relatively high degree of understanding and acceptance of external (or more cosmopolitan) standards of judgment and ways of thinking, along with relative receptivity to outsiders. (Attitude clusters entailing adherence to strongly localist views carried a negative weight on this measure.) Contrasts in modernization scores among members of the various occupational groups and among age classes within those groups showed up clearly, with a fairly consistent monotonic effect of age, the younger men being the more broadly oriented to the national life. We made use of these age differences within occupations when projecting distributions of elite views a decade hence. Similar projections were undertaken also for scores on the cluster of attitudes relating to human-development programs. The results present a more sanguine portrait of elite attitudes than a cross-sectional assessment of the present samples, although the magnitudes of shifts differed considerably from one occupational category to another. Particularly striking are the age differences in attitudes—and hence the projected shift toward modernization—among the local lawyers and physicians.

Within the professions and especially among the physicians and the non-Baptist clergy (virtually all of whom were college graduates) parental education proved significantly to affect judgments of the local mountain schools and to heighten awareness of the disadvantages faced by youth coming out of those schools to compete in labor markets outside the mountains. For most of the mountain elites, however, parents' education had been decidedly limited, as had been the education of the older bankers and public officials themselves.

Of more general importance than educational background were differences in nativity. This is both the simplest summary index of experience outside the mountains and a direct indicator of nonregional contributions to the current human resources of the area. To come from other than a mountain place proved to be one of the most important predictor variables on other characteristics among our elites; it was a comparatively good predictor both of differences in values and of the modes or patterns of participation in local community affairs. However, nativity was closely linked with occupation or profession; most of the non-natives actually were clergy. Furthermore, whereas the non-native clergy and physicians were more cosmopolitan in attitudes and in experience than their native confreres, among the administrative elites the few non-natives were often the most localist in outlook—a finding we ascribed to the dependency of administrative elites upon their local constituencies and the consequent greater need for an in-migrant aspirant to achieve strong local identification.

In any case it is clear that the localist attitudes that we found to prevail among the native leaders, especially those in the administrative elites, must inevitably foster inhospitality to that minority of outsiders whose activities are essential for modernization of eastern Kentucky. This regional ethnocentrism inevitably conditions the impact of most incoming communications, as it must weaken the nexus between the inner and the outer societies. At the same time the clear emergence of individuals who are of a broader culture and who display a relatively great potential for catalyzing further mobilization, takes us a long step toward understanding the social dynamics of regional modernization.

The Local Culture

In the immediately preceding remarks we have simply taken a difference between local and national cultures for granted, without comment on, let alone specification of, just what the local culture of Appalachian Kentucky is like. But the problematic nature of Appalachian modernization as seen in this study does not lie in the banal counterposing of local conservatives and cosmopolitan progressives. Cutting across such stereotypes is the culture of this region, in which a highly particularized and affective treatment of one's neighbors is still of vital importance. Hence conservatives often can act more freely and effectively, because they work within the culture, while progressives (whether native or foreign—and most of those who fell into our samples were foreign) have a record of short-lived achievements and long-lived mistrust. This conclusion is amply borne out by the experience of those antipoverty workers in community action programs who have attempted to mobilize support for multicounty planning units following federal guidelines. In so doing the workers have (usually unsuccessfully) challenged the local notion that interests could be aggregated legitimately under the umbrella of existing local political arrangements. In contrast to these experiences must be set the extensive development, however much faulted in practice, of pragmatic aid programs under the aegis of local public administrations: examples are the Work Experience and Training (referred to in our study by one of its pseudonyms, the "Unemployed Fathers' Program"), the Food Stamp, and the Head Start programs.

It is very clear that the pluralistic model of societal structure, with its complex and specialized input-output equilibrium, runs counter to the cultural and political norms of eastern Kentucky and of Appalachia generally. In the mountains established institutions are readier to absorb new functions than to make way for new institutions with new allegiances. When it became apparent that regional elites were challenged by wholly new organizations, with substantial payrolls financed by the federal government, the reaction of these elites was a countermove on behalf of the apparatus of local government, a move that eventuated in the passage of the 1967 Green amendment to the Economic Opportunity Act.

Whatever may be the observations of some writers concerning the motivational configurations of Appalachian society—and there are many stereotypical characterizations of fatalism, apathy, and abject dependency—we saw our elite respondents making discriminating choices. They do have strong commitments, both cultural and political; their attitudes are not simple defense-mechanisms to deny an unwelcome reality. Their attitudes have positive connotations also, and they reflect phenomenological realities of the mountain heritage: the characteristics of the pioneer or of the nineteenth-century entrepreneur are still held up to be admired; a man's virtue is still evident in his worldly success and the ambitious man need not stay poor; it is wiser to seek to transform the landscape than to try to change one's fellowmen. The home region arouses intense loyalty, and the out-group person is held in suspicion, while the world he comes from (with its big government, mass-media, and powerful economic interests) does unjustified violence to the mountain way of life.

Such broad sweeps of the brush, based upon answers to our questionnaires and upon comments respondents wrote on them,[2] mask a great variability in attitudes concerning local life, as in those relating to the larger national culture and eastern Kentucky's place in it. Nonetheless this simplified sketch of the traditional mountain ethos provides a benchmark in relation to which progressive development must be interpreted.

In view of the gerontocratic and strongly native character of the administrative elites, with their key position in local community affairs, the prevalence of unprogressive attitudes among them is one of the more serious stumbling blocks in the way of progressive change. The comparatively exceptional men among this group who take a broader view are all the more important on that account. Moreover, along with many of the nonadministrative elites and others who are outside of or who challenge the local establishment, they are on that account all the more frustrated. Indeed many of our respondents see themselves as living in a highly politicized environment, as abundant comments on our ques-

2. These comments are quantified insofar as it was possible in Chapter 6.

tionnaires or attention to local affairs in area newspapers quickly reveal. It is over problems connected with the allocation of power that the main social-political modernization efforts have foundered: administrative reorganization of education, effective involvement of the poor in community decision-making, giving outsiders (including federal administrators) key roles in building local social-action institutions, and in balancing between the short-term profit-taking of the strip mines and the long-term profits foregone that could have been derived (or might in the future be derived) from amenities of the area.

The Schools & the Cultural-Bridge Function

It has been proposed that the most promising way to bring together local and national cultures, and to promote a wider identity in Appalachian Kentucky in particular, is to make use of the educational system. The importance of schools for the development of productive capabilities (the formation of human resources) is usually taken for granted, but the implications of changing conditions for the performance of that function are not so fully appreciated. Nor can we separate this problem from the question as to how far mountain schools can carry out the broader socialization of youth for life in the nation at large; the answer to this question is critical in determining whether regional modernization efforts can ultimately succeed.[3]

If we look at those elites who are the products of the mountain schools, we find little ground for optimism concerning contributions of schooling to a wider awareness of life beyond the mountains or to skill in performing a cultural-bridge role. Taken by itself, the amount of schooling (wherever attained) was a much less reliable predictor of extent and type of participant behavior, or of attitudes and perceptions, than was occupation, age, or nativity. This should hardly surprise us; schools, after all, reflect their communities. In the relatively isolated subcultures in which many members of the mountain elites grew up, the schools shared both the values and the social isolation of their students. Furthermore what schools contribute may not be fully reflected in differential attitudes and behaviors of individuals who have had varying amounts of schooling: there may be some spillover from the more to the less educated among the elites.

It must be remembered also that circumstances obscure the contribution of education so far as our study is concerned. For one thing, educational variance was narrow within the elite occupations; public officials (and in lesser degree bankers) were the important exceptions. This means that our opportunity to observe the effects of differential amounts of education, and of local schooling in particular, was limited. Election to local political office favors the strongly localist orientations in eastern Kentucky as elsewhere, whatever a man's education may be. Second, on principle we did not sample by education. Clearly we can make no statements from our data about how representative groups of mountain people with various amounts of schooling would act. We have no evidence about the better-educated mountain men who have gone elsewhere to live, but only about those who remained—though it is the latter who are important so far as performance of a cultural-bridge role in today's society is concerned. At the same time, however, it must be noted that the least-educated men who were eligible for inclusion in our sample were highly selected from among their peers. Whether or not this blurs contrasts by schooling within our elites is not clear, but the question must be raised.

Third, while the men with the widest horizons were generally of relatively high educational attainment, whether they came from the mountains or elsewhere, not all well-educated men could see beyond the mountains. Moreover, among those schooled locally, the more educated by no means gave the most support to widened participation

3. In one study it was found that graduates of mountain high schools were better able to adjust themselves to the labor market in their home areas, but in those areas only. Migrants' economic status was not affected by the extent of their schooling, even though migration brought economic benefits to members of the sample studied. See H. K. Schwarzweller, "Education, Migration, and Economic Life—Chances of Male Entrants to the Labor-Force from a Low-Income Rural Area," *Rural Sociology*, 19 (June 1964).

by the poor or by the young in community decision-making. And finally there has indeed been change in the mountains, as age differentials in attitudes and in perceptions voiced by the elites attest. It would be impossible to draw inferences about the effects of what is happening in today's schools on adults and mountain communities of the future from our observations concerning effects of schooling among the mountain-reared of our sample.

More immediately pertinent information of other kinds is available, both from our study and from other sources, concerning the performance and potentials of the local schools as agencies for the enlargement of horizons and opportunities for the next generation. One type of evidence concerns experiences of young people currently coming out of the high schools, whether as dropouts or as graduates. The seniors in most mountain secondary schools have been performing poorly on statewide tests, despite the fact that they are a more selected set of individuals than are seniors elsewhere (being among a smaller proportion who have continued to high school completion in an area characterized by high dropout rates). The local exceptions, however, give evidence of the fact that a mountain community with the will to improve its schools and with leaders understanding what this can mean have indeed succeeded in bringing about remarkable changes.

No one should expect that a school can fully offset effects of deprived homes and neighborhoods. On the other hand it is equally clear that schools can reinforce subcultures or can operate to offset them. In the mountains, in contrast to city ghettos, teachers may have the advantage of working in a less hostile or rebellious classroom environment, which could mean more favorable conditions for moral or civic socialization and for preparation of the young to choose opportunities and to participate effectively in a wider future society. How far this enlightenment can and will be accomplished will depend, however, upon the "psychic mobility" of the teachers themselves and upon the support of their endeavors by school administrators and by members of the local elites. An earlier study of the region's elementary teachers revealed an educational culture of poverty, an educational system that was forced to live upon its own personnel and intellectual resources because of the small inflows of outside personnel and the weak support from informed public opinion.[4]

In the present study we found that male secondary teachers were considerably ahead of the administrative elites and of the Baptist clergy (though far behind the non-Baptist clergy) in modernization scores. This suggests, among other things, that these male teachers potentially could perform a cultural-bridge role and prepare mountain children to adapt to a wider environment, wherever the pupils may eventually come to live. Female teachers tended to have narrower horizons than the males. If we judge by age differentials in attitudes among members of the present teaching force, prospects for future improvement in orientations toward, or in capacity to reach out to, the wider society would appear gloomy, especially with respect to the female teachers. Female teachers seem likely to change less over the next decade than any other occupational group we have studied.

There is also dissatisfaction with mountain life among large fractions of just those teachers best qualified otherwise to exercise intermediary roles, and these are probably the men most likely to leave the mountains after a short tenure in a mountain school. In part this is inevitable. However, the consequences are serious where, as is most often the case, the teachers who do attain high integration in local community life have narrow horizons. That in many parts of the mountains key positions in the school system are political prizes, indeed that they are fundamental to local patronage systems, has been well described by others. Where this is the situation it must almost certainly alter the incentives for teachers and undermine their morale.

Quite as important as the contribution of those who staff the schools is the degree of involvement of the adult community in school affairs, and the extent of awareness among that community of both the existing situation in the schools and the

4. H. Dudley Plunkett, "The Elementary School Teacher as an Interstitial Person" (Ph.D. diss., University of Chicago, 1967).

needs and potentials for change. What is important is how prepared the general public is to support educational advances, whether this involves the provision of material resources or the accepting of new values and forms of school-community collaboration.

It would be expected that the most informed judgment concerning the schools, and the most articulate demand for changes in them, would come from the elites—that is, from those presumably more qualified to judge on the basis of background and of access to information from both local and wider sources. In fact most of the mountain elites were decidedly uncritical and strongly defensive of local schools. Generally this defensiveness was greater precisely in those localities where an observer could collect objective evidence showing extreme inadequacy of the schools for either conventional tasks or to meet newer challenges. The most emphatic in their insistence that "local schools are doing a good job" were the bankers, the Baptist clergy, and the manufacturers. There may be a slight basis for encouragement in the fact that a fifth of the local public officials were slightly critical of the local schools.[5] So were a fourth of the male teachers (fewer of the female teachers) and a third of the physicians and the non-Baptist clergy. Though few teachers (or Baptist clergy) were ready to admit that education given youth in mountain schools "failed to prepare them adequately for life elsewhere," large minorities or small majorities of all the other elites conceded this deficiency. However, the only criticism of local schools that characterized majorities of the administrative elites (public officials, bankers, and lawyers) was the proposition that local schools did not put enough emphasis on training for jobs in the mountains. The mixture of loyalties, frustrations, and limited knowledge reflected in these responses illuminates both the weakness and the ambivalence of support for school improvement in the mountain areas, but it points also to conceivable possibilities for real breakthroughs in school policy.

In some respects one of the more encouraging findings is that very little resistance was expressed to the importation of out-of-state teachers for mountain schools—a tolerance that contrasted sharply with attitudes toward other outsiders residing in the mountains. This receptivity (or, perhaps more correctly, this relative neutrality) with respect to the teacher from outside could be viewed cynically, as signifying that the teacher poses no threats to the elites, that teachers have no central position in the community and are in no position to make nuisances of themselves. There is certainly much truth in such an interpretation. Reactions to a question concerning (imaginary) nonlocal school administrators would undoubtedly have been quite different. But we may turn this logic around. Teachers who come into the mountains from other areas are very different from those outsiders that mountain men do most resent, different in several significant ways. The teachers come to settle in the mountains for a long enough time to share in mountain life, to listen to mountain people, to be genuine members of the community, even if not part of the ruling cliques. Their roles are familiar to the traditional society. In all these respects teachers can be assimilated quickly into mountain life. Furthermore, that the teachers stand apart from local power wielders means that they are also to a considerable degree insulated and freed from the latter; both the teachers' credibility and their room for maneuver gain from this fact.

In our judgment it would be a mistake to underestimate the improved "outreach" among mountain youngsters (and their parents) that could result from a great influx of outsiders to teach. One way in which this influx might be insured would be to arrange a rotation system that would provide for one- or for two-year replacements of in-service teachers in their home communities. If some of these incoming teachers came on loan from the communities to which mountain people most often migrate (whether in Kentucky or as far away as Chicago or Detroit), there would be a further advantage. Teachers who had lived in the mountains on such rotations would be able to carry back with them

5. It will be remembered that this was especially true of those public officials who were more active in nonpolitical affairs—that is, the businessmen politicians.

another exposure—an exposure to, and, one would hope, an empathic comprehension of, what migrant families bring with them from the mountains into their new urban environments. At the same time local teachers might be encouraged and given opportunity to extend their exposure and their cultural-bridge potential through increased in-service training on leave to other, more urban communities.

In general, what do our findings concerning the cultural-bridge potentials of teachers and of other elites mean for the development of human resources and for social modernization? Whether in schools or elsewhere, the relevance of education to regional modernization may be said to be threefold. There is first of all the socialization function, reflecting the social requirement of certain cognitive and attitudinal characteristics for effective participation in modern society, whether the person involved remains in Appalachia or becomes a migrant working in a metropolitan area. It is the socialization function with which the school as such is largely concerned, yet even here schools have only a limited autonomy. With favorable attitudes in the community the potential effects of both regular and compensatory educational programs are greatly multiplied. To be in the best position to exploit such opportunities, school systems need not only appropriate recruitment and in-service training policies but innovative approaches to school organization and to school-community relationships. There has been widespread and firm acceptance of the Head Start program among regional elites; such a situation amounts to an invitation to the agencies carrying out this program to work at a peculiarly sensitive point to compensate for the effects of social deprivation and to prepare for social change.

Second, even though young people in the mountains might have gained the capabilities that would admit them to a wide range of activities, and even though they might have acquired sufficient awareness or receptivity to the wider national culture, it does not necessarily follow that their recognition of alternatives open to them will match the objective opportunities. The perceptions by young people of roles (in either local or nonlocal life) will be conditioned not only by what they are deliberately taught but by the prevalent attitudes and practices with which they are surrounded in the communities where they live. Thus a wealth of research evidence tells us that pupil motivation is a function more of parental and peer-group attitudes than of teachers' attitudes or skills. The strength of tradition-bound perspectives in these matters suggests severe limitations of vocational horizons in the outlook of mountain youth.

Finally, educational agencies may perform quite another cultural-bridge function, not only for the oncoming generations of youth but also for contemporary adults. In part this may be a feedback or spillover effect whereby knowledge and attitudes acquired by schoolchildren and youth become part of the thoughts of their elders. But beyond this the schools and other institutions with manifest educational and training functions may share significantly in the more direct transmission to adults of modernizing attitudes and patterns for behavior. The extent to which a wide range of human-development programs will in fact reinforce one another in the mountains and contribute to modernization among mountain youth and adults is still problematic. Our study has, however, delineated some key features of the environmental context within which they operate. Among the elites, federal involvement is resisted less in human-development programs than in local planning at large. On the other hand, the human-development programs as a whole are very much less favored than are physical-resource development efforts.

Communication & Social Mobilization

The modernization of Appalachian Kentucky depends upon what the people of the region do, upon the nature and intensity of their social commitments and upon the experiences and attitudes of the more and the less active participants in community affairs. Some indicators of exposure to life and ideas beyond the mountains were discussed in Chapter 3, where we also introduced two activity indexes: the political and civic participation index and the youth-involvement index.

The first of these classified respondents into four categories: political and civic activists, civic activists, political activists, and inactives. The normal expectation of political scientists would be that these categories would scale (though the relative positions of the two intermediate categories would not be predicted), and that the scale would have social status correlates. In practice no such ordering occurred in our data. Furthermore educational correlates with political activity were quite unsystematic. In contrast, positive selection to civic activity was marked among the management-course participants and among men of other occupations whose education had been out-of-state. Political and civic activities were essentially different dimensions of behavior; the overlap of the two was confined to 13 percent of the whole sample of administrative elites and only 4 percent of the professionals (counting active men only, 19 and 13 percent, respectively).

High levels of civic activity and of youth involvement, on the other hand, were much more likely to occur together than combinations of civic and political activities, especially among the professionals. Moreover, evidence concerning attitude correlates tended to confirm that the civic activities reflected in our measures, with their requirements for comparative flexibility and innovative approaches, were more closely identified with modernization functions than were political activities.

Those members of our samples identified as civic activists are clearly among the most fully "mobilized" men in the mountains. They are on the whole characterized by attitudes that are sympathetic to modernization goals. Among other striking characteristics of this category of elites is the high proportion of the nonlocal element, in large part due to the high degree of civic activity among the more frequently "foreign" clergy. Moreover, those of the nonlocal clergy who expressed reservations about living in the mountains were no less active in civic affairs on that count. Thus the typically short-term commitment of the clergy to the area does not seem to be a bar to their performance of significant roles in modernization activities.

Still the fact remains that few civic activities give access to formal power, and formal power-holders (political activists) are disinclined to have civic involvements in our sense of the term. In this sense the political-civic activist category is the most strategically placed, and it is among these elites that modernizing attitudes could be expected to be most fruitful. Our data, however, indicate that no such pivotal group exists. Men in the political-civic activists category are by no means consistently among the most modernizing in their attitudes. In fact, in view of how infrequently the power-holding categories show modernizing attitudes and how often the civically active do so, we are obliged to draw the conclusion that political involvement in eastern Kentucky is associated with a negative propensity toward modernization, and that civic involvement carries a positive relationship to modernization, while passive persons frequently appear to fill an intermediate position. It may therefore be that we can interpret the special case of mixed political and civic involvements as representing at least as much "pork barrel" as modernization.

Almost inevitably this means that the widely reported local controversy over the procedures needed to implement new development policies is a prelude to more serious confrontations between the wielders of formal power and the social theorists—whether the latter be federal officials or clerical evangelists of the "social gospel." An alternative is that the machinery of antipoverty and other human-development programs will come under the control of the traditional local power-holders. In the present circumstances (1969) this new power to the local authorities could be deployed to resist big government, or it could be used to form an alliance of local and national paternalisms in dealing with problems of poverty. In either case the results would be to suffocate some of the local initiative of civic activists or modernization-minded inactives, not to mention effects on activities of nonelite groups. But these are not the only possibilities.

It is plain from our study that an altogether different strategy could be proposed, involving a purposive devolution of the power to originate social action. As far as the elites are concerned, we have already pointed out the low degree of social mobilization that characterizes many professionals. Among the physicians especially there is a lack of involvement in regional problems, in terms both of activity and of relevant attitudes—although there are very notable individual exceptions. We have also seen that lack of involvement ("inactive" on the political and civic involvement index and "low" on the youth involvement index) does not necessarily imply apathy; men categorized as inactives often had more positive attitudes than did those in the active categories.

The case is therefore strong for new policies to accommodate in modernization programs the criticisms made by many who have a positive interest in the programs' goals, but are dissatisfied with aspects of their administration, their results, or their byproducts.[6] It is misgivings of these types, we have suggested, that preclude general endorsement of human-development programs (as assessed, for example, through Index 1) even among more progressive groups in the mountains.

Such criticism may reflect regionalist interests, technical assessments, or ethical standards. For example, we have seen that the occupational groups closest to the working economy (the administrative elites and the management-course participants) are most likely to believe in economic benefits from Appalachian legislation. Whether this is a disinterested judgment is doubtful when it is seen beside the tendency of the same groups to regard national prosperity as of more benefit to the region than any special programs. These seemingly "all is grist that comes to the mill" attitudes contrast with the views of men who, while skeptical about the results that the special programs are achieving, believe that those programs are needed nevertheless. The concern of these latter respondents (judged from the comments they wrote on questionnaires) centers upon the threat of the demeaning of mountain people by technocratic outsiders who are oblivious of or inattentive to common human failures. Thus, maladministration and paternalism were charges that came through strongly in these comments, while many men favored greater efforts at dissemination of information as a backup to proliferating programs.

In sum it would appear that there is a substantial reserve of human potential that modernizing institutions can hope to draw upon. However, as things stand at the moment the utilization of such resources as the nonlocal professionals, the younger elements among the lawyers and male teachers especially (but also the young more generally, as the age-based projections of Chapter 5 suggested), the more educated but inactive management-course participants, and the more liberal clergy is unlikely to expand substantially or to have important cumulative effects. The mobilization of currently frustrated, and even alienated, groups could both infuse creativity into the activities of regional elites and extend the scope of effective performance. But the crux of the matter is that, while the availability of such hidden resources and their mobilization in regional institutions would seem to make a logical equation, our data in fact portray the frequent lack of correspondence between having modernizing attitudes and participating in institutions or agencies with modernizing functions.

Some common threads thus emerge from our analysis. In inventorying the *individual* characteristics of a representative sample of regional elites we also obtain information about the society at an *institutional* level. Conversely the effective communication of information, ideas, and attitudes (while having its institutional characteristics in, for example, educational and socioeconomic regional development programs) is finally dependent upon the social actions of individuals—that is, upon the propensities of the interstitial person to carry through with performance of cultural-bridge functions.

If we concern ourselves first, therefore, with the individual, it is clear that social exposure and social communication behavior are necessary but not sufficient conditions for performing modernizing functions. Passive exposure and active participation are given their significance by the

6. The clearest testimony to these remarks appears in the comments written on our questionnaires and reported in Chapter 6.

intention and values of the individual concerned. In this study we have sought to discover whether there is any systematic pattern in the distribution of these sets of traits. If the results are not amenable to any simple synthetic expression, this is because the patterns they reflect are not simple; it is not to say that they are of only theoretical concern. According to their aims, agencies of regional development will have to take into account not only a complex social structure but also the cultural elements that enter into the social dynamics of their target communities.

Attempts to shortcut regional planning by doing the "simple" physical tasks first have led to the unrealistic bifurcation of physical and human resource-development efforts, each having its own constituency in the mountains. Meanwhile attempts to cut the Gordian knot of poverty and dependency by applying the clinical skills of social engineering have demonstrated repeatedly that human resource development is less a technical than a cultural process.

Mountain society today appears to be characterized by several interrelated structural contradictions and conflicts of interests. These are only partially recognizable in studying, as we have done the upper layers of the social pyramid. There is first the paradox of the coexistence of a heritage of grassroots participation and the resistance of entrenched members of the local establishment to involvement of the poor or the young in the new-style maximum feasible participation. There is nothing distinctive to the mountains in such resistance; what is distinctive is the extent to which, despite some monolithic local power structures, the older view of men and of local democracy still has vitality. A further conflict emerges from the fact that there are many positive values in the face-to-face quality of traditional mountain culture, and many of those men who are ready and willing to move into the modern world in some respects are carefully counting the costs. Furthermore, though some of the threatened values concern everyone in a small-scale society (which can hardly be maintained), other values, and the anticipated costs, depend upon a man's favorable sociocultural background and economic status in the mountains and the degree to which he can exercise power or influence. Finally, opposed to the conservatism of those most inclined to count the costs, there is the implicit ultimatum of those who want to live or work in the mountains, but nevertheless, if they are not admitted to participate in choosing social goals of the future and in the vetting of area or community development programs, will vent their frustration by leaving or by withdrawing from local affairs. The consequence of such withdrawal is also a cost to the local communities and, in the longer run, to the conservatives; it is a cost in the depletion of effective resources for human leadership, in the reduced vitality of local life, and in the failure to mobilize popular commitment to improving the quality and viability of mountain communities of the future.

Each has, therefore, an interest in fostering communications and in learning about the characteristics and values of others with an interest or a stake in mountain life. This applies to elites in relation to nonelities, to administrative in relation to professional elites, and, perhaps above all, to outsiders in relation to insiders. But the nurturing of communications must be a long-term process to allow for the diffusion against ecological, social, and cultural resistances, of crucial motivational and institutional change.

Tables

TABLE 1. Factor Analysis of Ecological Data for Eastern Kentucky Extended

			Factor	
		I	II	III
Percentage of variance explained: }	23 Factors	43.7	55.5	66.1
	3 Factors	66.1	83.9	100.0
Variable name	**Commonality**	**Factor loadings**		
Percentage of adults with schooling:				
More than 8 years, 1950	.94	.94	.22	.08
More than 8 years, 1960	.93	.89	.17	.10
High school graduate, 1960	.95	.96	.14	.12
Illiterate	.75	-.84	.16	-.09
Current school retention rates:				
To 9th grade or more	.68	.58	-.04	.59
To 12th grade	.81	.14	.20	.86
To 12 grade, adjusted	.91	.37	-.24	.85
Percentage of males employed:				
In agriculture	.87	-.50	-.88	-.08
In white-collar jobs	.76	.59	.60	.23
In mining	.87	-.45	.80	.16
Percentage of adult females in active labor force	.85	.92	.10	.02
Income per capita	.93	.95	.12	.09
Income per square mile	.92	.84	.42	.21
Fertility rates	.53	-.69	.14	-.19
Rate of population change, 1950 to 1960	.80	.84	-.22	-.23
Proportion of employed commuting to work outside county	.29	.11	.08	-.52
Population density	.90	.73	.55	.24
Road mileage to nearest city of 20,000 population	.75	-.76	.39	.13
Percentage of residences with telephones	.88	.93	-.04	.16

TABLE 2. Summary of Samples Studied

	Sampling ratio	Total sample list*	Returns obtained	Return rates (percentage)
Secondary teachers by mail	.33	798	541	67.8
Other elites by mail				
Clergy	1.00[a]	236	173	73.3
Management courses	1.00	311	153	49.2
Other elites by interview				
Bankers	1.00[b]	111	79	71.2
Lawyers	.50[c]	141	90	63.8
Physicians	.50[c]	122	80	65.6
Public officials	....[d]	159	97	61.0[e]
Total nonteachers		1,080	672	62.2
Manufacturing entrepreneurs	....[f]	....[f]	57	....[f]

*Includes individuals in fact no longer resident. This amounted to approximately a fifth for teachers and was high for clergy also. For the total interview sample of 533 (excluding manufacturers) those who had left or died numbered at least 43, with a possible maximum of 113, or between 8 and 21 percent but closer to the former. In sampling we did not substitute new names to replace those no longer living in eastern Kentucky (or deceased).

[a]Regular denominations only. For Baptists we used a $3,000 salary cutoff to exclude the numerous part-time clergymen.

[b]President or manager and next most senior executive.

[c]Where there were more than 12 in one town, this ratio was reduced to 25 percent, provided at least 6 persons were included.

[d]All county judges, mayors, and chairmen of boards of trustees for cities to and including the sixth class. For magistrates we took a ratio of .50.

[e]The low return rate in this group is attributable to the difficulties encountered by interviewers in locating magistrates in the valleys and hollows, together with special problems encountered in one county.

[f]The manufacturers were interviewed primarily for other purposes. Of a total of 173 interviews 57 included a trial set of attitude questions, most of which were later used on the form for other groups and are therefore comparable.

TABLE 3. Age Distributions of Respondents by Occupation

Occupation	N	Percentage Distribution by Age						Percentage under 40	Percentage 50 and over
		Total	Under 30	30-39	40-49	50-59	60+		
Public officials	97	100	...	8	36	32	24	8	56
Bankers	79	100	...	5	15	22	58	5	80
Lawyers	90	100	9	12	26	20	33	21	53
Clergy: Baptist	74	100	8	32	35	16	8	40	24
Clergy: non-Baptist	99	100	13	34	23	18	11	47	29
Physicians	80	100	5	22	22	29	21	27	50
Management course participants	151[a]	100	7	31	37	20	5	38	25
Manufacturing entrepreneurs	95[b]	100	15	11	34	22	18	26	40
Teachers: male	314[c]	100	38	31	19	10	2	69	12
Teachers: female	226	100	30	14	22	30	4	44	34

[a]Excluding 2 cases not responding on age

[b]Excluding 19 cases not responding on age

[c]Excluding 1 case not responding on age

TABLE 4. Proportions Native to Eastern Kentucky by Age and Occupation[a]

Occupation	Age					
	Under 40	40-49	50-59	60+	N	NR
Public officials	100*	94	100	100	95	2
Bankers	100*	100	100	91	77	2
Lawyers	84	91	88	93	90	1
Clergy: Baptist	37	32	25	33*	73	1
Clergy: non-Baptist	8	17	22	18	96	3
Physicians	73	56	65	76	78	2
Management course participants	88	84	73	88*	151	2
Manufacturing entrepreneurs[b]	92	88	55	67*	54	3
Teachers: male	82	92	97	83*	311	4
Teachers: female	79	82	75	53	225	1

*Less than ten in this age category.

[a]Identifying themselves as native to the mountains in response to the question "In what place would you consider yourself a native?" (See the first item on the questionnaires.)

[b]Proportions born in the county of present residence (attitude subsample).

TABLE 5. Cumulative Percentages Completing Selected Levels of Education by Occupation

	Educational level reached							
	Graduate work	College graduate	Some college	High school graduate	Some high school	Elementary	N	NR
Public officials	4	12	31	57	81	100	93	4
Bankers	6	24	62	79	96	100	77	2
Lawyers	53	80	95	98	99	100	89	1
Clergy: Baptist	53	64	85	89	93	100	74	0
Clergy: non-Baptist	87	92	97	97	100		95	4
Physicians	95	100					79	1
Management course participants	9	30	63	88	97	100	151	2
Manufacturing entrepreneurs	- 11	-	33	65[a]	76[b]	100	63	1
Teachers: male	32	99	100				315	0
Teachers: female	24	99	100				226	0

[a]Another two cases (3 percent) may have had some higher education.

[b]Another seven cases (11 percent) may have had some high school, but were recorded as elementary school only.

TABLE 6. Educational Attainments by Occupation and Age

	Age	N	Percentage distribution by schooling				
			Total	College completion or more	Some college	High school graduate	Less than high school graduate
Public Officials	<50	42	99	12	7	40	40
	50+	51	100	12	29	14	45
Bankers	<50	16	100	38	56	6	-
	50+	61	100	20	32	20	28
Lawyers	<50	42	100	98	2	-	-
	50+	48	100	63	33	2	2
Clergy: Baptist	<50	56	100	70	18	5	7
	50+	18	99	44	33	-	22
Clergy: non-Baptist	<50	68	100	96	3	1	-
	50+	27	100	82	11	7	-
Physicians	<50	39	100	100	-	-	-
	50+	40	100	100	-	-	-
Management course participants	<50	113	100	28	36	26	10
	50+	37	100	30	27	27	16
Manufacturing entrepreneurs	<50	39	100	13	26	42	19
	50+	24	99	8	26	18	47

TABLE 7. Percentage Distributions of Education of Respondents' Parents

Respondent's Occupation	Neither completed high school	One or both completed high school	One or both some college	One completed college	Both completed college	NR
Public officials	60	12	7	1	2	18
Bankers	47	15	15	5	-	18
Lawyers	43	17	12	9	3	16
Clergy: Baptist	76	4	12	3	-	5
Clergy: non-Baptist	46	22	11	8	4	8
Physicians	35	17	19	15	4	10
Management course participants	51	24	11	7	1	6
Teachers: male	63	17	15	4	-	1
Teachers: female	54	12	26	5	1	2

TABLE 8. Paternal Occupations by Occupation and Age of Respondent

Respondent's occupation	N	Father's occupation: percentage distribution					
		Total	Mining	Farming	Trade	Profession	Other
				Age under 50			
Public officials	41	100	17	41	15	7	20
Bankers	14	100	7	7	43	14	29
Lawyers	40	100	15	20	25	25	15
Clergy: Baptist	56	100	14	41	13	14	18
Clergy: non-Baptist	69	100	4	26	15	17	38
Physicians	39	100	8	15	16	38	23
Management course participants	109	101	17	16	36	9	23
Manufacturing entrepreneurs	38	100	5	13	8	13	61
Teachers: male	267	100	19	24	19	14	24
Teachers: female	146	100	11	23	24	19	23
				Age 50 and over			
Public officials	53	100	6	47	19	9	19
Bankers	61	100	8	39	23	15	15
Lawyers	44	100	2	41	9	32	16
Clergy: Baptist	17	101	18	59	6	6	12
Clergy: non-Baptist	28	100	0	32	32	11	25
Physicians	39	101	3	36	15	26	21
Management course participants	37	99	22	16	29	16	16
Manufacturing entrepreneurs	18	100	-	17	17	11	55
Teachers: male	35	100	6	52	15	18	9
Teachers: female	68	99	5	39	21	18	16

TABLE 9. Percentage Distributions of Responses Indicating Feelings about the Area

Feelings about the area[a]	Public officials	Bankers	Lawyers	Clergy: Baptist	Clergy: non-Baptist	Physicians	Management course participants	Teachers: male	Teachers: female
This has been my home, these are my kind of people, and I am happier living here than anywhere else.	93	82	80	23	15	59	62	62	55
Where I grew up was different, but I have grown to love this community and regard it as my permanent home.	4	14	10	32	39	27	23	11	21
I want to live here for a while, but would not want to spend the major part of my life here.	1	1	4	38	35	9	4	14	11
I would rather live somewhere else, but there are compensations in living here.	1	3	6	8	9	5	10	11	11
I definitely do not like living here.	--	--	--	--	2	--	1	2	2

[a]The question asked was, "Which of the following most nearly describes your feeling about the area where you live and work? (Check one only.)"

TABLE 10. Feelings about Living in the Area by Age and Occupation

Occupation	Content (responses 1 and 2)		Reservations (all others)		Percentage with reservations	
	Age <50	Age 50+	Age <50	Age 50+	Age <50	Age 50+
Public officials	41	53	2	-	4	-
Bankers	13	61	3	-	18	-
Lawyers	36	44	5	3	12	6
Clergy: Baptist	29	7	22	8	43	53
Clergy: non-Baptist	36	17	34	11	49	39
Physicians	31	37	8	3	21	7
Management course participants	91	34	17	3	16	8
Teachers: male[a]	145	16	42	7	22	30
Teachers: female[a]	65	46	21	10	24	18
Total	487	215	154	45	32	21
Total excluding clergy and teachers	202	119	35	9	17	8

[a]Sample responding on supplementary questionnaire.

TABLE 11. Percentage Distributions of Nativity-Identification Categories by Major Occupation Sets

Nativity	Identification (feelings about the mountains)	Administrative elites	Professional elites	Management course participants
Local:	Content	88	53	77
	Reservations	5	2	11
Nonlocal:	Content	6	23	8
	Reservations	1	22	4
Total:	Percentage	100	100	100
	Number	343	394	138

TABLE 12. Percentage Distributions of Education-Identification Categories by Major Occupation Sets

Education	Identification (feelings about the mountains)	Administrative elites	Professional elites	Management course participants
High school or less:	Content	43	4	32
	Reservations	-	1	5
Some college:	Content	29	3	30
	Reservations	1	2	4
College completion or more:	Content	24	63	23
	Reservations	3	27	6
Total:	Percentage	100	100	100
	Number	238	316	145

TABLE 13. Exposure to Nonmountain Life by Occupation

Occupational groups	Percentages with given types of exposure				
	College out-of-state	Work out-of-state (a year or more)	Military Service	Work in city of 15,000 or more	Work in city of 50,000 or more
Administrative elites (weighted average)	14	27	51	41	28
Public officials	2	34	44	39	30
Bankers	15	19	36	20	15
Lawyers	19	26	61	46	33
Professional elites (weighted average)	47	52	50	54	47
Clergy: Baptist	37	61	28	53	47
Clergy: non-Baptist	62	69	16	57	44
Physicians	44	38	60	54	49
Management course participants	18	35	47	42	31
High school teachers:					
Male	11	29	49	30	23
Female	20	25	5	24	15

TABLE 14. Exposure to Nonmountain Life by Age and Nativity: Administrative and Professional Elites and Businessmen

	Percentages with given types of exposure			
	College out-of-state	Work out-of-state (a year or more)	Military service	Work in city of 15,000 or more
A. Elite category and nativity				
Administrative elites:				
Native	12	24	51	37
Non-native	33*	57*	54*	64*
Professional elites:				
Native	27	27	57	39
Non-native	64	74	45	67
B. Elite category and age				
Administrative elites:				
Under 40	34	36	54	63
40-49	11	30	77	42
50-59	10	28	44	45
60 and over	9	20	35	22
Professional elites:				
Under 40	42	52	44	63
40-49	46	56	78	51
50-59	54	54	40	62
60 and over	54	43	32	30
Management course participants				
Under 40	13	28	66	46
40-49	15	43	76	38
50-59	25	33	43	33
60 and over	**	**	**	71*

**Denominator under 10

*Denominator 10 to 24

TABLE 15. Indexes of Current Contacts outside the Mountains by Occupation

	Read an urban daily newspaper	Visited 5 or more major cities in past year
	Percentages	
Administrative elites:	90	39
Public officials	77	29
Bankers	96	29
Lawyers	93	49
Professional elites:	83	64
Clergy: Baptist	73	59
Clergy: non-Baptist	83	71
Physicians	89	62
Management course participants	90	51
High school teachers:		
Male	78	32
Female	82	39

TABLE 16. Organizational Participation of Teachers by Sex: Percentage Distributions of Degree of Involvement

	Active members		Inactive members	No such affiliations reported	NR	Total
	Very active	Attend meetings				
	Males (N = 300)					
Educational organizations:						
National or regional	13	41	35	7	3	99
Local	26	45	8	19	3	101
Religious organizations	29	14	5	49	4	101
Civic organizations	23	10	2	61	4	101
	Females (N = 217)					
Educational organizations:						
National or regional	12	41	37	5	4	99
Local	25	47	15	9	4	100
Religious organizations	37	21	3	35	4	100
Civic organizations	24	8	6	58	4	100

TABLE 17. Types of Very Active Participation: Percentage Distributions of Teachers by Sex

	Male teachers	Female teachers
Single activities		
In educational organizations only	12	11
In religious organizations only	13	16
In civic organizations only	7	7
Multiple activities		
In both educational and religious organizations	6	9
In both educational and civic organizations	5	5
In religious and civic (whether or not in educational) organizations	5	7
No high levels of activity reported	45	41
Total	99	101

TABLE 18. Community Involvement of Teachers: Percentages Discussing Community Affairs with Designated Other Elites

Occupations of discussion partners	Male teachers	Female teachers
1. Superintendent of schools	54	48
2. County agents	36	23
3. Business leaders: local	53	35
4. Business leaders: in other counties	15	12
5. Bankers, lawyers, and/or journalists: local	36	24
6. Bankers, lawyers, and/or journalists: in other counties	11	7
7. Local doctor	31	30
8. Minister of a church other than your own	34	29
9. None of the above	16	24
Selected combinations:		
Any businessman (3 and/or 4)	55	37
Nonlocal businessman, banker, lawyer, and/or journalist (4 and/or 6)	21	16
Businessmen only	4	3
Superintendent only	8	9

TABLE 19. Persons Consulting with Teachers Concerning Children Other Than Their Own, as Reported by Teachers

Occupational group	Percentage of teachers consulted by members of the designated groups	
	Male teachers	Female teachers
A. Doctor, clergyman, and/or public official	37	23
B. Local school superintendent and/or member of a college faculty	40	29
C. Welfare worker	48	40
D. Other nonschool persons	11	18
E. No one	30	37
<u>Selected combinations</u> (mutually exclusive)		
A only	5	2
A and D, not B or C	1	1
A and B, not C	5	5
A and C (with or without B and/or D)	26	15
C only	14	15
C and B; C and D; C, B, and D	8	10
D only	3	6
B only or B and D	8	9
No one	30	37

TABLE 20. Consultations with Teachers as Reported by Other Respondents; Percentage Distributions within Elite Categories

Frequency and job-relatedness of consultations	Administrative elites*	Professional elites*	Management course participants
Rarely or never	39	24	34
In regular work only	31	47	25
Voluntary only	17	12	33
In regular work and as a voluntary activity	14	18	8
Number	344	331	141

*Weighted samples.

TABLE 21. Percentages of Elites with Local Youth Contacts, by Occupation

	Youth-related contacts with parents		Direct contacts		
	In regular work	In volunteer activities	Individual youth only	Youth groups	Total
Administrative elites	53	26	48	27	75
Public officials	53	33	49	31	80
Bankers	39	31	51	26	77
Lawyers	58	24	46	25	71
Professional elites	86	30	42	42	84
Clergy: Baptist	86	37	40	56	96
Clergy: non-Baptist	92	32	27	70	97
Physicians	81	25	52	22	74
Management course participants	32	23	36	29	65

TABLE 22. Percentage Distributions of Youth Involvement within Age, Education, and Nativity Classes for Main Elite Categories

	Degree of youth involvement		
	High	Medium	Low
Administrative elites*	21	35	44
Professional elites*	25	50	25
Management course participants	20	35	45
Administrative elites*			
Native	21	36	43
Non-native	24	24	52
Age under 50	24	35	41
Age 50 and over	14	38	48
Education under 16 years	21	31	48
Education 16 years plus	22	37	41
Professional elites*			
Native	21	50	29
Non-native	27	50	23
Age under 50	29	49	22
Age 50 and over	17	52	31
Education under 16 years	23	61	16
Education 16 years plus	25	48	27

*Weighted samples.

TABLE 23. Percentage Rates on Social Exposure Indexes within Elite and Youth Involvement Categories

	Degree of youth involvement		
	High	Medium	Low
Attended college outside of Kentucky:			
Administrative elites	6	21	13
Professional elites	56	49	35
Worked for a year or more in a city of 15,000 or over:			
Administrative elites	40	43	34
Professional elites	56	52	60
Visited five or more major cities during the preceding year:			
Administrative elites	52	45	33
Professional elites	76	61	60

TABLE 24. Percentages Participating in Local Government and Community Affairs by Occupation

	Political office (past or present)	Officeholder or committee member (past or present)			Other significant active roles
		Area development	Economic opportunity	Civic clubs	
Administrative elites[a]	63	16	11	21	28
Public officials	100	26	22	17	22
Bankers	38	13	5	28	41
Lawyers	60	11	7	21	25
Professional elites[a]	10	20	15	23	37
Clergy: Baptist	11	24	17	21	28
Clergy: non-Baptist	3	26	25	28	54
Physicians	15	14	9	20	32
Management course participants	23	16	10	37	35

[a]Weighted samples.

TABLE 25. Percentage Rates of Participation in Local Government and Community Affairs: Elite Categories by Age, Education, and Nativity

	Political office				More than one civic activity		
	Administrative elites						
	All*	Bankers and lawyers	Professional elites*	Management course participants	Administrative elites	Professional elites	Management course participants
Age:							
Under 40	46	39	10	14	22	31	16
40-49	70	54	6	31	20	25	38
50-59	75	63	9	27	21	23	33
60 and over	67	49	22	25	15	16	@@
Education (years completed)							
12 years or less	71	44	0@	21	15	14@	16
Some college	63	48	5	22	26	14	24
16 or more	60	56	11	27	18	26	45

*Weighted samples.

@@Denominator under 10.

@Denominator 10 to 24.

TABLE 26. Combinations in Political and Civic Participation: Activity Type Percentage Distributions within Elite Categories

Activity types	Administrative elites			
	All*	Bankers and lawyers	Professional elites*	Management course participants
Inactive	31	41	69	61
Civically active	6	8	21	16
Politically active	50	43	6	12
Both	13	8	4	11
Total	100	100	100	100
Percentages of:				
Politically active who are civically active	20	16	43	49
Politically inactive who are civically active	16	16	23	21
Civically active who are politically active	69	50	18	40
Civically inactive who are politically active	62	51	8	16

*Weighted samples.

TABLE 27. Combinations in Political and Civic Participation: Activity Type Percentage Distributions within Elite and Age, Education, and Nativity Categories

	Activity types					
	Inactive	Active civic	Active political	Active both	Total	N
Age under 50						
Administrative elites@	32	6	47	15	100	143
Professional elites@	69	23	3	5	100	206
Management course participants	61	16	12	11	100	113
Age 50 and over						
Administrative elites@	30	6	52	12	100	213
Professional elites@	70	16	10	4	100	126
Management course participants	56	18	13	13	100	138
Education 12 years or less						
Administrative elites@	25	4	60	11	100	104
Professional elites@	86*	14*	-	-	100	14
Management course participants	71	7	13	9	100	56
Education over 12 years						
Administrative elites@	32	7	47	14	100	244
Professional elites@	69	21	6	4	100	312
Management course participants	55	21	12	12	100	95
Native of eastern Kentucky						
Administrative elites@	30	6	51	13	100	326
Professional elites@	67	18	10	5	100	144
Management course participants	61	17	11	11	100	127
Not native of eastern Kentucky						
Administrative elites@	42	4	46	8	100	24
Professional elites@	70	23	3	4	100	180
Management course participants	56	16	16	12	100	25

@Weighted samples.

*Denominator 10 to 24.

TABLE 28. Social Exposure by Political and Civic Participation

Activity types	Administrative elites[a]	Professional elites[a]	Management course participants
Percentages who have been to college outside Kentucky			
Inactive	20	47	14
Civically active	5*	59	20
Politically active	10	22*	28*
Both	15	31*	20*
Percentages who have worked in a city of 15,000 or more			
Inactive	33	55	43
Civically active	37*	57	42
Politically active	42	36*	29*
Both	36	53*	53*
Percentages who have visited five or more major cities in the past year			
Inactive	37	62	48
Civically active	58*	77	54
Politically active	33	38*	44*
Both	59	67*	65*

[a]Weighted samples.

*Denominator 10 to 24.

TABLE 29. Relationships between Activity Type and Youth Involvement of Administrative Elites

Participation scores		Total administrative elites*			Bankers and lawyers only		
		Degree of youth involvement					
Civic	Political	High	Medium	Low	High	Medium	Low
		Activity percentages					
High	High	22	15	6	7	9	7
High	Low	6	7	6	7	11	7
Low	High	55	52	45	59	44	38
Low	Low	17	26	43	27	36	48
	Total	100	100	100	100	100	100
		Ratios to expectancy					
High	High	1.83	1.25	.50	.88	1.13	.88
High	Low	1.00	1.16	1.00	.88	1.38	.88
Low	High	1.10	1.20	.90	1.37	1.00	.88
Low	Low	.53	.81	1.34	.66	.88	1.17

*Weighted sample.

TABLE 30. Relationships between Activity Type and Youth Involvement of Professional Elites[a]

Participation scores		Degree of youth involvement		
Civic	Political	High	Medium	Low
		Activity percentages		
High	High	10	3	2
High	Low	39	18	9
Low	High	4	7	7
Low	Low	47	72	81
Total		100	100	100
		Ratios to expectancy		
High	High	2.00	.60	.40
High	Low	1.85	.85	.42
Low	High	.67	1.16	1.16
Low	Low	.69	1.04	1.17

[a]Weighted sample.

TABLE 31. Relationships between Activity Type and Youth Involvement of Bankers, Lawyers, Clergy, and Physicians Combined

Participation scores		Degree of youth involvement		
Civic	Political	High	Medium	Low
	I. All four groups combined: activity percentages			
High	High	9	5	5
High	Low	28	16	8
Low	High	22	18	25
Low	Low	41	61	62
Total		100	100	100
	II. All four groups combined: ratios to expectancy*			
High	High	1.69	.89	.44
High	Low	1.75	.93	.50
Low	High	.95	.90	1.11
Low	Low	.68	1.06	1.16
	III. Bankers and lawyers: ratios to expectancy*			
High	High	1.17	1.50	1.17
High	Low	.44	.69	.44
Low	High	2.68	1.95	1.73
Low	Low	.47	.63	.84
	IV. Clergy and Physicians: ratios to expectancy*			
High	High	1.67	.50	.33
High	Low	2.44	1.13	.56
Low	High	.18	.32	.32
Low	Low	.84	1.26	1.42

*Expectancies are derived from marginal distributions for all four occupational categories combined, using weighted samples.

TABLE 32 A. Percentage (and Number) of Respondents Agreeing on Opinionnaire Items Concerning Mountain Culture and the Outsider: Mountain Culture and Yesterday's People

	Public officials	Bankers	Lawyers	Clergy: Baptist	Clergy: non-Baptist	Physicians	Management course participants	Manufacturing entrepreneurs	Teachers: male	Teachers: female
1. If a young man really has ambition, he can make a success of his life no matter how poor or ignorant his family may have been.	94 (87)	93 (71)	92 (82)	97 (73)	77 (74)	94 (73)	97 (146)	96 (54)	89 (148)	88 (114)
2. Public assistance has made people into lazy loafers and they won't work even when a job is offered them.	72 (71)	90 (71)	70 (64)	90 (65)	67 (65)	84 (67)	90 (138)	93 (51)	. . .	. . .
3. Mountain men are good workers if you understand how to get along with them.	98 (94)	94 (77)	90 (81)	85 (63)	79 (73)	87 (67)	89 (131)	94 (50)	. . .	. . .
4. Labor strife has kept a lot of business out of East Kentucky.	62 (59)	77 (58)	73 (65)	61 (46)	63 (61)	68 (54)	82 (121)	84 (46)	65 (142)	61 (93)

TABLE 32A. (Continued)

	Public officials	Bankers	Lawyers	Clergy: Baptist	Clergy: non-Baptist	Physicians	Management course participants	Manufacturing entrepreneurs	Teachers: male	Teachers: female
5. One of the most serious problems in the mountains is that too many people are suspicious.	39 (36)	48 (35)	37 (34)	59 (44)	53 (51)	27 (21)	36 (53)	. . .	39 (85)	30 (45)
6. Having representatives selected by the poor on planning committees retards long-term development.	39 (36)	45 (32)	40 (33)	30 (21)	34 (31)	50 (40)	49 (70)	. . .	45 (100)	37 (56)
7. You will rarely get decisions that are realistically geared to the problems of the poor unless the poor have their own representatives.	66 (62)	41 (30)	51 (44)	70 (52)	66 (62)	54 (43)	48 (70)	. . .	70 (153)	75 (114)

8. Youth newly out of school are not given a chance to participate actively in community affairs.	60 (56)	40 (30)	51 (44)	60 (43)	66 (62)	44 (35)	44 (65)	. . .	53 (116)	48 (72)
9. The elementary school teacher's training equips him or her to take a part in community development planning.	74 (69)	70 (51)	73 (64)	82 (60)	63 (59)	74 (58)	67 (100)	82 (41)	62 (137)	66 (100)

TABLE 32 B. Percentage (and Number) of Respondents Agreeing on Opinionnaire Items Concerning Mountain Culture and the Outsider: Local Loyalties and "Inside" versus "Outside"

	Public officials	Bankers	Lawyers	Clergy: Baptist	Clergy: non-Baptist	Physicians	Management course participants	Manufacturing entrepreneurs	Teachers: male	Teachers: female
10. Mountain people are proud and they don't like outsiders coming in and trying to change the way they do things.	66 (63)	63 (47)	58 (51)	71 (52)	75 (72)	75 (57)	67 (98)	62 (31)	52 (113)	67 (98)
11. Our local schools are doing a good job.	78 (74)	91 (70)	76 (68)	84 (63)	65 (62)	65 (52)	73 (110)	85 (46)	72 (158)	78 (116)
12. One of the biggest problems in trying to plan and coordinate local development efforts is that the Feds don't understand the situation here.	78 (73)	81 (61)	76 (65)	59 (43)	69 (66)	65 (50)	71 (105)	52 (25)	70 (154)	76 (115)
13. The journalists who have been publicizing mountain problems in the national press do a lot of harm.	62 (57)	75 (57)	58 (51)	72 (53)	58 (56)	67 (53)	79 (117)	58 (29)	60 (133)	67 (100)

14.	It would be better if the young volunteers who come in to help were all local; outsiders don't belong and mountain people often resent their interference.	52 (50)	66 (45)	48 (43)	59 (44)	39 (38)	53 (42)	47 (72)	38 (18)	54 (119)	54 (84)
15.	East Kentucky has been exploited by outside capitalists.	63 (56)	50 (38)	71 (62)	73 (53)	75 (71)	73 (58)	54 (79)	46 (21)	64 (141)	66 (100)

TABLE 32 C. Percentage (and Number) Agreeing on Opinionnaire Items Concerning Mountain Culture and the Outsider: Interstitial Persons and the Cultural Bridge Role

	Public officials	Bankers	Lawyers	Clergy: Baptist	Clergy: non-Baptist	Physicians	Management course participants	Manufacturing entrepreneurs	Teachers: male	Teachers: female
16. Some of the money now spent by the federal government on new projects would be better spent in bringing greater understanding of programs and policies to the community as a whole.	80 (75)	55 (41)	53 (45)	53 (39)	55 (52)	58 (46)	61 (88)	. . .	69 (152)	63 (95)
17. Establishment of a development discussion or planning group is in itself an important step toward community betterment.	83 (76)	83 (64)	77 (63)	90 (65)	91 (86)	87 (68)	78 (112)	. . .	. . .	. . .

18.	Business and professional people serve the common welfare best by concentrating their efforts on developing as fully as possible their own firm or practice.	61 (59)	61 (48)	57 (52)	57 (61)	37 (36)	53 (42)	61 (94)	. . .	. . .	. . .
19.	Men with my educational background should actively encourage programs that will help bring mountain people into closer contact with ideas and events outside the mountains.	92 (84)	82 (65)	89 (81)	89 (63)	95 (92)	92 (74)	84 (129)	. . .	. . .	. . .
20.	An educated preacher can contribute more than anyone else to help mountain people bridge the gap between mountain life and the outside world.	53 (51)	58 (46)	40 (36)	67 (50)	58 (57)	45 (36)	47 (72)	66 (33)	36 (86)	40 (62)
21.	An out-of-state teacher is more of a problem than an asset to most local elementary schools.	21 (20)	27 (21)	21 (29)	15 (11)	16 (16)	18 (14)	19 (29)	22 (11)	19 (43)	22 (34)

TABLE 32 C. (Continued)

	Public officials	Bankers	Lawyers	Clergy: Baptist	Clergy: non-Baptist	Physicians	Management course participants	Manufacturing entrepreneurs	Teachers: male	Teachers: female
22. Local bankers know only the traditional kinds of local enterprise; they won't back a man with new ideas.	54 (52)	23 (18)	44 (40)	40 (29)	43 (41)	42 (34)	44 (68)	27 (14)	. . .	. . .
23. Local bankers know people as individuals and can serve local businessmen better than the impersonal city bankers.	67 (61)	88 (68)	57 (50)	77 (56)	62 (61)	65 (52)	53 (79)	50 (26)	. . .	. . .

TABLE 33. Percentage of Each Occupation Category Who Strongly Agree on Items 18 and 19

Occupation	Item 18	Item 19	Item 19 minus item 18
Public officials	43	79	36
Bankers	48	60	12
Lawyers	39	72	33
Clergy: Baptist	26	62	36
Clergy: non-Baptist	16	74	58
Physicians	34	63	29
Management course participants	34	57	23

TABLE 34 A. Percentage (and Numbers) of Respondents Agreeing on Opinionnaire Items Concerning Prospects and Policies for Modernization: Economic Prospects and Priorities

	Public officials	Bankers	Lawyers	Clergy: Baptist	Clergy: non-Baptist	Physicians	Management course participants	Manufacturing entrepreneurs	Teachers: male	Teachers: female
24. Rising national prosperity would do more for the mountains right now than all the special programs for their economic development.	52 (47)	62 (45)	40 (33)	34 (24)	25 (24)	39 (31)	37 (54)	52 (27)	37 (80)	33 (47)
25. Interstate pacts or national legislation with teeth in it to control strip mining and require land rehabilitation would just put more mountain men out of jobs.	28 (26)	25 (19)	28 (24)	10 (7)	12 (11)	20 (16)	14 (21)	. . .	12 (28)	14 (22)
26. The new East Kentucky turnpike and planned "development highways" will move people out of the mountains more than bring business or industry in.	10 (9)	19 (14)	14 (12)	14 (10)	19 (18)	14 (11)	16 (24)	21 (12)	. . .	. . .

27.	Development highways are essential and it's about time the back country got its share.	96 (91)	100 (76)	98 (88)	95 (69)	94 (89)	96 (75)	95 (138)	94 (50)	94 (205)	92 (137)
28.	A well-planned program to foster tourism could put the mountain economy back on its feet.	86 (83)	91 (68)	78 (67)	65 (47)	69 (65)	78 (62)	81 (121)	73 (43)	. . .	. . .
29.	Technological progress is going to hurt more than help the futures of children now in mountain schools.	27 (25)	21 (16)	17 (15)	27 (19)	29 (27)	22 (17)	21 (30)	15 (7)	20 (43)	15 (22)
30.	Too many young people have been emigrating from East Kentucky without adequate reason.	42 (39)	46 (35)	28 (25)	28 (21)	24 (23)	29 (23)	24 (36)	. . .	17 (36)	23 (36)
31.	It is unfair to ask a man who has grown up in the mountains to leave his friends and kinfolk in order to get a job.	38 (35)	38 (27)	36 (32)	29 (22)	24 (23)	23 (18)	28 (42)	. . .	27 (59)	25 (35)
32.	The next million dollars for Appalachian programs would be better put into water, sewage, access roads, etc., than into efforts to develop the economic potential of the working population.	76 (72)	79 (58)	74 (61)	55 (39)	54 (50)	69 (55)	68 (100)	. . .	59 (129)	45 (67)

TABLE 34 B. Percentage (and Numbers) of Respondents Agreeing on Opinionnaire Items Concerning Prospects and Policies for Modernization: Human Resource Development Policies and Programs

	Public officials	Bankers	Lawyers	Clergy: Baptist	Clergy: non-Baptist	Physicians	Management course participants	Manufacturing entrepreneurs	Teachers: male	Teachers: female
33. The education given young people in mountain schools does not prepare them for life elsewhere.	54 (50)	47 (35)	45 (40)	31 (23)	53 (50)	53 (42)	46 (69)	54 (28)	37 (70)	30 (45)
34. Local vocational schools don't put enough emphasis on training for work in the mountains.	65 (60)	57 (43)	64 (55)	51 (38)	49 (47)	51 (40)	46 (68)	63 (30)	43 (93)	36 (53)
35. The main deficiencies in mountain labor are attributable more to lack of opportunity to acquire know-how on-the-job than to inadequate school learning.	79 (73)	81 (61)	82 (72)	71 (53)	47 (44)	54 (43)	67 (98)	. . .	68 (148)	60 (90)

36.	There would be less "welfarism" in the mountains if the proportion of time the schools devoted to vocational courses were greater.	89 (84)	87 (65)	81 (72)	81 (59)	80 (76)	84 (67)	79 (119)	. . .	84 (185)	88 (133)
37.	Kentucky school systems need more of programs like Head Start for the preschool age child.	79 (75)	70 (53)	62 (54)	60 (45)	88 (77)	52 (41)	66 (97)	. . .	78 (162)	75 (114)
38.	The inclusion of classes for unemployed fathers is a major advance over old relief programs.	71 (69)	60 (47)	73 (66)	76 (57)	82 (80)	69 (55)	75 (115)	78 (42)	54 (73)	65 (100)
39.	The job corps camp program will do a lot for East Kentucky youth.	72 (70)	46 (36)	46 (41)	53 (40)	47 (46)	51 (41)	39 (60)	54 (26)	51 (114)	58 (90)
40.	The kind of adult education that could accomplish most in the mountains would be long programs (a year or more) in basic reading, writing, and arithmetic.	80 (75)	70 (52)	72 (65)	74 (54)	66 (63)	54 (43)	67 (99)	71 (36)	36 (78)	71 (108)

TABLE 34 C. Percentage (and Number) of Respondents Agreeing on Opinionnaire Items Concerning Prospects and Policies for Modernization: Local Development and the Federal Government

	Public officials	Bankers	Lawyers	Clergy: Baptist	Clergy: non-Baptist	Physicians	Management course participants	Manufacturing entrepreneurs	Teachers: male	Teachers: female
41. Recent national education bills will bring too much federal intervention in local schools.	40 (38)	54 (41)	51 (46)	62 (45)	25 (24)	51 (41)	55 (80)	. . .	43 (94)	41 (61)
42. Generous federal financial assistance in local development saps local initiative.	55 (49)	68 (50)	57 (50)	77 (56)	64 (60)	80 (61)	67 (99)	. . .	72 (157)	73 (109)
43. The federal government often gives so much technical assistance and advice on development projects that local people lose interest in thinking things out for themselves.	52 (47)	72 (53)	60 (52)	63 (46)	59 (57)	70 (56)	66 (97)	. . .	70 (155)	63 (97)

TABLE 35. Percentage Distribution of Responses on Opinionnaire: Total Mountain Sample

	Factor loading	Agree strongly	Agree mildly	No opinion	Disagree mildly	Disagree strongly	No response
Mountain factor 1: Support of federal-local cooperation and compensatory human development activities							
37. Kentucky school systems need more of programs like Head Start for the preschool age child.	-.605	40.6	28.3	3.9	10.7	13.9	2.6
38. The inclusion of classes for unemployed fathers is a major advance over old relief programs.	-.582	35.4	32.2	14.4	7.5	9.6	0.9
39. The job corps camp program will do a lot for East Kentucky youth.	-.575	18.2	33.1	13.3	17.7	15.2	2.5
42. Generous federal financial assistance in local development saps local initiative.	.523	36.1	29.7	2.8	14.3	13.0	4.0
43. The federal government often gives so much technical assistance and advice on development projects that local people lose interest in thinking things out for themselves.	.496	30.9	32.0	5.5	17.2	11.9	2.5
41. Recent national education bills will bring too much federal intervention in local schools.	.491	20.6	24.2	9.5	23.4	19.6	2.7

TABLE 35. (Continued)

	Factor loading	Agree strongly	Agree mildly	No opinion	Disagree mildly	Disagree strongly	No response
40. The kind of adult education that could accomplish most in the mountains would be long programs (a year or more) in basic reading, writing, and arithmetic.	(-.355)	35.7	31.4	5.8	15.5	9.3	2.3
Mountain factor 2: Defense of ordinary folk							
6. Having representatives selected by the poor on planning committees retards long-term development.	.550	16.9	23.1	15.7	23.7	16.3	4.3
4. Labor strife has kept a lot of business out of East Kentucky.	.498	41.0	25.6	6.3	13.2	11.7	2.1
30. Too many young people have been emigrating from East Kentucky without adequate reason.	.415	11.2	14.9	4.4	25.1	42.3	2.1
24. Rising national prosperity would do more for the mountains right now than all the special programs for their economic development.	.404	14.9	23.3	7.1	25.0	24.5	5.3
5. One of the most serious problems in the mountains is that too many people are suspicious.	.387	11.2	27.4	6.5	25.6	26.3	3.1

20.	An educated preacher can contribute more than anyone else to help mountain people bridge the gap between mountain life and the outside world.	(.326)	15.9	30.7	7.5	23.3	19.4	3.2
Mountain factor 3: Critical view of local schools								
33.	The education given young people in mountain schools does not prepare them for life elsewhere.	-.665	15.9	24.5	2.3	27.3	27.2	2.8
11.	Our local schools are doing a good job.	.657	31.3	42.4	1.1	13.3	10.2	1.6
9.	The elementary school teacher's training equips him or her to take a part in community development planning.	.543	29.5	37.1	8.5	14.8	7.5	2.7
Mountain factor 4: Favoring grassroots participation								
7.	You will rarely get decisions that are realistically geared to the problems of the poor unless the poor have their own representatives.	-.682	30.1	29.9	5.0	18.9	13.1	3.1
16.	Some of the money now spent by the federal government on new projects would be better spent in bringing greater understanding of programs and policies to the community as a whole.	-.584	29.1	31.3	12.0	14.6	9.8	3.2

TABLE 35. (Continued)

	Factor loading	Agree strongly	Agree mildly	No opinion	Disagree mildly	Disagree strongly	No response
8. Youth newly out of school are not given a chance to participate actively in community affairs.	-.511	21.7	28.1	6.3	24.7	16.1	3.1
Mountain factor 5: Burden of disadvantaged backgrounds of mountain children							
36. There would be less "welfarism" in the mountains if the proportion of time the schools devoted to vocational courses were greater.	.574	50.6	31.2	5.2	7.5	3.2	2.2
29. Technological progress is going to hurt more than help the futures of children now in mountain schools.	-.514	8.8	11.6	10.4	25.1	40.0	4.1
1. If a young man really has ambition, he can make a success of his life no matter how poor or ignorant his family may have been.	.437	64.4	18.3	0.1	4.3	3.6	9.2
Mountain factor 6: Local receptivity to outsiders							
10. Mountain people are proud and they don't like outsiders coming in and trying to change the way they do things.	.714	29.7	34.7	1.5	20.4	10.2	3.4

14. It would be better if the young volunteers who come in to help were all local; outsiders don't belong and mountain people often resent their interference.	.571	24.7	26.5	4.4	25.3	15.7	3.4
21. An out-of-state teacher is more of a problem than an asset to most local elementary schools.	.517	8.2	11.5	8.7	29.0	40.3	2.3
12. One of the biggest problems in trying to plan and coordinate local development efforts is that the Feds don't understand the situation here.	.465	35.7	34.0	5.8	15.6	5.9	2.9
13. The journalists who have been publicizing mountain problems in the national press do a lot of harm.	.400	39.7	24.9	4.7	17.1	11.4	2.3
Mountain factor 7: Localist antimigration syndrome							
31. It is unfair to ask a man who has grown up in the mountains to leave his friends and kinfolk in order to get a job.	-.641	13.2	15.1	2.4	24.1	43.2	2.1
35. The main deficiencies in mountain labor are attributable more to lack of opportunity to acquire know-how on-the-job than to inadequate school learning.	-.511	33.1	31.9	3.1	15.9	13.0	3.0
30. Too many young people have been emigrating from East Kentucky without adequate reason.	(-.349)	11.2	14.9	4.4	25.1	42.3	2.1

TABLE 35. (Continued)

	Factor loading	Agree strongly	Agree mildly	No opinion	Disagree mildly	Disagree strongly	No response
34. Local vocational schools don't put enough emphasis on training for work in the mountains.	(-.324)	21.9	25.5	16.7	18.8	13.5	3.6
Mountain factor 8: Skepticism about physical development potentials							
27. Development highways are essential and it's about time the back country got its share.	.617	69.2	22.9	1.8	2.1	1.0	3.0
32. The next million dollars for Appalachian programs would be better put into water, sewage, access roads, etc., than into efforts to develop the economic potential of the working population.	.495	41.0	19.2	4.2	15.8	15.8	4.0
15. East Kentucky has been exploited by outside capitalists.	.403	36.5	26.2	9.2	13.2	12.0	3.0
25. Interstate pacts or national legislation with teeth in it to control strip mining and require land rehabilitation would just put more mountain men out of jobs.	-.382	8.3	8.1	8.1	18.5	54.6	2.4

TABLE 36. Attitude Variation by Occupation: Deviations from Median of Occupation Scores

	Median of occupation scores (all groups)	Mean score, administrative and professional elites	Occupation groups: Administrative elites			Professional elites				Teachers		Subcategories of Public officials	
			Public officials	Bankers	Lawyers	Clergy: Baptist	Clergy: non-Baptist	Physicians	Management course participants	Male	Female	Business-political	Pure political
Attitudes implying externalized criteria													
Index 3. Critical view of local schools	36	37	0	-4	0	-7	+9	+5	+3	-1	-4	+5	-8
Index 5. Burden of disadvantaged environment of mountain children	20	21	-1	0	0	0	+10	+1	-1	+2	-1	-4	+1
Index 6. Receptivity to outsiders	42	44	0	-4	+5	0	+5	0	-1	+3	0	+4	-2
Localism and the antimigration syndrome													
Index 7. The antimigration syndrome	44	50	+12	+11	+10	+5	0	-2	0	-2	-3	+8	+18

TABLE 36. (Continued)

	Median of occupation scores (all groups)	Mean score, administrative and professional elites	Occupation groups: Administrative elites: Public officials	Administrative elites: Bankers	Administrative elites: Lawyers	Professional elites: Clergy: Baptist	Professional elites: Clergy: non-Baptist	Professional elites: Physicians	Management course participants	Teachers: Male	Teachers: Female	Subcategories of public officials: Business-political	Subcategories of public officials: Pure political
Attitudes entailing positive orientations to the general run of local people													
Index 2. Defense of (favorable orientation to) ordinary folk	52	51	-4	-8	0	-1	+3	+1	-4	+4	+6	-5	-1
Index 4. Fostering of grassroots participation	61	58	+7	-9	-7	+2	0	-7	-7	+3	+2	+7	+7
Development prospects and policy													
Index 8. Skepticism about physical development potential	25	24	-1	+1	-1	0	+1	-2	+1	0	+5	-2	0
Index 1. Local-federal cooperation and compensatory education	52	52	+9	-4	0	-3	+7	-5	-3	0	+2	+11	+8

TABLE 37. Mean Attitude Scores and Variation by Nativity, Age, Education, and Exposure

	Median of occupation scores (all groups)	Mean score, administrative and professional elites	Differences in index scores (administrative and professional elites)				
			Non-native minus native	Age under 40 minus age 50+	College graduate minus high school or less	Worked in city of 50,000 minus did not	Visited 5 major cities minus did not
Attitudes implying externalized criteria							
Index 3. Critical view of local schools	36	37	+6	+4	+7	+5	+9
Index 5. Burden of disadvantaged environment of mountain children	20	21	+5	+5	+3	+1	+3
Index 6. Receptivity to outsiders	42	44	+5	+8	+7	+5	+4
Localism and the antimigration syndrome							
Index 7. The antimigration syndrome	44	50	-10	-10	-12	-7	-7
Attitudes entailing positive orientations to the general run of local people							
Index 2. Defense of ordinary folk	52	51	+4	+9	+8	+5	+2
Index 4. Fostering of grassroots participation	61	58	-1	+2	-7	-3	-2

TABLE 37. (Continued)

	Median of occupation scores (all groups)	Mean score, administrative and professional elites	Differences in index scores (administrative and professional elites)				
			Non-native minus native	Age under 40 minus age 50+	College graduate minus high school or less	Worked in city of 50,000 minus did not	Visited 5 major cities minus did not
Development prospects and policy							
Index 8. Skepticism about physical development potential	25	24	+5	-1	-3	+2	-1
Index 1. Local-federal cooperation and compensatory education	52	52	+3	+5	-5	a	0

[a]Difference under 0.5.

TABLE 38. Age Differences in Attitude Scores within Occupations

	Public officials	Bankers	Lawyers	Clergy: Baptist	Clergy: non-Baptist	Physicians	Management course participants	Teachers: male	Teachers: female
Number in sample by age									
Under 40	8	4	19	30	47	22	58	145	55
40-49	35	12	23	26	23	18	55	41	33
50-59	31	17	18	12	18	23	30	24	41
60+	23	46	30	6	11	17	8	6	15
	Scores for Age Under 40 Minus Age 50-59								
Attitudes implying externalized criteria									
Index 3. Critical view of local schools	-0.1	+3.5	-0.4	+3.7	+6.3	+5.5	+10.8	+3.8	+6.3
Index 5. Burden of disadvantaged environment of mountain children	+9.6	+0.9	+1.5	+2.7	+4.3	+6.7	+2.6	+2.0	+1.3
Index 6. Receptivity to outsiders	-7.0	+15.3	+3.7	+5.5	+11.5	+16.3	+3.5	+2.3	-2.6
Localism and the antimigration syndrome									
Index 7. The antimigration syndrome	-4.4	-20.3	-10.2	-12.8	-3.0	-5.9	-1.0	-7.6	-2.0

TABLE 38. (Continued)

	Public officials	Bankers	Lawyers	Clergy: Baptist	Clergy: non-Baptist	Physicians	Management course participants	Teachers: male	Teachers: female
Attitudes entailing positive orientations to the general run of local people									
Index 2. Defense of ordinary folk	+5.1	+5.7	+13.5	+10.5	+10.9	+7.4	+3.3	+5.1	-2.8
Index 4. Fostering of grassroots participation	+7.8	-28.0	+5.6	+1.9	-1.8	+2.0	-1.2	-6.7	+9.6
Development prospects and policy									
Index 8. Skepticism about physical development potential	+0.8	+6.0	-7.2	-3.8	-1.0	+2.8	+5.3	+10.4	+4.5
Index 1. Local-federal cooperation and compensatory education	-10.0	+4.0	+5.9	-0.4	+16.8	+8.0	-0.5	+4.2	-8.9
	Scores for Age 40-49 Minus Age 60+								
Attitudes implying externalized criteria									
Index 3. Critical view of local schools	+7.9	+9.7	+6.2	+0.3	+10.5	-1.1	+7.4	+9.8	+1.8

Index 5. Burden of disadvantaged environment of mountain children	+5.7	+0.6	+4.3	+7.3	+3.5	+2.0	+8.6	+5.6	+12.6
Index 6. Receptivity to outsiders	+6.5	-2.7	+13.8	+0.9	+3.0	+13.3	+20.0	+2.3	+5.5
Localism and the antimigration syndrome									
Index 7. The antimigration syndrome	-6.6	-7.9	-9.1	-4.1	-1.3	-20.3	-34.1	+0.8	-6.7
Attitudes entailing positive orientations to the general run of local people									
Index 2. Defense of ordinary folk	+1.4	+9.1	+13.6	+3.8	+18.7	+16.6	+18.2	-5.2	+15.1
Index 4. Fostering of grassroots participation	-9.8	-10.3	+5.7	-4.2	-2.2	-6.5	-16.2	+13.3	-14.7
Development prospects and policy									
Index 8. Skepticism about physical development potential	+11.5	+5.0	+2.5	+9.4	-1.4	+12.0	-0.4	+9.9	-6.8
Index 1. Local-federal cooperation and compensatory education	+4.6	-9.1	+12.1	+1.1	+5.0	+12.3	-6.9	-5.9	-2.9

TABLE 39. Attitude Patterns by Youth Involvement

	Youth involvement		
	High	Medium	Low
Attitudes implying externalized criteria			
Index 3. Critical view of local schools	41	37	35
Index 5. Burden of disadvantaged environment of mountain children	19	22	22
Index 6. Receptivity to outsiders	46	43	43
Localism and the antimigration syndrome			
Index 7. The antimigration syndrome	48	50	49
Attitudes entailing positive orientations to the general run of local people			
Index 2. Defense of ordinary folk	53	53	49
Index 4. Fostering of grassroots participation	58	58	56
Development prospects and policy			
Index 8. Skepticism about physical development potential	23	25	25
Index 1. Local-federal cooperation and compensatory education	54	53	51

TABLE 40. Attitude Patterns by Political and Civic Participation

	Participation scores			
	Active both	Active political	Active civic	Neither
<u>Attitudes implying externalized criteria</u>				
Index 3. Critical view of local schools	38	35	47	36
Index 5. Burden of disadvantaged environment of mountain children	18	18	25	23
Index 6. Receptivity to outsiders	42	41	50	44
<u>Localism and the antimigration syndrome</u>				
Index 7. The antimigration syndrome	54	54	47	47
<u>Attitudes entailing positive orientations to the general run of local people</u>				
Index 2. Defense of ordinary folk	53	49	56	51
Index 4. Fostering of grassroots participation	60	57	55	58
<u>Development prospects and policy</u>				
Index 8. Skepticism about physical development potential	23	24	22	26
Index 1. Local-federal cooperation and compensatory education	60	51	60	49

TABLE 41. Attitude Characteristics by Youth Involvement and Participation Combinations (Administrative and Professional Elites: Weighted Samples)

	High youth involvement				Low youth involvement			
	Civic and political (N=20)	Political (N=34)	Civic (N=28)	Neither (N=39)	Civic and political (N=9)	Political (N=54)	Civic (N=13)	Neither (N=101)
Index 3. Critical view of local schools	40	31	57	40	38	38	41	33
Index 5. Burden of disadvantaged environment of mountain children	16	14	24[a]	24	18	18	25	23
Index 6. Receptivity to outsiders	46	40	48	48	50	38	53	45
Index 7. Localism and the antimigration syndrome	51	52	45[b]	47	59	54	44	47
Index 4. Fostering of grassroots participation	60	55	52	63	65	56	48	57
Index 1. Local-federal cooperation and compensatory education	54	52	56	53	59	52	56	50

[a]Although generally the non-natives in any participation category score higher on this factor than those born in eastern Kentucky, the relationship in this cell is reversed; the non-natives in this instance are predominantly Baptist clergy.

[b]Although generally the natives score higher on this factor than the non-natives, the relationship is reversed in this cell.

APPENDIX A

The ESLS Questionnaire

(Used for all samples except teachers and mountain manufacturers)

ECONOMIC AND SOCIAL LEADERSHIP STUDY

A. BACKGROUND INFORMATION

1. In what place would you call yourself a native? (Check one)

    ____1. Same county as present residence

    ____2. Another Kentucky county (name)

    ____

    ____3. Outside Kentucky

    Town______________________

    County_________State_________

2. What is your age?

    ____1. Under 25

    ____2. 25-29

    ____3. 30-39

    ____4. 40-49

    ____5. 50-59

    ____6. 60 or over

3-4. What is your present occupation? (If you have more than one, put a 1 beside the occupation on which you spend the most time, and a 2 beside any other occupations you may have.)

    ____1. Banker

    ____2. Insurance agent

    ____3. Practicing attorney

    ____4. Coal operator

    ____5. Proprietor or manager of a business (specify nature of business)

    ____

    ____6. Newspaper editor

    ____7. Clergyman

    ____8. Physician

    ____9. Public official (specify office)

    ____

    ____

    ____

    ____10. Other (specify)

    ____

5. Have you been in military service?

    Yes_____ No_____

6. Excluding military service have you ever worked outside Kentucky?

    ____1. Never

    ____2. For 3 months or less

    ____3. For 4 to 12 months

    ____4. For more than 1 but under 5 years

    ____5. For 5 years or more

7. Excluding military service have you worked for a year or more elsewhere in Kentucky? Yes____ No____

    If yes, name the county or counties

    ____

8. Check the types of places in which you have worked for a year or more

    ____1. A city of over 50,000 people

    ____2. A city of 15,000 to 50,000 people

    ____3. A city or town of 1,000 or more, but under 15,000

    ____4. A small town of less than 1,000

    ____5. In the country

9. Check the one of the following that comes closest to describing your father's principal occupation.

    ____1. Coal miner

    ____2. Coal mine operator

    ____3. Farmer

    ____4. Retail trade proprietor or manager

    ____5. Other business management or proprietorship (give type of business)

    ____

    ____6. Teacher

    ____7. Other profession (specify)

    ____

    ____8. Other occupation (specify)

    ____

10. Have you any relatives or close friends who have professional positions in the local school system or in any local educational institution? Yes____ No____

11. If yes, please give the following information for each:

Sex	Relationship to you	Position	If a principal or teacher, type or level of school
_____	_____________________	____________	__________________________
_____	_____________________	____________	__________________________

12-15. Check the highest level of education reached by yourself and each of your parents:

	Self	Father	Mother
1. Elementary	___	___	___
2. Some high school	___	___	___
3. Completed high school	___	___	___
4. Some regular college	___	___	___
5. Degree from a four-year college	___	___	___
6. Beyond college completion	___	___	___

16. If you had post-graduate education, specify what it was and indicate any certificate or degree received.

____

____

17-18. What schools or training programs have you attended outside the county of your present residence?

___1. High school (Give town and state)

___2. College (Give name, location and date)

____

____

___3. Special training programs (Include "short courses." Specify nature and length of program as well as where.)

____

____

___4. None

19-28. Check those of the following cities you have visited during the past year and the approximate number of times in each:

	Number of times		
	1-4	5-9	10 or more
Lexington..........	___	___	___
Louisville.........	___	___	___
Cincinnati.........	___	___	___
Ashland-Huntington.	___	___	___
Knoxville..........	___	___	___
Pittsburgh.........	___	___	___
Dayton, Ohio.......	___	___	___

More distant major cities and foreign countries (list)

____

____

29-34. Indicate the newspapers you read and how often you read them:

	Daily	Once or twice a week	Occa-sion-ally
1. County or local town.............	___	___	___
2. Lexington.........	___	___	___
3. Louisville........	___	___	___
4. Knoxville.........	___	___	___
5. Ashland-Huntington.......	___	___	___
6. Other (specify)			
___________________	___	___	___
___________________	___	___	___

35. Which of the following most nearly describes your feeling about the area where you live and work? (Check one)

___1. This has been my home, these are my kind of people, and I am happier living here than anywhere else.

___2. Where I grew up was different, but I have grown to love this community and regard it as my permanent home.

___3. I want to live here for a while, but would not want to spend the major part of my life here.

___4. I would rather live somewhere else, but there are compensations in living here.

___5. I definitely do not like living here.

36-37. Do you have direct contacts with local youth other than relatives? (Check any statements that fit you.)

___1. I participate in community service activities with youth groups. (specify these) ________________

____

___2. I have frequent occasion to talk with individual young people about their personal, school or job problems.

___3. Rarely with either individuals or groups, except in casual conversations.

38-39. Do you have conversations or consultations with teachers or other school people about programs or problems involving children or youth? (Check any that fit you)

___1. Rarely or never

___2. Often in the course of my regular work

___3. Frequently in connection with my activities in PTA

___4. As a member of a school board

___5. In connection with other community or public services (specify) ________________

____

___6. Informally with school teachers (or other school people) who are friends or relatives

40-41. Do you have conversations or consultations with other adults about their children or young people?

___1. Often in the course of my regular work

___2. In connection with community or public service activities (specify nature of these)

____

___3. Very frequently in informal situations

___4. Occasionally, in conversations with friends

___5. Rarely or never

42-48. Do you play an active role in community affairs? Yes___ No___

If yes, indicate below the nature and extent of your participation:

___1. Holder of political office currently (specify)________________

___2. Holder of political office in the past (specify)________________

___3. Member of planning or zoning commission

___4. Holder of office in a civic club (specify club and office)

____

___5. Office-holder or committee member in county or area development council

___6. Office-holder or committee member in county or area economic opportunity organization

___7. Other community activities to which you give a significant amount of time (specify)________________

____

49. What changes do you expect the activities of researchers and social planners will bring in the lives of people in Appalachia? (Check one)

___1. No change of importance

___2. Changes mainly for the better

___3. Changes mainly for the worse.

B. VIEWS CONCERNING MOUNTAIN PROSPECTS, DEVELOPMENT PROGRAMS AND LEADERSHIP

There are many differences of opinion concerning mountain prospects and development programs. After each of the following statements, check your degree of agreement or disagreement.

	agree strongly	agree mildly	disagree mildly	disagree strongly	no opinion
1. Rising National prosperity would do more for the mountains right now than all the special programs for their economic development............................	☐	☐	☐	☐	☐

	agree strongly	agree mildly	disagree mildly	disagree strongly	no opinion
2. The next million dollars for Appalachian programs would be better put into water, sewage, access roads, etc., than into efforts to develop the economic potential of the working-age population...........	☐	☐	☐	☐	☐
3. Establishment of a development discussion or planning group is in itself an important step toward community betterment.........	☐	☐	☐	☐	☐
4. Generous federal financial assistance in local development saps local initiative..	☐	☐	☐	☐	☐
5. The new East Kentucky turnpike and planned "development highways" will move people out of the mountains more than bring business or industry in...........	☐	☐	☐	☐	☐
6. A well-planned program to foster tourism could put the mountain economy back on its feet...............................	☐	☐	☐	☐	☐
7. Having representatives selected by the poor on planning committees retards long-term development...................	☐	☐	☐	☐	☐
8. Interstate pacts or national legislation with teeth in it to control strip mining and require land rehabilitation would just put more mountain men out of jobs...	☐	☐	☐	☐	☐
9. The federal government often gives so much technical assistance and advice on development projects that local people lose interest in thinking things out for themselves.............................	☐	☐	☐	☐	☐
10. Business and professional people serve the common welfare best by concentrating their efforts on developing as fully as possible their own firm or practice......	☐	☐	☐	☐	☐
11. The elementary schoolteacher's training equips him or her to take a part in community development planning...........	☐	☐	☐	☐	☐
12. You will rarely get decisions that are realistically geared to the problems of the poor unless the poor have their own representatives on the committees that make these decisions.....................	☐	☐	☐	☐	☐
13. Youth newly out of school are not given a chance to participate actively in community affairs........................	☐	☐	☐	☐	☐
14. Local bankers know only the traditional kinds of local enterprise; they won't back a man with new ideas................	☐	☐	☐	☐	☐
15. Some of the money now spent by the federal government on new projects would be better spent in bringing greater understanding of programs and policies to the community as a whole......	☐	☐	☐	☐	☐

C. VIEWS CONCERNING RELATIONS BETWEEN MOUNTAIN AND NON-MOUNTAIN PEOPLE AND GROUPS

How do you feel about each of these statements?

	agree strongly	agree mildly	disagree mildly	disagree strongly	no opinion
16. An out-of-state teacher is more of a problem than an asset to most local elementary schools........................	☐	☐	☐	☐	☐
17. The journalists who have been publicizing mountain problems in the national press do a lot of harm..........................	☐	☐	☐	☐	☐
18. Mountain people are proud and they don't like outsiders coming in and trying to change the way they do things.............	☐	☐	☐	☐	☐
19. An educated preacher can contribute more than anyone else to help mountain people bridge the gap between mountain life and the outside world.........................	☐	☐	☐	☐	☐
20. East Kentucky has been exploited by outside capitalists.......................	☐	☐	☐	☐	☐
21. One of the biggest problems in trying to plan and coordinate local development efforts is that the Feds don't understand the situation here........................	☐	☐	☐	☐	☐
22. It would be better if the young volunteers who come in to help were all local; outsiders don't belong and mountain people often resent their interference...........	☐	☐	☐	☐	☐
23. Local vocational schools don't put enough emphasis on training for work in the mountains................................	☐	☐	☐	☐	☐
24. Development highways are essential and it's about time the back country got its share....................................	☐	☐	☐	☐	☐
25. Local bankers know people as individuals and can serve local businessmen better than the impersonal city bankers...........	☐	☐	☐	☐	☐

26. Do most businessmen you know feel encouraged in their long-run business prospects by the new national interest in Appalachian development?

___1. Mostly encouraged

___2. Mostly think it won't make any difference

___3. Have no idea

27-31. Thinking of the importance of their services to the community, how would you rank the following occupations? (Give the most important a rank of 1, the second 2, and so on to the least important with a rank of 5)

	Rank
Resident clergyman	____
Local newspaper editor	____
High school principal	____
Doctor	____
Businessman with 100 employees	____

32-36. Again thinking of the importance of their services to the community, how would you rank the following occupations? (Again rank from 1 to 5)

	Rank
Nurse	____
Newscaster on radio or TV	____
Elementary school teacher	____
Traveling buyer or salesman	____
Small Business Administration representative	____

D. PEOPLE AND WORK

How do you feel about the following statements?

	agree strongly	agree mildly	disagree mildly	disagree strongly	no opinion
37. Mountain men are good workers if you understand how to get along with them..................................	☐	☐	☐	☐	☐
38. The main deficiencies in mountain labor are attributable more to lack of opportunity to acquire know-how on-the-job than to inadequate school learning.........	☐	☐	☐	☐	☐
39. Public assistance has made people into lazy loafers and they won't work even when a job is offered them................	☐	☐	☐	☐	☐
40. If a young man really has ambition he can make a success of his life no matter how poor and ignorant his family may have been..................................	☐	☐	☐	☐	☐
41. One of the most serious problems in the mountains is that too many people are suspicious................................	☐	☐	☐	☐	☐
42. Too many young people have been emigrating from East Kentucky without adequate reason...........................	☐	☐	☐	☐	☐
43. The inclusion of classes for unemployed fathers is a major advance over old relief programs...........................	☐	☐	☐	☐	☐
44. Labor strife has kept a lot of business out of East Kentucky..........................	☐	☐	☐	☐	☐
45. It is unfair to ask a man who has grown up in the mountains to leave his friends and kinfolk in order to get a job.............	☐	☐	☐	☐	☐

E. EDUCATION AND TRAINING

Finally, how far do you agree or disagree with the following?

	agree strongly	agree mildly	disagree mildly	disagree strongly	no opinion
46. Our local schools are doing a good job.....	☐	☐	☐	☐	☐
47. The education given young people in mountain schools does not prepare them for life elsewhere.........................	☐	☐	☐	☐	☐
48. The kind of adult education that could accomplish most in the mountains would be long programs (a year or more) in basic reading, writing, and arithmetic.................................	☐	☐	☐	☐	☐
49. The job corps camp program will do a lot for East Kentucky youth...............	☐	☐	☐	☐	☐
50. Recent national education bills will bring too much federal intervention in local schools...................	☐	☐	☐	☐	☐
51. Kentucky school systems need more of programs like Head Start for the pre-school-age child...........................	☐	☐	☐	☐	☐

	agree strongly	agree mildly	disagree mildly	disagree strongly	no opinion
52. Men with my educational background should actively encourage programs that will help bring mountain people into closer contact with ideas and events outside the mountains..............................	☐	☐	☐	☐	☐
53. There would be less 'welfarism' in the mountains if the proportion of time the schools devoted to vocational courses were greater...............................	☐	☐	☐	☐	☐
54. Technological progress is going to hurt more than help the futures of children now in mountain schools....................	☐	☐	☐	☐	☐

If this questionnaire has raised issues on which you would like to comment, we hope you will use the remaining space on this questionnaire for that purpose. Any comments you may have to make will be read with very great interest.

APPENDIX B

The TC Questionnaire

(Mountain Teachers)

To avoid duplication and confounding with extraneous data used in a special analysis of teachers but not in the foregoing monograph, the opinionnaire items for the TC Questionnaire have not been reproduced. They followed that questionnaire as presented here.

STUDY OF THE TEACHER AND THE COMMUNITY

A. BACKGROUND INFORMATION

1. In what place would you call yourself a native?

   ___1. Same county as present residence

   ___2. Another Kentucky county (which?)

   ____

   ___3. Outside Kentucky

   Town ______________________

   County ___________ State _____

2. When were you born? (Year) __________

3-6. Check the highest level of regular schooling reached by yourself and each of your parents

	Self	Father	Mother
1. Elementary	___	___	___
2. Some high school	___	___	___
3. Completed high school	___	___	___
4. Some regular college	___	___	___
5. Degree from a four-year college	___	___	___
6. Beyond college completion	___	___	___

7. Check the types of places in which you have worked for a year or more.

   ___1. City of over 50,000 people

   ___2. City with 15,000 to 50,000 people

   ___3. City or town of 1,000 or more but under 15,000

   ___4. Small town of less than 1,000

   ___5. In the country

8. Have you, <u>during the past year</u>, visited any other classroom or school in order to compare teaching methods?

   ___1. No

   ___2. Yes, in this school only

   ___3. Yes, in one other school

   ___4. Yes, in more than one other school

9. Marital status

   ___1. Single

   ___2. Married

   ___3. Widowed, separated, or divorced

10-12. What schools or training programs have you attended outside the county of your present residence?

   ___1. None

   ___2. High school (give town and state)

   ____

   ___3. College during regular academic year (give names, locations and dates)

   ____

   ____

   ___4. College or university summer schools (give names, locations and dates)

   ____

   ____

   ___5. Other special training programs and short courses (Specify length and nature of program as well as where)

   ____

   ____

13-14. Check the one of the following that comes closest to describing your father's principal occupation. (If he is retired or is deceased, check what his principal occupation used to be)

___1. Coal miner
___2. Coal mine operator
___3. Farmer
___4. Retail trade proprietor or manager
___5. Other business management or proprietorship (give type of business) ______________
___6. Teacher
___7. Other profession (specify) ______________
___8. Other occupation (specify) ______________

15. Excluding military service, have you ever worked outside Kentucky?

___1. Never
___2. For 3 months or less
___3. For 4 to 12 months
___4. For more than 1 but under 5 years
___5. For 5 years or more

16-17. Excluding military service, have you held jobs for a year or more elsewhere in Kentucky?

Yes ___ No ___

If yes, name the county or counties in which you have worked.

____

____

18-28. Check those of the following cities you have visited <u>during the past year</u> and the number of times in each:

	Number of times			
	1	2-4	5-9	10+
1. Lexington	___	___	___	___
2. Louisville	___	___	___	___
3. Cincinnati	___	___	___	___
4. Ashland-Huntington	___	___	___	___
5. Knoxville	___	___	___	___
6. Pittsburgh	___	___	___	___
7. Dayton, Ohio	___	___	___	___

	Number of Times			
	1	2-4	5-9	10+
More distant major cities (list)				
______________	___	___	___	___
______________	___	___	___	___
______________	___	___	___	___
______________	___	___	___	___

29. Have you been in military service?

Yes ___ No ___

30-33. Indicate the newspapers you read and how often you read them:

	Daily	Once or twice a week	Occasionally
1. County or local town	___	___	___
2. Lexington	___	___	___
3. Louisville	___	___	___
4. Knoxville	___	___	___
5. Ashland-Huntington	___	___	___
6. Other (specify)	___	___	___
______________	___	___	___
______________	___	___	___

34. Which of the following most nearly describes your feeling about the area where you live and work? (Check one only)

___1. This has been my home, these are my kind of people, and I am happier living here than anywhere else.
___2. Where I grew up was different, but I have grown to love this community and regard it as my permanent home.
___3. I want to live here for a while, but would not want to spend the major part of my life here.
___4. I would rather live somewhere else, but there are compensations in living here.
___5. I definitely do not like living here.

35-45. Which of the following facilities are available in your high school?

___35. Permanent guidance counselor
___36. Tape recorder
___37. Laboratory for pupils' chemical experiments

___38. Teachers' lounge

___39. TV for instructional use

___40. Projector and moving pictures

___41. Subject-matter clubs

___42. School newspaper

___43. Regular faculty meetings

___44. Chapter of Future Teachers of America

___45. Trip for graduating seniors to an important city

46. About how many books do you own personally?

___1. Under 24

___2. 25-49

___3. 50-99

___4. 100-200

___5. Over 200

47. Do you feel that most of your pupils' parents expect you to be better informed than they are about county or state affairs?

___1. Yes, on most matters

___2. Yes, on some matters

___3. Rarely or never

___4. Uncertain

48. How often do you read journals of education?

___1. One journal or less a month

___2. Two journals a month

___3. More than two journals a month

49. With how many individual parents of your pupils have you had conversation <u>during the past month</u>?

___1. None

___2. Less than five

___3. Five to nine

___4. Ten to fourteen

___5. Fifteen or more

B. PEOPLE AND ORGANIZATIONS

1-6. Do you belong to or participate in programs of any national, state, or local community organizations? If so, list below at the left the names of the organizations to which you belong and check how actively you participate in EACH such organization

Educational organizations (as NEA, KEA, County EAs, etc.)	Very active	Attend meetings	Just belong
Please specify: ____________________	___	___	___
____________________	___	___	___
____________________	___	___	___
Other organizations (civic, church, etc.)			
Please specify: ____________________	___	___	___
____________________	___	___	___

7-11. Thinking of the importance of their services to the community, how would you rank the following occupations? (Give the most important a rank of 1, the second 2, and so on to the rank 5.)

	Rank
7. Resident clergyman	___
8. Local newspaper editor	___
9. High school principal	___
10. Doctor	___
11. Businessman with 100 employees	___

12-16. Again thinking of the importance of their services to the community, how would you rank the following occupations?

	Rank
12. Nurse	___
13. Newscaster on radio or TV	___
14. Elementary school teacher	___
15. Traveling buyer or salesman	___
16. Small Business Administration representative	___

17-23. Which of the following have been most helpful or useful to you in providing new ideas to improve your teaching, or, if you are a principal, your school? (Mark three only, ranking them 1, 2, 3.)

		Rank
17.	Meetings of educational organizations	___
18.	Teaching experience	___
19.	Books and journals	___
20.	Superintendent	___
21.	Local colleagues	___
22.	Your principal	___
23.	Contacts at colleges	___

24-25. Which of the following describes the person from whom you would get the best advice in making your job plans for the future?

___1. No one or only your immediate family

___2. A local fellow teacher or principal

___3. Superintendent

___4. A member of a college faculty

___5. Another person in education (give his or her job)_________

___6. Another person not in education (give his or her job)_________

26. How many times have you attended a PTA meeting in the past year? (Check one)

___1. This community has no PTA

___2. Never attend meetings

___3. Attend some meetings

___4. Attend most meetings

27. What changes do you expect the activities of researchers and social planners will bring in the lives of people of Appalachia?

___1. No changes of importance

___2. Changes mainly for the better

___3. Changes mainly for the worse

28. Have you participated with any non-school people in planning youth programs in your community since June 1, 1965?

Yes ____ No ____

If yes, what sort of program or programs?

____

29-37. During this school year, have you consulted or been consulted by any of the following concerning particular pupils who were NOT their own children? (Check any that apply. If none of these, check 37.)

___29. A doctor

___30. A clergyman

___31. A social welfare worker

___32. Member of a college faculty

___33. A public official

___34. A member of a college faculty

___35. Your local school superintendent

___36. Some other non-school person or persons (give job or position)

____

☐ 37. No one

38-46. Have you, during the past year, discussed any aspect of community affairs with any of the following persons? (In each case indicate the approximate number of times.)

		Number of times
38.	Superintendent of schools	___
39.	County agent	___
40.	Local business leader	___
41.	Business leader in ANOTHER county	___
42.	Minister of a church other than your own	___
43.	Local doctor	___
44.	Local banker, lawyer or journalist	___
45.	Banker, lawyer or journalist in ANOTHER county	___
46.	None of these (check if applies)	☐

47. Do most local teachers you know feel encouraged in their work by the new national interest in Appalachia?

___1. Most feel encouraged

___2. Most do not feel encouraged

___3. Have no idea

48. From your experience, how is a teacher's social standing in the local community affected by having contacts and friends outside the county? (Check one)

___1. Standing is increased

___2. Standing is decreased

___3. Standing is not affected

APPENDIX C

Attitude Factor Scores & Their Correlates

The material included here was shifted from the body of the book to this appendix for two reasons. First, exclusion of this more technical material facilitates reading for those whose interest and background incline them to more "literary" discourse with intuitively simple quantitative analysis. But, second, there has also been an expression of interest in this phase of our work and its methodology. By setting it apart we could present it in a fashion that would better serve such interests, without concern that digressions to explain methods would interrupt the flow of thought—or that omission of such explanations would prove frustrating. That the analysis presented in these pages is important for evaluation of the findings reported in Chapters 4 and 5 will be evident enough to those who are interested in a more intensive critical assessment. We regret, however, that our resources did not allow us to go on to regression analyses using the index instead of the factor scores as the dependent variables. The use of components analysis as a way of analyzing the patterning of responses on attitude items and of selecting variables for the construction of attitude indexes was discussed in Chapter 5, which also presented mean index values by occupation, age, participation variables, and several other traits. We observed systematic differences in expressed attitudes, but it was evident also that there was substantial similarity of attitudes among categories of the sampled population, whatever the basis of classification. However, none of the discussion in the main body of this book has incorporated formal statistical tests of the significance of associations between background or personal characteristics, or participation variables, and the attitudes expressed by respondents. Also, the number of characteristics that could be simultaneously related to attitudes was necessarily few in the absence of any constraining assumptions such as the linearity of relationships assumed in conventional regression analysis. This appendix reports the results of multiple regressions in which the scores of respondents on each of seven factors are treated as dependent variables.

The Methodology

The methodology is basically simple. We used multiple regressions with one or more sets of categorical independent variables ("dummy sets"), though in a few equations we included one or more cardinal independent variables as well. Numerous equations were tested out, but we always forced in all variables within a dummy set when any member of that set was included.[1] In all cases the factor scores used as dependent variables were those obtained in components analysis that had included the mountain teachers. However, many of the regressions were run excluding teachers—usually with better results than those in which teachers were included.[2] This difference reflected the large number of teachers in the sample and the high variance in attitudes among the teachers. Also important is the fact that it was not until after the regressions including teachers were run that we realized the importance of splitting the clergy into two categories, Baptist and non-Baptist. This split was made in all subsequent programs.

Concerning Dummy Variables

Since the use of dummy variables in multiple regression analysis is a relatively unfamiliar technique, a few further words concerning such analysis are in order here. We may begin by taking a simple example in which the only inde-

1. In fact we literally forced them in on the regressions that included teachers, but used a very low F criterion in the regressions that excluded teachers. This was due to the fact that in running the former regressions we were using a MESA program, whereas on the latter we used BIMED. The analysis is identical otherwise.

2. Regressions for Factor 2 are the notable exception.

pendent variables are age categories. Note that age could have been used in cardinal form, but we treated age as a dummy set nevertheless, dividing the initial cardinal age variable into age categories, each of which is treated as a variable. In the particular case this became a dummy set of six variables, as follows:

- A_2 Under 30 years of age (the "omitted dummy")
- A_3 Age 30–39
- A_4 Age 40–49
- A_5 Age 50–59
- A_6 Age 60 and over
- A_0 Age unknown

There are several advantages in this procedure. First, by setting up age categories, we eliminate linearity assumptions so far as the form of the relationship between age and attitudes is concerned. Moreover, the use of a dummy set for age allowed us to treat nonresponse on age as a separate category; there was no need to eliminate cases in which there was no response on age or, alternatively, to assign age estimates to those cases. Note also that unlike age many of our independent variables—most notably occupation—were categorical to start with and could not have been converted to cardinal or ordinal form.

Each of the categorical age variables specified above takes a value of 1 if it applies to the individual, a value of zero if it does not. One of the categorical variables in each dummy set must be omitted from the regression to prevent overdetermination of the results. We chose to treat the youngest age category as the omitted dummy of the age set.[3] The estimated value for the omitted dummy appears in the intercept of a regression equation, and the metric regression coefficient on each other dummy of the set is accordingly the estimated difference between the mean factor score of those under age thirty and the mean factor score of those in the designated age category. Taking the age variables only, and assuming a regression analysis for scores on Factor 7, the antimigration syndrome, as the dependent variable, we may write the regression equation:

$$V^7 = K^7 + b^7_3 A_3 + b^7_4 A_4 + b^7_5 A_5 + b^7_6 A_6 + b^7_0 A_0$$

where V^7 is the score on Factor 7 and all superscripts refer to the fact that this is an equation with Factor 7 scores as the dependent variable. K is the intercept and hence the estimate for the omitted age dummy A_2 (since no other dummy sets were included). The other independent variables, A_3, A_4, and so on, are as listed above in specification of the categorical age variables. In the regression excluding teachers the estimated parameters of this equation, together with T values (shown in parentheses) were as follows:

$$\begin{array}{l} V^7 = -.166 - .027\,A_3 + .125\,A_4 + .375\,A_5 \\ \quad (-1.055) \quad (-.208) \quad (.720) \quad (2.110) \\ \quad + .683\,A_6 - .224\,A_0 \\ \quad (3.824) \quad (-.304) \\ R^2 = .064 \qquad F = 9.07 \end{array}$$

Ignoring for the moment the T values, coefficient of correlation, and F values, what does this equation tell us? It states that the estimated mean value for the Factor 7 score for men under thirty (the intercept) is a negative –.166 when (as in the above equation) only age characteristics are taken into account. It says also that men in their thirties are very like those below thirty (a difference of only .027) in Factor 7 scores, but each successive age category has a higher factor score and the beta values rise more sharply between A_5 and A_6 than in any other age interval. The mean Factor 7 score for men of sixty or more is $(-.166 + .683) = .517$; that for men in their fifties is $(-.166 + .375) = .209$, and so on. It is clear, among other things, that the form of the age relationship to Factor 7 is nonlinear. But this is essentially the kind of information we already presented in our estimates of mean scores on Index 7 by age categories, the differences between taking factor scores and index values as the dependent variable aside.

Still looking at the simple equation using age categories but no other independent variables, we can of course take the further step of evaluating the significance of the regression coefficients. This is standard procedure, as in any

3. This was an unfortunate choice. Interpretations would have been simplified had we taken as the omitted dummy an age category that was better represented across other classifications.

multiple regression analysis, but with the important difference that it must be remembered that the beta coefficients refer not to deviations from the overall mean but to the differences (in Factor 7 attitude scores) between the means for each age category and that for the age category "omitted"—i.e., left in the intercept. The T values must of course be interpreted accordingly. In the particular illustration, b_5 and b_6 turn out to be significant at the .05 and .001 levels, respectively, and the coefficient of determination is significant above the .001 level of probability. Nevertheless age differences on Factor 7 explain only 6.4 percent of the variance in scores ($R^2 =$ .064). Age makes a difference, indeed, but it accounts for only a small part of the variation in Factor 7 scores when age dummies are the only independent variables.

Orders of Entry & Forced Entry by Dummy Sets

When independent variables include more than one dummy set, there is very little point in the use of stepwise regressions. Instead of using that procedure, we simply programmed a large number of equations. In doing this it was of course possible to reverse orders of entry. For example in all cases we included equations using the occupation set only, the age set only, and the two sets combined. This allowed us to examine sensitivity both of the regression coefficients on occupations to inclusion of age and of coefficients on age to inclusion of occupations. Analysis of this sort is critical in spotting situations in which one variable may be acting in large measure as proxy for another, and as a preliminary indicator of where we must look for multicollinearity and identification problems. We did not, however, undertake any direct statistical measurement of interaction.[4]

Regression Results & Their Interpretation: The Example of Factor 3

Overall the regression analyses yielded "highly significant" results but only very modest coefficients of determination. At the highest R^2 got up to around .20, explaining a fifth of the variance. This was for Factor 7; for the other factors our analysis provided explanations of more like 10 percent of the variance. Nevertheless the patterning of relationships was interesting and distinctive as among the dependent variables (as indeed it should be, given the nature of components analysis to start with).

Only a few selected equations are reproduced in tables that follow. Our criteria in making this selection were both relative performance in explaining the variance of scores on the factor taken as dependent variable and the matching of closely related equations to permit examination of how regression coefficients are affected by other variables included. The numbers by which equations are designated refer first to the dependent variable and then to the particular equation for that variable. When the equation is run on the sample inclusive of teachers this is indicated by addition of a "T" to the designation of equation number. Thus, for example, the first equation run on the ESLS sample only (that is, excluding teachers) and with Factor 3 scores as the dependent variable is designated equation (3.1); the results of running this equation are summarized in the first column of Table 42, part A. Equations using essentially the same sets of independent variables to explain Factor 3 scores, but including teachers in the sample, are numbered to match the numbering on similar equations that excluded teachers. Thus equation (3.1T), shown in the first column of Table 42, part B, resembles equation (3.1) in that both of these equations refer to scores on Factor 3 and both include as independent variables the occupation dummy set only. It should be noted, however, that while the classifications on other sets of dummy variables—as the age or the education sets—are identical for the all-mountain sample and for that

4. So far as interactions between age and occupation are concerned, some indirect indication of what is involved may be gleaned from a study of the mean index values on crossed age-occupation cells, shown in Chapter 5. Other tables and charts in Chapter 5 present what could be interpreted as interaction profiles involving, for example, occupation and participation types as they affect or are associated with one attitude complex or another. However, no sort of validity or significance test was incorporated in that presentation.

including teachers, the occupation dummy sets differ through the inclusion of teachers and the dividing of the clergy.

Discussion of the regressions for Factor 3, which we described as a critical view of local schools, makes a convenient starting point for several reasons. The common element in items loading high on this factor was easily identified and Factor 3 can be readily understood. At the same time the regressions for Factor 3 are among those that raise questions of interpretation because of associations between age and occupation and between nativity and occupation with their possible interactive effects vis-à-vis associations with the dependent variable; such problems arise for some of the other dependent variables (factors), but for some they do not. And finally the regressions for Factor 3, with those for Factors 7 and 1, have some special interest on account of the performance of variables concerned with localist identification (NAT and the ID set) and/or participation, and the insights into the nature of the factor itself that observation of such relationships may provide. Discussion of the results of the Factor 3 regressions is presented in more detail, and with more supporting equations than for subsequent factors, not only because of its intrinsic interest but also because in examining these results first we are also engaged in exposition of the potentials and problems of interpretation with our methodology.

Regressions Confined to the ESLS Sample

The results of the Factor 3 regressions using the ESLS sample only are presented selectively in part A of Table 42. Five of these equations included the set of occupation variables. In the first of these, where occupations alone are used, the importance of the split between Baptist and non-Baptist clergy is immediately evident, so far as analysis of Factor 3 scores is concerned. Moreover the coefficients for the Baptists and for the non-Baptists both deviate significantly from values for the omitted dummy (lawyers), with the Baptists decidedly supportive of the local schools, the non-Baptists decidedly the most inclined to view them critically. In fact the coefficients for equation (3.1) set the non-Baptist clergy clearly apart from all other groups. After the lawyers, otherwise the most ready to criticize, come management course participants and physicians and then, going down the scale on Factor 3 scores, the public officials, the bankers, and finally the Baptist clergy. This is reasonably consistent, though not identical, with the ranking of occupations in mean scores on Index 3, reported in Chapter 5, Table 36.[5] But how far do these results stand up when other variables are taken into account?

When the set of dummy variables on age is included in the regression, with or without F-M (the parental education index) as well, there are several, generally minor modifications of the regression coefficients on the various occupations. Most interesting of these is the raising of the significance of the negative deviation among Baptist clergy and the reduction of the positive coefficient for the non-Baptists. Both groups of clergy are relatively young, and relatively young men tended generally to have somewhat more critical views of the mountain schools (if we exclude those under thirty). But this means that if we accept the assumption of independence in operation of the age and the occupation variables with respect to scores on Factor 3, the Baptist clergy may be seen as even more uncritical of the schools, age-for-age, than appeared to be the case when age was not taken into account. The non-Baptist clergy, on the other hand, stand out less sharply in contrast to other occupation groups when their age composition is taken into consideration. The greater negative value for the management-course participants in equation (3.2) as compared with (3.1) is also a reflection of their comparative youth. In fact the effects of introducing the age variables into an equation along with the occupation dummy variables is consistently just what we might expect on account of differences in age composition of the various occupational groups on the assumption

5. We should not expect perfect correspondence for a number of reasons. The indexes include only those items with the highest loading on a factor, whereas factor scores are computed using all items. Furthermore the weights implicit in the method of deriving factor scores are quite different. Results can be quite sensitive to both of these important differences.

TABLE 42. Regression Analysis for Factor 3: Critical Views of Local Schools

	A. Sample excluding teachers; equations excluding ID variables								
Equation numbers	(3.1)	(3.2)	(3.3)	(3.4)	(3.5)	(3.6)	(3.7)	(3.8)	(3.9)
R^2	.040	.065	.076	.050	.059	.063	.089	.111	.102
F	4.61***	4.15***	4.50***	3.44***	3.74***	4.45***	3.75***	3.37***	3.35**
Intercept	.101	.115	-.126	-.252	-.394	-.282	-.340	-.186	-.135
	Regression coefficients								
Independent variables@									
Occupation set									
O-L	z	z	z				z	z	
O-B	-.280	-.204	-.199				-.161	-.151	
O-M	-.025	-.150	-.119				-.082	-.197	
O-CB	-.389*	-.485**	-.414*				-.405*	-.506**	
O-CNB	.331*	.247	.267				.294	.150	
O-PH	-.006	-.037	-.064				-.047	-.062	
O-PO	-.164	-.179	-.129				-.003	.011	
Age set									
A-2		z	z	z	z	z	z	z	z
A-3		.205	.258	.172	.222	.212	.250	.229	.185
A-4		.148	.209	.116	.166	.153	.201	.176	.139
A-5		-.082	-.031	-.045	-.061	-.090	-.037	-.051	-.069
A-6		-.180	-.066	-.150	-.074	-.116	-.052	-.074	-.032
A-0		1.646*	1.702*	1.710*	1.785*	1.562*	1.879*	2.067**	2.101**

Education set							
E-12		z	z		z	z	z
E-3		.171	.054		.059	.039	.024
E-4		.356*	.317*		.351*	.368*	.289*
E-5		.305*	.233		.237	.232	.201
E-6		.389**	.305*		.226	.177	.240
F-M (parental education)	.052**		.050**	.051**	.046*	.042*	.049**
NAT (nativity)						.067	.039
School experience elsewhere set							
WHRS-1				z			
WHRS-4				.079			
WHRS-5				-.013			
WHRS-7				.352**			
WHRS-0				.178			
Location set							
LOC-1						-.150	-.115
LOC-2						-.284*	-.274*
LOC-3						z	z
LOC-4						-.218	-.267
LOC-5						-.287*	-.339*
LOC-6						-.151	-.163
LOC-7						.632*	.559
Community contact and participation indexes							
CIV							.102
POS-AD							-.178
POS-T							-.206*
YOUTH							-.108

*Significant at P=.05
**Significant at P=.01
***Significant at P=.001

[@]A glossary defining these variables is provided at the end of this appendix.
[z]Omitted dummy.

TABLE 42. (Continued)

	B. Sample including teachers; regressions excluding ID variables						
Equation numbers	(3.1T)	(3.2T)	(3.5T)	(3.6T)	(3.9T)	(3.10T)	(3.11T)
R^2	.013	.024	.036	.043	.048	.038	.054
F	1.95	2.10	3.92***	4.71***	3.69***	5.89***	3.27***
Intercept	-.007	.022	-.287	-.206	-.259	-.275	-.516
	Regression coefficients						
Independent variables[a]							
Occupation set							
O-TM	z	z					z
O-FM	-.179	-.120					-.187
O-L	.108	.218					.169
O-B	-.172	.015					.064
O-M	.084	.109					.142
O-CB; O-CNB	.134	.165					b
O-PH	.102	.188					.035
O-PO	-.005	.049					.240
Age set							
A-2		z	z	z	z	z	z
A-3		.017	.079	.066	.053	.096	.044
A-4		-.020	.054	.046	.030	.072	.019
A-5		-.176	-.122	-.141	-.153	-.102	-.141
A-6		-.313*	-.178	-.195	-.217*	-.161	-.202
A-0		-.147	-.217	-.214	-.210	-.247	-.182

Education set					
E-12	z		z		z
E-3	.049		.040		.045
E-4	.306*		.250*		.333*
E-5	.122		.069		.277
E-6	.236*		.122		.306*
E-0	b		b		.043
F-M (parental education)	.049***	.044***	.043***	.048***	.040**
NAT (nativity)				.079***	.086***
School experience elsewhere set					
WHRS-1		z	z		
WHRS-4		.076	.024		
WHRS-5		.080	.035		
WHRS-7		.364***	.307**		
WHRS-0		.095	.066		

*Significant at P=.05. **Significant at P=.01. ***Significant at P=.001.
[@]For definitions see glossary, end of this appendix.
[z]Omitted dummy.
[b]Deleted by regression.

TABLE 42. (Continued)

	C. Equations including ID variables			
	Sample excluding teachers			Sample including teachers
Equation numbers	(3.12)	(3.13)	(3.14)	(3.14T)
R^2	.048	.109	.117	.077
F	6.65***	3.80***	3.72***	3.55***
Intercept	-.091	-.241	-.366	-.520
	Regression coefficients			
Independent variables@				
Occupation set				
O-TM		x	x	z
O-FM		x	x	-.194
O-L		z	z	.192
O-B		-.163	-.192	.063
O-M		-.137	-.148	.126
O-CB		-.644***	-.581**	{-.038
O-CNB		.042	.086	
O-PH		-.072	-.074	.069
O-PO		.003	-.007	.250
Age set				
A-2		z	z	z
A-3		.226	.272	.058
A-4		.179	.227	.040
A-5		-.023	.016	-.117
A-6		-.067	.011	-.155
A-0		1.664*	1.745*	-.107

Education set				
E-12		z	z	z
E-3		.045	.039	.036
E-4		.353*	.320*	.317*
E-5		.238	.174	.241
E-6		.231	.142	.249
E-0		-.127	-.212	.051
F-M (parental education)			.044*	.041**
NAT (nativity)			.000	.055
Identification set				
ID-1	z	z	z	z
ID-2	.202*	.166	.141	.095
ID-3	.456***	.491***	.462***	.259*
ID-4	.604***	.478**	.473**	.375**
ID-5	1.813**	1.537**	1.600**	1.472***
ID-0	-.049	.063	.060	-.140

*Significant at P=.05. **Significant at P=.01. ***Significant at P=.001.

[@]For definitions see glossary, end of this appendix.

[x]Excluded from sample.

[z]Omitted dummy.

that there is no age-occupation interaction in associations with Factor 3 scores. Turning this analysis around, we see that the age coefficients are remarkably stable across the equations presented in Table 42, part A, and on other equations not reproduced. This does not prove absence of serious multicollinearity problems, of course, and we did not go on to test statistically for interaction. However, analysis of index differences by age within occupation categories, presented in Chapter 5, lends support to the judgment that with respect to attitudes toward the local schools we may be justified in assuming independence in the effects of age and occupation.

In most respects the effect of introducing nativity (NAT) into the regressions is similar to, and reinforces, the effects of including the age dummies. While we did not reproduce equations matched in all respects except nativity, the contrast between equations (3.8) and (3.7) in their coefficients for the Baptist and the non-Baptist clergy were in fact matched in an equation that omitted the LOC dummy set. A check on the mean values of Index 3 within occupation-nativity cells also gives general presumptive support to the independence hypothesis. The important exception is the irrelevance or even the inverted effect of nativity within the category of public officials—an effect that is quite unimportant overall because non-native public officials are the rare exception. This is one of the reasons, of course, why introducing NAT makes so little difference in the beta coefficients of O-PO.

In view of the nature of the attitude cluster represented by Factor 3, it must be of special interest to look into associations between factor scores and educational indicators. Better educated men are indeed more critical than others: this shows up consistently across all equations containing the education dummy set, although men who had completed college (E-5) were no more inclined to be critical of mountain schools than were those with some college (but not college completion); the coefficients on E-4 and E-5 in equation (3.4) are both significantly different from E-12 at the .05 probability level, but they differ very little from each other and that for E-5 is actually the lesser. In fact the coefficient on E-4 retains its significance even when other variables in the regression include the occupation dummy set and/or the F-M index of parental education. Of the equations reproduced in Table 42, those most useful in tracing effects of introducing education variables on the occupational coefficients and vice versa are (3.2), (3.3), (3.5), and (3.7). Inclusion of the education dummy set seems to have very little effect on occupational differentials in Factor 3 scores except for the public officials, who have far more than their share in the lower education categories, and especially among those who had not graduated from high school (the omitted dummy, E-12). In fact the education category E-12 comes very close to being a subgroup made up of the least educated public officials only, and it is hardly surprising that the effect of the education dummies on the beta coefficients for public officials is not reflected, inversely, in any substantial alteration of the differentials between the betas on E-3 and E-4 as between equations (3.5) and (3.7). The behavior of the coefficients on E-6, referring to graduate education, is another matter, given their high sensitivity to and likely interaction with effects of memberships in the professions.

This brings us to the effects of parental education, the F-M index, which was important in the Factor 3 regressions but in no others. No matter what else was in a regression for scores on Factor 3 as the dependent variable, the regression coefficient for F-M is significant, and in most cases at the .01 level (.001 in the regressions including teachers). The coefficient for F-M drops to a .05 significance level only when the equation includes *both* the occupation and education dummy sets. The association between high scores on F-M and college graduation or more on the part of the respondent is reflected in the dampening of coefficients on E-5 and, more especially, on E-6 when F-M is included in the equation. On the other hand the coefficient on F-M is remarkably robust. At the same time—and this is particularly interesting—the coefficient on WHRS-7 (high school and college attendance outside of Kentucky) remains significant at a .01 level even in an equation that includes F-M provided the occupation and education dummy sets are not also simultaneously included. WHRS-7 is the only variable among those available to us as indicators of exposure that came through significantly in the regression analyses for Factor 3. This is undoubtedly because of the particularly relevant kind of exposure entailed, with its clear educational component. Indeed WHRS does better than the education dummy set in an equation with age and F-M, as a comparison between equations (3.5) and (3.6) shows.

The last two equations in part A of Table 42 include dummy sets for location. The pattern of coefficients on these locations was stable in its essentials across other equations as well. Consistently the coefficient for LOC-7, which is the Bluegrass margin, was the highest, followed by the omitted dummy, LOC-3, which is the counties of the upper Kentucky River basin (Knott, Leslie, Letcher, Perry). The coefficient on LOC-7 has an extremely high standard error, however—so much so that when occupations are not included in the equation even a coefficient of .559 is not significant at the .05 level. Attitudes toward the schools among the residents of LOC-7 are extremely diverse, reflecting the counter influences of a schooling situation in fact superior to most in the mountains, but a standard of comparison that was also decidedly higher. It must be remembered that the comparison measured by the coefficient is with LOC-3, and the respondents residing in LOC-3 were the second most critical of their schools. Compared with any location other than LOC-3, the men of LOC-7 were significantly the more critical. Interpretation of the contrasts between LOC-3 attitudes and those in the Upper Sandy River basin or the Harlan-Cumberland area or the southwestern counties (LOC-2, 4, and 5) is hazardous, and we refrain from injecting into this discussion intuitions or hypotheses on this matter that we have not had the time or opportunity to check. One thing at least is clear, however: locational differences in attitudes toward local schools cannot be explained by present objective differences among areas in what the schools have to offer.

Factor 3 Regressions for the Total Mountain Sample (Including Teachers)

In no case did regression equations for the total mountain sample inclusive of teachers (part B of Table 42) explain as high a proportion of the variance in Factor 3 scores as was explained for the ESLS sample only—although, given the enlarged sample, the F values were higher for some of the equations on the total sample inclusive of teachers. The poorest performance relative to that on the ESLS runs was in the failure of occupational categories to discriminate. This reflects two facts. First, as already noted, the runs including teachers did not split clergy into Baptist and non-Baptist, and this was precisely the contrast that proved to be most important with respect to Factor 3 scores in the ESLS runs. Equally important is that the male teachers differed very little from other occupational groups in their attitudes toward local schools.

So far as the coefficients are concerned, the disinclination of the most youthful nonteachers to criticize local schools was notable, and this gave the entire structure of Factor 3 age coefficients on A-3 through A-6 in the ESLS regressions an upward boost as compared with coefficients on A-3 through A-6 when teachers were included in the sample. It is unfortunate that we chose the youngest age group for the omitted dummy; this does not alter the evidence, but it makes interpretation more awkward.

Education also behaves in essentially the same way for the all-mountain sample as for the ESLS sample regressions on Factor 3, but with two minor exceptions that are again of more methodological than substantive interest. First, the category E-5, college graduates, is less differentiated from those with the least education in the all-mountain regressions (compare equation 3.5T with 3.5). This unquestionably reflects the large numbers of teachers with education at level E-5 together with teacher biases in favor of the mountain schools. When occupations are included in the regression, as in equation (3.11T), the coefficient on E-5 looks more like coefficients on this education level in part A of Table 42. Statistical interaction is involved, certainly, but it is also relatively easy to interpret the data; the identification problem in this case is not a difficult one. The second contrast between the performance of the education dummy set in Part 2 versus part A of Table 42 is a similar but less marked contrast between coefficients on E-6; compare equations (3.5T) and (3.5) for example.

F-M, the index of parental educational attainment, carries coefficients slightly smaller than in comparable regressions using the ESLS sample, but it is significant at the .001 level in most equations, and is conspicuous also because it does so much more than anything else except WHRS 7 and NAT. NAT carried notably more weight in the all-mountain runs on Factor 3 than in runs on the ESLS sample only. For example, NAT added virtually nothing to the results of equation (3.7), if we except its effect on the coefficients of O-CB and O-CNB. On the other hand it proved to be a highly significant variable when added to a similar equation that included teachers (3.11T).

Mountain Identification & Factor 3 Scores

Part C of Table 42 explores the extent to which scores on Factor 3 may be associated with degrees of identification with the mountains, whatever a man's occupation, age, or education may be. The implications of these equations will be best understood if we compare them not only with each other, but with selected equations from parts A and B of Table 42 as well. In making such comparisons, we are dealing with quite a different sort of question than those raised on the immediately preceding pages, however. Interest is not so much in the question of independence or interaction in the effects of independent variables on Factor 3 scores. Instead we are interested in using these findings as a shortcut to checking on the extent to which responses on Factor 3 may be associated with, and even part of, an attitude complex that is measured also by responses indicating degrees of self-identification with the mountain region.

The first question, therefore, is how far the ID dummy set taken by itself may relate to Factor 3 scores. Equation (3.12) provides an answer for the ESLS sample; taken by itself, the ID dummy set explains 5 percent of the variance in Factor 3 scores for that sample. Though hardly impressive (despite its high level of significance), this is better than what we could do with an occupation dummy set alone, and it is approximately what we obtained using the age and education dummy sets without any other variables. The coefficients on the ID dummies progress systematically upward, and as soon as we reach the point, with ID-3, at which any sort of reservation is expressed, the coefficients become highly significant (at the .001 probability level or higher). This remains the critical breaking point in a regression that includes occupation, age, and education dummy sets. Finally equation (3.14) adds F-M and NAT, though NAT is wholly washed out by the ID set, which takes over whatever effect nativity may have. Equation (3.14) includes the same variables as (3.8) except that the ID set is substituted for the LOC set, with a slight improvement in results, given the other variables in these equations. (ID alone is much more effective than LOC alone.) Equation (3.14T), the parallel equation to (3.14) but including teachers, gives poorer results not only because (as by now we should expect) the variables other than the ID set are less powerful, but also because the ID set itself is less potent among the teachers. The ID dummies do more than anything else in equation (3.14) nevertheless, and the significance of the differences in coefficients is neatly ordered from ID-2 (not significant) to ID-5 (at the .001 level of significance).

One of the limitations of the effectiveness of the ID dummies in explaining variance in Factor 3 scores is evidently the distinctive pattern of attitudes of the Baptist clergy. In an equation with age, education, and ID dummy sets the beta coefficient for the Baptist clergy becomes a highly significant —.644, while the coefficients for the non-Baptist clergy and the public officials become virtually zero, bringing them together with the lawyers. This seems to make it abundantly clear that the position of the Baptist clergy, with their strong defenses of the local mountain schools, is very closely bound up with their professional roles even when these ministers perceive themselves as temporary residents of the Kentucky mountains. But it brings out another fact as well: even when they do not define themselves as strictly local mountain men, a large proportion of the Baptist clergy come from quite similar Appalachian areas and many anticipate that if or when they leave the Kentucky mountains it will be to go to other parts of rural Appalachia. The non-Baptist clergy have generally quite different experiences and expectations. At the same time, even if there were no variance at all in Factor 3 scores of men in ID categories 3, 4, and 5, the ID dummy set would be limited in its explanatory power because of the large numbers of respondents who identify themselves as strongly local and among whom there is considerable variation in degree of pride or defensiveness with respect to mountain schools. Variance in these attitudes among the strongly native members of the mountain elites is in fact one of the optimistic inferences from our data, as are the high unexplained variances generally, both on Factor 3 and on others. It should be noted, however, that it is primarily on Factors 3 and 7 (the anti-migration syndrome) that the ID dummy variables are significant.

Analyses of Regressions for Other Factors

Factor 5

Perception of mountain children as suffering from disadvantaged backgrounds was rare among our respondents, even when reference was specifically to the run-of-the-mill folk. In fact there was just one occupational group whose members showed any signs of such recognition —the non-Baptist clergy. This shows up clearly in Table 43. No matter what else may be entered in a regression, the contrast between the non-Baptist clergy and the lawyers is significant at the .001 or the .01 level. Though the age coefficients are quite stable, given inclusions of the occupational dummies, there is no very striking relationship with age. Even the coefficients for A-5, which deviate most from the omitted dummy (the non-response category, A-O, aside) did not reach a .05 level of significance. It is notable that controlling for occupation and age it is the least educated who were most inclined to perceive the disadvantages of youngsters growing up in the mountains. Those respondents who had been to college (but had not graduated) were the most inclined to deny emphatically the existence of such disadvantages. Other variables that were of particular interest in the Factor 3 regressions were generally useless on Factor 5: F-M told nothing, and NAT did not even affect the coefficients for Baptist or non-Baptist clergy. The WHRS set added to equation (5.3) did raise the R^2 from .077 to .087, but even WHRS 7, which did the work, was significant at a .05 level only; WHRS was no good as a substitute for the education dummy set in equation (5.3), or in any other. The regressions including teachers were quite uninteresting on Factor 5, and discussion is therefore limited to the ESLS runs on this factor.

Of particular importance in regressions on Factor 5 were the LOC dummies, the county MOD indicator, and interactions between these. MOD is itself a factor score, but for counties, not individuals. (As explained in Chapter 1, it was derived in an earlier study by one of the authors.) High-loading variables on MOD included, for example, variables relating to educational attainments of adult males over twenty-five years of age, female labor-force participation rates, per capita incomes in the county, proportions of residences with telephones, and so forth (Table 1). The ways in which MOD and the LOC dummy set operate with respect to Factor 5 is easily seen by comparing equations (5.2), (5.4), (5.5), and (5.6). The first of these includes as independent variables the occupation and age sets only. Equation (5.4), which adds MOD, raises the value of R^2 only slightly, and MOD itself is barely significant at the .05 level. Equation (5.5), with LOC dummies but not MOD, gives very nearly the same R^2, but none of the differences between localities are significant, and we have lost a substantial number of degrees of freedom. But when MOD and the LOC set are put together in the same equation, as they are in (5.6), R^2 goes up to .093 and the coefficient on MOD triples, reaching significance at better

TABLE 43. Regression Analysis for Factor 5: Disadvantaged Backgrounds of Mountain Children

Equation number	(5.1)	(5.2)	(5.3)	(5.4)	(5.5)	(5.6)	(5.7)	(5.8)
R^2	.053	.063	.077	.069	.071	.093	.106	.108
F	6.22***	4.07**	3.41**	4.07**	2.93*	3.72***	3.34***	3.96***
Intercept	.055	.204	.403	.011	.380	.001	.222	.154
Independent Variables@	Regression coefficients							
Occupation set								
O-L	z	z	z	z	z	z	z	z
O-B	-.147	-.106	-.085	-.091	-.092	-.043	-.030	-.092
O-M	-.207	-.233	-.189	-.282	-.260	-.371**	-.333*	-.435**
O-CB	.047	.004	-.014	.005	.012	.042	.024	-.069
O-CNB	.508***	.467**	.397**	.467***	.464***	.502***	.443**	.406**
O-PH	-.009	-.007	-.078	-.023	.002	-.021	-.084	-.128
O-PO	-.166	-.144	-.208	-.131	-.139	-.107	-.177	-.004
Age set								
A-2		z	z	z	z	z	z	z
A-3		-.044	-.041	-.060	-.032	-.031	-.028	-.008
A-4		-.089	-.067	-.104	-.072	-.062	-.041	-.016
A-5		-.277	-.270	-.300	-.260	-.276	-.271	-.225
A-6		-.198	-.191	-.236	-.165	-.190	-.188	-.163
A-0		-1.057	-1.195	-1.004	-.969	-.827	-.977	-.907
Education set								
E-12			z				z	
E-3			-.221				-.230	
E-4			-.373**				-.386**	
E-5			-.298				-.306	
E-6			-.131				-.160	
E-0			.090				.061	

MOD (county modernization)	1.490*		4.088***	4.081***	3.929**
Location set					
LOC-1		-.269	-.560***	-.598***	-.577**
LOC-2		-.263	-.411**	-.397**	-.402**
LOC-3		z	z	z	z
LOC-4		-.195	-.442***	-.448**	-.435**
LOC-5		-.247	-.559***	-.550***	-.524***
LOC-6		-.221	-.396**	-.421*	-.332*
LOC-7		-.103	-1.029**	-1.091**	-1.006**
Participation indexes					
POL					-.205**
CIV					-.062

*Significant at P=.05
**Significant at P=.01
***Significant at P=.001
[@]For definitions see glossary at end of this appendix.
[z]Omitted dummy.

than the .001 level. There can be no question that, purified of special subarea features by the inclusion of the LOC (multicounty) dummy variables in the regression, the more educated a population and the more developed its communications with urban centers (as represented in MOD scores) the more likely are its residents to perceive the disadvantages suffered by children living in impoverished areas where communication is poor. At the same time the control for MOD sharpens the contrasts among the regression coefficients for the LOC set. Location 7, which is made up of counties at the upper range in county MOD scores, looks very different on Factor 5 scores when controlled for county MOD, which eliminates the confounding effect of LOC-7 on the Factor 5 regressions. But that is not all. The contrast between LOC-3 and all other locations now appears as highly significant, with men of LOC-3 expressing an unusual degree of concern about problems of mountain children relative to the scoring of LOC-3 counties on the MOD analysis. Incidentally this is the more interesting in view both of the importance of this location as one of the major coal centers of eastern Kentucky and the relatively high intercept values for this location with respect to scores on Factor 3—i.e., the relative readiness of respondents of this area to take a constructively critical view of the situation in local schools.

The last two equations of Table 43 compare the effects of adding either the education dummy set or the POL and CIV variables to the regressions. In either case we reach a coefficient of determination of 10 to 11 percent. Otherwise equation (5.7) is interesting primarily as it demonstrates the stability of the education and of the MOD and LOC coefficients in comparisons with equations (5.3) and (5.6) respectively. Equation (5.8) brings out the fact that, with controls for other traits, men who rate high in political involvement are even less inclined than others to perceive mountain children as handicapped.

Factor 6

Results of the regressions for Factor 6 were impressive not for anything they explained but for their utter lack of significance, and we have reproduced only three equations (Table 44), all from the ESLS sample. Those for the sample including teachers were even weaker. Taking equation (6.1), which used the occupation dummy set only, about all we can say is that the Baptist clergy are decidedly less oriented to the attitudes picked up by Factor 6 than were the lawyers, who were the most favorably inclined (the coefficients for all other occupations are negative). Correspondence with rankings on the associated Index 6 scores (Table 36) is only moderate. Baptist clergy do indeed have the lowest scores in Table 36 and the largest negative coefficient on equation (6.1), and lawyers are at the top in both cases, but the non-Baptist clergy do not look at all remarkable for their receptivity to outsiders in the Factor 6 regressions—especially when controls for age are introduced. What we are observing in fact is a very low between-occupation variance (except possibly for contrasts between lawyers at one extreme and Baptist clergy at the other) and an associated high degree of sensitivity of occupation means to differences between the items and implicit weights in the indexes and in the derivation of factor scores on Index 6 and Factor 6. Negative values for the older men (over sixty) as contrasted with younger men seem clear, but at the best, in equation (6.2), this contrast is significant at the .05 level only, even though it does indeed show up clearly enough in the index comparisons of Chapter 5 as well. Barely significant also, this time on the plus side, is the coefficient for WHRS 7. This is shown in our "best" equation for Factor 6—i.e., equation (6.3).

In view of the disappointing results of regressions on Factor 6, which came as something of a surprise, we rechecked all relevant computations on the related Index 6 and reexamined the printouts of input programs for the regressions. Turning up no errors in this process, we reexamined the loadings on Factor 6 with a view to reconsidering our interpretation of that factor. There are indeed two types of responses bearing high Factor 6 loadings: those that express the respondent's attitudes and those that express how

TABLE 44. Regression Analysis for Factor 6: Receptivity to Outsiders

Equation number	(6.1)	(6.2)	(6.3)
R^2	.017	.038	.070
F	1.65	2.33*	2.33*
Intercept	.174	.316	-.007
		Regression coefficients	
Independent variables@			
Occupation set			
O-L	z	z	z
O-B	-.208	-.107	-.208
O-M	-.121	-.252	-.162
O-CB	-.420**	-.535***	-.465*
O-CNB	-.294*	-.400**	-.410*
O-PH	-.218	-.266	-.266
O-PO	-.095	-.116	.005
Age set			
A-2		z	z
A-3		.081	.105
A-4		-.020	.019
A-5		-.089	-.068
A-6		-.386*	-.328
A-0		.655	.777
School experience elsewhere set			
WHRS-1			z
WHRS-4			.228
WHRS-5			.055
WHRS-7			.312*
WHRS-0			-.118
Location set			
LOC-1			.225
LOC-2			.230
LOC-3			z
LOC-4			.087
LOC-5			-.038
LOC-6			.263
LOC-7			-.077

*Significant at P=.05 **Significant at P=.01 ***Significant at P=.001

@For definitions see glossary at end of this appendix.

zOmitted dummy.

he feels *other* people feel. There was nothing in the results of this examination that could suggest why the non-Baptist clergy should be comparatively high on the index-score estimates but not in the Factor 6 regressions, but it does raise questions concerning the interpretation of Factor 6 in one as against another role context and analytical perspective.[6] The best that could be said of it is that on the whole the rankings of the index scores (if not the factor scores) associated with high-loading items on Factor 6 were consistent with a priori expectations. Differences among group means on Index 6 were small enough that they played only a minor part in the determination of the modernization scores (not to be confused with county MOD) that were developed and analyzed in Chapter 5.

Factor 7

Factor 7 turned out to be all that Factor 6 was not—remarkably neat and unambiguous in its interpretation and its intergroup patterning, both in the regression analysis and in the associated indexes of Chapter 5. In this case also we have omitted analysis of regressions using the entire mountain sample, including teachers. Those regression results resembled very closely the results using the ESLS sample only, but with slightly lower values of R^2 and slightly higher F values. The coefficients on teachers were close to those for clergy and O-M.

Equation (7.1), Table 45, displays a sharp demarcation between those we classified as members of the administrative elites and members of the professional elites. Bankers and public officials stand with the lawyers in their positive scores on the antimigration syndrome. (Note that the intercept—in this case the mean score for lawyers—is a highly significant .456.) The physicians, both clergy groups, and, behind them, the management-course participants are strongly negative as compared with lawyers; all the coefficients on these occupation groups were significant at the .001 probability level.

It might be expected that men who reported themselves as natives of the mountains would be more inclined to display attitudes in line with Factor 7 than would those who had come to the mountains from elsewhere, and the coefficients on NAT are indeed significant—very highly significant in equations that do not include education dummy sets. Age and NAT taken together (7.3) give exactly the same coefficient of determination, with the same F value, as the dummy set for occupations. Also evident in equation (7.3) is a distinct contrast between younger men and those in their fifties or, especially, those aged sixty or over.

A comparison of equation (7.2) with (7.1) brings out immediately the effects of associations between nativity outside of the mountains and membership in the clergy, Baptist or otherwise. But note that here again an essentially similar effect is created by introducing age controls, as in equation (7.4). In either case it is now the physicians above all who stand out in their opposition to (negative scores on) the antimigration syndrome. There is also, unambiguously, the strong effect of education on the Factor 7 scores. The progression is smooth and systematic in the rise of negative coefficients with increase in amount of education from men who had not completed high school (the omitted dummy) on to E-6, or men with graduate education. The men of LOC 3 are distinctive once again, this time for their relative indifference to migration and associated aspects of Factor 7 attitudes. In equations not reproduced here we obtained significant coefficients on POL (always positive) but not on CIV.[7]

Factors 2 & 4

Factor 2, roughly labeled as an attitude cluster in "defense of ordinary folk," is the only case in which the regressions using the all-mountain sample (inclusive of teachers) gave higher coefficients of determination than did those using the ESLS sample only. One of the main reasons is easily observed in Table 46: teachers were at the upper end of the continuum in scores on this factor. At the other extreme were bankers and management-course participants, followed by

6. Some of the problems may be intuitively evident in examination of some of the item-by-item responses shown in Table 32.

7. When, but only when, both occupation and age variables were in the regression, YOUTH hovered around a negative value at the .05 significance level for Factor 5 scores.

public officials. The age coefficients shown in equation (2.2) are almost identical with those in an equation that contained age dummies only and in an equation that substituted the WHRS dummy set for the occupation set—equations yielding R^2 values of .056 and .073 respectively. The age patterning of scores on Factor 2 is unmistakable in the ESLS runs. It is less clear in the runs including teachers, as we have noted with several other factors, although even in equations (2.2T) and (2.3T) the break between those under and those over fifty years of age is evident enough. The education dummy sets contributed little in regressions for Factor 2 scores, and equations including education dummy variables have therefore been omitted. In fact the only independent variable that consistently claimed attention in regressions for Factor 2 was CIT-W (which was unimportant for other dependent variables); the more urban a man's prior working experience, the less affirmative were his responses on the attitudes that make up Factor 2. Also acting as a dampener in this respect was high parental education, with moderately significant negative coefficients on F-M, not shown in Table 46.

That defensive attitudes concerning ordinary folk did not necessarily imply support of active participation of the poor or the young in community decision-making is underlined by the very fact that the components analysis brought out, as distinct and independent factors, the cluster of traits picked up in Factor 2 and the grassroots participation theme that is central to Factor 4. This contrast is further evidenced in a comparison of Table 47 with Table 46. There are common features to be sure. The teachers, for example, score high on both factors; but the lawyers and non-Baptist clergy occupy quite different positions in the two sets of regressions—with the lawyers taking an exceptionally affirmative stance on Factor 2 but a quite skeptical relative position on the question of extending participant roles in community decision-making to folk they regard as presumptively unqualified for such roles. Perhaps the most striking contrast between response patterns on Factors 2 and 4 are the age relationships displayed in the runs on the ESLS sample (excluding teachers). Whereas coefficients became increasingly negative with increasing age in the Factor 2 regressions, the oldest respondents gave the most support to grassroots participation. No changes in the other variables included in an equation altered these age patterns on either the Factor 2 or Factor 4 regressions.

Among all other variables tried, the only interesting results on either Factor 2 or Factor 4 were from the LOC dummy set, and again the contrast between those two factors is clear. The most favorable to ordinary folk (Factor 2 scores) were respondents living in LOC-6, along the middle Kentucky River in the rural heart of the mountains. That area stood out in marked contrast to all others in the ESLS Factor 2 regressions, and it carried the highest scores on regressions including teachers as well. But there was nothing distinctive about the LOC-6 coefficients so far as responses relating to grassroots participation were concerned. In fact it was the very different Bluegrass-margin area, LOC-7, in which we found both the highest coefficients on Factor 4 and the lowest ones on Factor 2.

Factor 1

This factor, it will be remembered, brought together a large number of high-loading items relating to compensatory human development activities, and to federal-local cooperation in such endeavors. Observation of distributions of responses on the relevant individual items and analysis of mean Index 1 scores for various groupings of the population (presented in Chapters 4 and 5) led us to suggest that what this factor was picking up was essentially an orientation to community activity. The regression results for Factor 1 scores support this notion. It is the non-Baptist clergy and the public officials who consistently score the highest on Factor 1, as on Index 1. Regardless of whether the occupation dummy sets were included in the regression or not, the age patterns indicated within each sample in Table 48 were repeated. In the ESLS sample the youngest men (under thirty) are distinctively the most supportive of human development programs and federal help in their implementation, but whether a respondent is forty or fifty or over sixty years of age makes no

TABLE 45. Regression Analysis for Factor 7: Anti-Migration Syndrome

Equation number	(7.1)	(7.2)	(7.3)	(7.4)	(7.5)	(7.6)	(7.7)	(7.8)
R^2	.112	.129	.112	.137	.153	.156	.168	.180
F	13.96***	14.08***	14.00***	9.52***	9.93***	7.59***	7.78***	6.19***
Intercept	.456	.646	.247	.263	.430	.745	.827	.683
				Regression coefficients				
<u>Independent variables</u>[@]								
Occupation set								
O-L	z	z		z	z	z	z	z
O-B	.098	.082		-.015	-.029	-.205	-.189	-.196
O-M	-.524***	-.479***		-.393**	-.352**	-.611***	-.545***	-.556***
C-B	-.583***	-.345*		-.459**	-.232	-.528***	-.321	-.321
C-NB	-.702***	-.409*		-.594***	-.312	-.539***	-.302	-.282**
O-PH	-.840***	-.728***		-.806***	-.699***	-.712***	-.634***	-.641***
O-PO	.099	.014		.060	.023	-.231	-.224	-.202
Age set								
A-2			z	z	z	z	z	z
A-3			-.025	-.029	-.007	-.033	-.014	-.026
A-4			.078	.007	.034	-.017	-.009	.002
A-5			.300	.247	.264	.228	.247	.232
A-6			.559**	.435*	.446*	.337	.361*	.330
A-0			-.367	-.260	-.267	-.016	-.029	-.184
Education set								
E-12						z	z	z
E-3						-.113	-.089	-.113
E-4						-.257	-.237	-.251
E-5						-.387*	-.338*	-.367*
E-6						-.550***	-.476**	-.484**
E-0						-.627*	-.599*	-.621*

NAT (nativity)	-.139***	-.181***		-.135***		-.116*	-.123**
Location set							
LOC-1							.193
LOC-2							.345**
LOC-3							z
LOC-4							.225
LOC-5							.213
LOC-6							.068
LOC-7							.395

*Significant at P=.05.
**Significant at P=.01.
***Significant at P=.001.
@For definitions see glossary at end of this appendix.
zOmitted dummy.

TABLE 46. Regression Analysis for Factor 2: Defense of Ordinary Folk

	Sample excluding teachers			Sample including teachers		
Equation number	(2.1)	(2.2)	(2.3)	(2.1T)	(2.2T)	(2.3T)
R^2	.033	.081	.088	.063	.099	.111
F	3.78***	5.30***	5.33***	9.93***	9.54***	9.92***
Intercept	.045	.496	.650	.257	.167	.439
	Regression coefficients					
Independent variables[@]						
Occupation set						
O-TM	x	x	x	z	z	z
O-FM	x	x	x	.051	.095	.092
O-L	z	z	z	-.211	-.057	-.109
O-B	-.502***	-.345*	-.314*	-.713***	-.443**	-.456**
O-M	-.309*	-.451***	-.447***	-.520***	-.520***	-.568***
O-CB	-.123	-.263	-.266	{-.229*	{-.197	{-.254*
O-CNB	.061	-.066	-.067			
O-PH	-.166	-.190	-.211	-.378**	-.265*	-.342*
O-PO	-.329	-.323*	-.302*	-.540***	-.416***	-.442**
Age set						
A-2		z	z		z	z
A-3		-.256	-.237		.173	.158
A-4		-.218	-.198		.185	.173
A-5		-.554***	-.538**		-.116	-.130
A-6		-.759***	-.728***		-.331**	-.328**
A-0		-.292	-.323		.683**	.683**

Work in city		
CIT-W	-.075*	-.090**

*Significant at P=.05.
**Significant at P=.01.
***Significant at P=.001.
[@]For definitions see glossary at end of this appendix.
[x]Excluded from sample.
[z]Omitted dummy.

TABLE 47. Regression Analysis for Factor 4: Grassroots Participation

	Sample excluding teachers				Sample including teachers	
Equation number	(4.1)	(4.2)	(4.3)	(4.4)	(4.1T)	(4.3T)
R^2	.059	.037	.073	.092	.051	.063
F	6.98***	5.18***	4.69***	4.17***	7.937***	5.834***
Intercept	-.258	.255	-.520	-.263	.122	.210
			Regression coefficients			
Independent variables[@]						
Occupation set						
O-TM	x		x	x	z	z
O-TF	x		x	x	.077	.099
O-L	z		z	z	-.380**	-.394**
O-B	-.026		-.102	-.152	-.406**	-.461**
O-M	-.067		-.008	-.038	-.447***	-.403**
C-B	.542***		.590***	.510***	{ .038	{ .062
C-NB	.326*		.377*	.283		
O-PH	.050		.071	-.018	-.330*	-.305*
O-PO	.532***		.546***	.416*	.152	.190
Age set						
A-2			z	z		z
A-3			.254	.281		-.096
A-4			.200	.244		-.151
A-5			.149	.173		-.267*
A-6			.450*	.456*		.089
A-0			.008	.191		-.067

Education set		
E-12	z	z
E-3	-.378*	-.231
E-4	-.365*	-.209
E-5	-.744***	-.554***
E-6	-.291*	-.172
E-0	-.331	-.266

*Significant at P=.05.
**Significant at P=.01.
***Significant at P=.001.
[@]For definitions see glossary at end of this appendix.
[x]Excluded from sample.
[z]Omitted dummy.

TABLE 48. Regression Analysis for Factor 1: Human Development Programs

	Sample excluding teachers						Sample including teachers		
Equation number	(1.1)	(1.2)	(1.3)	(1.4)	(1.5)	(1.6)	(1.2T)	(1.4T)	(1.5T)
R^2	.059	.067	.082	.068	.077	.092	.048	.042	.052
F	6.90***	6.78***	6.60***	4.37***	4.56***	4.75***	6.54***	3.77***	4.38***
Intercept	-.052	-.180	-.127	.314	.194	.223	.206	.064	-.081
	Regression coefficients								
Independent variables@									
Occupation set									
O-TM	x	x	x	x	x	x	z	z	z
O-TF	x	x	x	x	x	x	.117	.169	.129
O-L	z	z	z	z	z	z	.024	.050	.059
O-B	-.147	-.136	-.206	-.105	-.095	-.167	-.112	-.092	-.072
O-M	-.163	-.194	-.300*	-.172	-.201	-.295*	-.170	-.100	-.122
O-CB	.100	.060	-.169	.086	-.078	-.171	{ .140	{ .353***	{ .180
O-CNB	.450**	.253	.084	.413**	.210	.055			
O-PH	-.215	-.291	-.384*	-.206	-.283	-.367*	-.268*	-.150	-.227
O-PO	.370*	.394**	.447**	.413**	.440**	.484**	.418***	.440***	.473***
Age set									
A-2				z	z	z		z	z
A-3				-.321	-.337	-.341		-.179	-.168
A-4				-.412*	-.431*	-.435*		-.233*	-.224*
A-5				-.431*	-.443*	-.430*		-.154	-.145
A-6				-.406*	-.415*	-.391*		-.160	-.154
A-0				-.364	-.360	-.282		-.112	-.162

NAT (nativity)	.094*	.084*		.097*	.089*	.091***		.094***
Participation indexes								
POL		-.160*			-.144			
CIV		.119**			.123**			

*Significant at P=.05.
**Significant at P=.01.
***Significant at P=.001.
[@]For definitions see glossary at end of this appendix.
[x]Excluded from sample.
[z]Omitted dummy.

difference. Also, no matter what other variables are included in the regression, the positive coefficients on CIV (civic participation index) were significant at the .01 level. The coefficients on POL (political participation index) reached barely significant negative values in some regressions. Note, however, that it would not be legitimate to interpret either CIV or POL as control variables in estimating the occupational regression coefficients. While the statistics do not in themselves tell us what interaction problems may be involved, it seems clear enough that the predominant direction of influence is from occupational role to community participation and Factor 1 attitudes. NAT raises questions that are formally similar, but with the difference that the variable NAT is a background characteristic of the individual, not in itself a behavioral or attitude trait.

The relatively strong positive values on the NAT index suggest a disinclination among natives of the mountains to recognize or, possibly, to accept the idea that human development may constitute at once a major problem and an important potential for mountain society and people. Unquestionably it is also indicative of some degree of resistance to the intrusion of federal agencies in mountain affairs. Controlling for occupations, all NAT coefficients are significant at the .05 level at least, and for the all-mountain regressions they are significant at the .001 level. But the statistical multicollinearity and identification problems introduced by consideration of the place of NAT in regressions for Factor 1 scores are more difficult to disentangle and probably more serious than in the regressions for Factor 3. A better understanding of just what is involved here would require a further, more direct exploration of the statistical interaction effect between NAT and O-CNB, especially, as these variables are associated with scores on Factor 1.

Summary Remarks

One of the main purposes of this appendix has been to pursue some questions further than cross-tabulations, with or without attitude indexes, could carry us. Generally the regressions have confirmed conclusions inferred from other ways of organizing the evidence. The most important exception is instructive, however: this was the disparities in implied rankings of the non-Baptist clergy on Factor 6 and Index 6. That conflict underlines the facts that (1) explained variance on Factor 6 was extremely small and (2) very substantial discrepancies are possible between an index score that is built up from responses on high-loading variables only as against scores on a factor, which incorporate weightings of all variables in the factor analysis in delineation of the factor. At the same time, this result underlines a substantive fact stressed in Chapters 5 and 7 as well—the fact that attitudes among mountain men are not nearly as predictable from their ages, occupations, or schooling as common stereotypes might suggest.

On the other hand, where factor scores and index scores proved to be more fully in accord (as was generally the case), the regression analysis also yielded a number of clear-cut positive results. It was only in the regression analysis, for example, that we were able to establish that education of their parents had a significant effect on respondents' attitudes toward the schools, even with controls for occupation and respondent's education. Another example on Factor 3 was the distinctiveness of the Baptist clergy, which became increasingly evident when tested in several multiple regression equations. Also of special interest, but not mentioned in the body of this book, was the importance of the county factor MOD, the dummy set LOC, and their interaction with respect to attitude Factor 5. While use of factor scores as independent variables might be regarded as even more questionable than their use as dependent variables, this particular finding is a tantalizing one. Even though it is far from decisive, those results invite further explorations into the ecology of social and economic development and lag.

Glossary of Independent Variables Used in the Regressions

In this glossary the independent variables are grouped by topic rather than form, with cardinal variables and dummy sets under the same heading when they belong together for substantive reasons.

Location dummies & county factor scores:

LOC-1 . . . LOC-7 dummy set. (Locations as designated by these numbers in Figure 10.) The omitted dummy is LOC-3.

MOD. See Table 1. This is factor scores for counties.

Personal characteristics:

Occupation dummy set:

O-B	Bankers
O-L	Lawyers (omitted dummy on second set of regressions)
O-M	Management-course participants
O-CB	Baptist clergy
O-CNB	Non-Baptist clergy
O-PH	Physicians
O-PO	Public officials
O-TM	Male secondary school teachers (omitted dummy on first set of regressions)
O-TF	Female secondary school teachers

Age dummy set:

A 2	Age under 30 (omitted dummy)
A 3	Age 30–39
A 4	Age 40–49
A 5	Age 50–59
A 6	Age 60 and over
A 0	Age not reported

Education dummy set:

E 12	Did not complete high school (omitted dummy)
E 3	High school completion
E 4	Some college
E 5	Completed four years of college
E 6	Post-college education
E 0	Education not reported

Background and exposure variables:

NAT = Nativity index. Values of the variable are treated as if cardinal.

1	Same county as present residence
2	Other eastern Kentucky
3	Other Kentucky, non-metropolitan
4	Other state, non-metropolitan
5	Metropolitan

F-M = Index of parental education, treated as if cardinal.

1	Both completed eighth grade or less.
2	At least one had some high school; neither completed high school.
3	One completed high school, other did not.
4	Both completed high school.
5	One some college, other did not complete high school.
6	One or both some college; both at least completed high school.
7	One completed college; other did not complete high school.
8	One completed college; other completed high school or some college.
9	Both completed college.

WHRS dummy set (school experience elsewhere):

WHRS 1	No high school outside East Kentucky (omitted dummy)
WHRS 4	High school and college elsewhere in Kentucky
WHRS 5	High school out of state, college in Kentucky; *or*

	high school in Kentucky, college out of state
WHRS 7	High school and college out of state
WHRS 0	Non-response

CIT-W = Index of largest size of place in which respondent had worked for one year or more. Values of the variable, treated as cardinal, are:

1 A city of over 50,000
2 City of 15,000 to 50,000
3 A city or town of 1,000 or more but less than 15,000
4 A small town of under 1,000
5 In the countryside

(The use of the 1,000 division instead of the more standard 2,500 was a choice made after careful analysis of mountain settlement patterns.)

COMMUNITY CONTACTS & PARTICIPATION INDICATORS:

POS-AD Dummy variable for close family or personal contacts with administrative personnel in the local school system. Value is 1 if such contacts, zero otherwise.

POS-T Index of association with school teachers (treated as cardinal)

POL Index of political participation (past and present offices held). The index is constrained to values from 0 to 3 for number of past and present positions held. (Note that in Chapters 3 and 5 this is treated as a dichotomous variable: holds or has held a political office versus no such offices.)

CIV Number of kinds of civic activities. Code ranges from 0 to maximum value of 4. Its construction is explained in Chapter 3; see page 35. This variable also is used as a dichotomy in Chapters 3 and 5; the split is for index values or 2 or more versus values of 0 or 1.

YOUTH Both detailed and truncated indexes of degree of involvement with youth were included in some of the regressions, but in no case did this aspect of participant behavior display clearly significant associations with any of the dependent variables: this negative result could not have been expected a priori, but it is entirely consistent with the findings reported in Chapter 5. In view of the poor performance of this variable, we omit the details of its specification.

ATTITUDE VARIABLES:

ID (Identification with the mountain area) dummy set. These dummy variables are numbered according to answers on the following question (discussed in Chapter 2):

Which of the following most nearly describes your feeling about the area where you live and work? (Check one.)

ID 1 This has been my home, these are my kind of people, and I am happier living here than anywhere else.

ID 2 Where I grew up was different, but I have grown to love this community and regard it as my permanent home.

ID 3 I want to live here for a while, but would not want to spend the major part of my life here.

ID 4 I would rather live somewhere else, but there are compensations in living here.

ID 5 I definitely do not like living here.

ID 0 No response.

There were very few nonresponses on any of the independent variables or dummy sets. However, where this occurred on variables treated as cardinal, the value was set at the mean for the entire nonteacher sample. No cardinal variables were used in the regressions in which teachers were included, excepting variables on which there were no nonresponses.

FIGURE 10.
County Groupings,
Eastern Kentucky & Adjacent Bluegrass

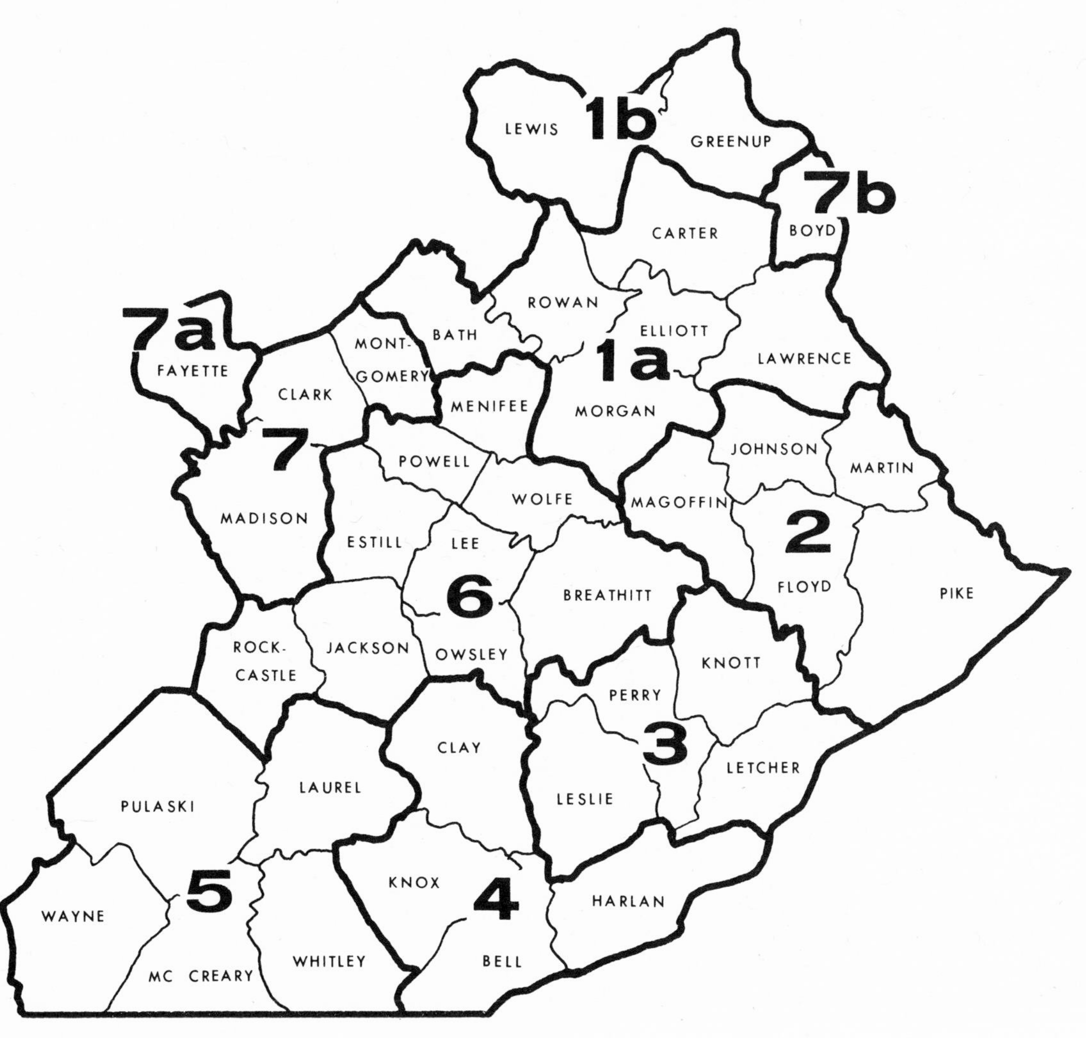

Index